Our Daily Bread.

2016 ANNUAL GIFT EDITION

For Personal and Family Devotions • Since 1956

Contents   Page

COVER PHOTO
Lake District, United Kingdom, Kevin Gregory © Our Daily Bread Ministries

WRITERS

Dave Branon	Chek Phang Hia	David H. Roper
Anne M. Cetas	Cindy Hess Kasper	Jennifer Benson Schuldt
Poh Fang Chia	Alyson Kieda	Joseph M. Stowell
William E. Crowder	Randy K. Kilgore	Marion Stroud
Mart DeHaan	Albert Lee	Marvin L. Williams
David Egner	Julie Ackerman Link	Philip D. Yancey
H. Dennis Fisher	David C. McCasland	

POEM CREDITS

Jan. 9, by Keith and Melody Green. © 1982 Birdwing Music. *Jan. 15*, by Ira F. Stanphill. © Renewal 1978. Singspiration. *Jan. 25*, by Lelia Morris. © Renewal 1940. Hope Publishing. *Feb. 8*, by Julia Johnston. © Renewal 1938. Hope Publishing. *Feb. 14*, by Fredrick Blom. © 1968 Singspiration. *Feb. 19*, by Edward H. Bickersteth. © 1968 Singspiration. *Feb. 23*, by Frederick M. Lehman. © Renewal 1945. Nazarene. *Feb. 24*, by Linda Lee Johnson. © 1979 Hope Publishing. *Mar. 6*, by Alfred H. Ackley. © 1952 The Rodeheaver Co. *Mar. 22*, by John W. Peterson. © 1957 Singspiration. *Mar. 27*, by J. Wilbur Chapman. © Renewal 1938. The Rodeheaver Co. *Apr. 11*, by Rich Mullins. © 1988 Edward Grant. *Apr. 23*, by Virgil P. Brock. © Renewal 1964. The Rodeheaver Co. *Apr. 28*, by Norman J. Clayton. © Renewal 1973. Norman J. Clayton. *May 7*, by William J. Gaither. © 1963 William J. Gaither. *May 16*, by Haldor Lillenas. © Renewal 1951. Lillenas Publishing. *June 4*, by Thomas Chisholm. © Renewal 1951. Hope Publishing. *June 21*, by Austin Miles. © Renewal 1940. The Rodeheaver Co.

ARTICLE CREDITS

Jan. 9, *Apr. 25*, excerpted and adapted from *The Jesus I Never Knew*; *Feb. 4*, *Mar. 5*, *Apr. 5*, *Prayer: Does It Make Any Difference?*; *May 17*, *Rumors of Another World: What on Earth Are We Missing?*; *July 11*, *Finding God In Unexpected Places*; *Aug. 18*, *Sept. 29*, *Oct. 15*, *Nov. 29*, *Grace Notes* by Philip D. Yancey, © Zondervan. Published by permission of Zondervan.

Introduction

We want to hear from God, don't we? To be near Him, to know more about Him, to be known by Him. This 2016 Annual Gift Edition has been produced to help you in that desire. It will guide you through the Bible so that you might hear from His heart.

There's a special story on page 187 about a young woman who questioned God's love for her. She wondered, *Is God's love a generic sort of love for humanity as a whole, or does He desire a unique love relationship with each of us?* Perhaps Christy Bower's story can help you or someone you know.

You may also want to consider obtaining more copies of this book to share with loved ones.

Please contact us if we can serve you.

The staff at Our Daily Bread Ministries 🌱

LOVE *Our Daily Bread?*
Then get it on your phone!

Download the *Our Daily Bread* app, and our other apps, now!

And you can get the *Our Daily Bread* booklet, along with ministry updates and offers, sent to your home address every 3 months. Just contact your nearest Our Daily Bread Ministries office (see page 381).

31 Days of Thanks

January, according to many US calendars, is National Thank You Month. This, of course, is easily transferable everywhere, so perhaps it should be Global Thank You Month.

In order to make the best use of this celebration of gratitude, let's begin by seeing what Scripture says about thankfulness.

TODAY'S READING
Psalm 136:1-16, 26

Oh, give thanks to the Lord of lords! v. 3

One place to start is Psalm 136, which begins and ends with the words, "Oh, give thanks" (VV. 1,26). Again and again in this chapter we are reminded of a single, overriding reason to bestow our gratitude on our great God: "His mercy endures forever." We could spend the whole month learning about gratitude from Psalm 136.

The psalmist reminds us of God's "great wonders" (V. 4). He tells us of God's creative work brought on by His wisdom (V. 5). He moves on to rehearse the great exodus of His people (VV. 10-22). As we think through these pictures of creation and deliverance found in Psalm 136, we can easily find something to thank God for every day of this Thank You Month.

What better way to start off a new year than to concentrate on conveying gratitude to our Lord! "Oh, give thanks to the Lord, for He is good! For His mercy endures forever" (V. 1). 🌿

DAVE BRANON

How good it is to thank the Lord,
And praise to Thee, Most High, accord,
To show Thy love with morning light,
And tell Thy faithfulness each night! PSALTER

When you think of all that's good, give thanks to God.

No Appetite

When I was battling a bad cold recently, I lost my appetite. I could go through an entire day without eating much food. Water would suffice. But I knew I couldn't survive long on water alone. I needed to regain my appetite because my body needed nourishment.

When the people of Israel came back from exile in Babylon, their spiritual appetite was weak. They had departed from God and His ways. To get the people back to spiritual health, Nehemiah organized a Bible seminar, and Ezra was the teacher.

TODAY'S READING
Nehemiah 8:1-12

As newborn babes, desire the pure milk of the word, that you may grow thereby. 1 Peter 2:2

Ezra read from the book of the law of Moses from morning until midday, feeding the people with the truth of God (NEH. 8:3). And the people listened attentively. In fact, their appetite for God's Word was so stirred that the family leaders and the priests and Levites met with Ezra the following day to study the law in greater detail because they wanted to understand it (V. 13).

When we feel estranged from God or spiritually weak, we can find spiritual nourishment from God's Word. "As newborn babes, desire the pure milk of the word, that you may grow thereby" (1 PETER 2:2). Ask God to give you a renewed desire for relationship with Him, and begin feeding your heart, soul, and mind with His Word. ❀ *POH FANG CHIA*

Break Thou the Bread of life, dear Lord, to me,
As Thou didst break the loaves beside the sea;
Beyond the sacred page I seek Thee, Lord,
My spirit pants for Thee, O living Word. LATHBURY

Feeding on God's Word keeps us strong and healthy in the Lord.

Help from His Spirit

Many of us make promises to ourselves to mark the beginning of a new year. We make pledges such as I'm going to save more, exercise more, or spend less time on the Internet. We begin the year with good intentions, but before long old habits tempt us to take up our old ways. We slip up occasionally, then more frequently, and then all the time. Finally, it's as if our resolution never existed.

TODAY'S READING
Micah 6:3-8

What does the LORD require of you but to do justly, to love mercy, and to walk humbly with your God? Micah 6:8

Instead of choosing our own self-improvement goals, a better approach might be to ask ourselves: "What does the Lord desire of me?" Through the prophet Micah, God has revealed that He wants us to do what is right, to be merci-ful, and to walk humbly with Him (MIC. 6:8). All of these things relate to soul-improvement rather than self-improvement.

Thankfully, we don't have to rely on our own strength. The Holy Spirit has the power to help us as believers in our spiritual growth. God's Word says He is able to "strengthen you with power through his Spirit in your inner being" (EPH. 3:16 NIV).

So as we begin a new year, let's resolve to be more Christlike. The Spirit will help us as we seek to walk humbly with God. 🌿

JENNIFER BENSON SCHULDT

Truthful Spirit, dwell with me;
I myself would truthful be;
And with wisdom kind and clear
Let Thy life in mine appear. LYNCH

He who has the Holy Spirit as his resource has already won the victory.

Situation Excellent

At the First Battle of the Marne during World War I, French lieutenant general Ferdinand Foch sent out this communiqué: "My center is giving way, my right is retreating. Situation excellent. I am attacking." His willingness to see hope in a tough situation eventually led to victory for his troops.

Sometimes in life's battles we can feel as if we are losing on every front. Family discord, business setbacks, financial woes, or a decline in health can put a pessimistic spin on the way we look at life. But the believer in Christ can always find a way to conclude: "Situation excellent."

> **TODAY'S READING**
> **Philippians 1:3-14**
>
> **The things which happened to me have actually turned out for the furtherance of the gospel.** v. 12

Look at Paul. When he was thrown in prison for preaching the gospel, he had an unusually upbeat attitude. To the church at Philippi he wrote, "I want you to know, brethren, that the things which happened to me have actually turned out for the furtherance of the gospel" (PHIL. 1:12).

Paul saw his prison situation as a new platform from which to evangelize the Roman palace guard. In addition, other Christians became emboldened by his situation to preach the gospel more fearlessly (VV. 13-14).

God can use our trials to work good in spite of the pain they bring (ROM. 8:28). That's just one more way He can be honored. ❧   *DENNIS FISHER*

Comfort us, Lord, when life's trials assail—we fail and
stumble so often. Renew us, and help us to grow so that
others may also know Your goodness and comfort.

Trials can be God's road to triumph.

Adoption

My wife, Marlene, and I have been married for over 35 years. When we were first dating, we had a conversation I have never forgotten. She told me that at 6 months old she had been adopted. When I asked her if she ever wondered about who her real parents were, she responded, "My mom and dad could have selected any of a number of other babies that day, but they chose me. They adopted me. They are my real parents."

That strong sense of identification and gratitude she has for her adoptive parents should also mark our relationship with God. As followers of Christ, we have been born from above through faith in Him and have been adopted into the family of God. Paul wrote, "He chose us in Him before the foundation of the world, that we should be holy and without blame before Him in love, having predestined us to adoption as sons by Jesus Christ to Himself, according to the good pleasure of His will" (EPH. 1:4-5).

> TODAY'S READING
> **Ephesians 1:3-12**
>
> **He chose us in Him . . . having predestined us to adoption as sons by Jesus Christ to Himself.** vv. 4-5

Notice the nature of this transaction. We have been chosen by God and adopted as His sons and daughters. Through adoption, we have a radically new relationship with God. He is our beloved Father!

May this relationship stir our hearts to worship Him— our Father—with gratitude. ❦ *BILL CROWDER*

Loving Father, thank You for making me Your child and giving me a place in Your family. With a grateful heart, I thank You for making me Yours.

God loves each of us as if there were only one of us. AUGUSTINE

The Night No One Came

One winter night composer Johann Sebastian Bach was scheduled to debut a new composition. He arrived at the church expecting it to be full. Instead, he learned that no one had come. Without missing a beat, Bach told his musicians that they would still perform as planned. They took their places, Bach raised his baton, and soon the empty church was filled with magnificent music.

> TODAY'S READING
> **Matthew 6:1-7**
>
> **Do not do your charitable deeds before men, to be seen by them.** v. 1

This story made me do some soul-searching. Would I write if God were my only audience? How would my writing be different?

New writers are often advised to visualize one person they are writing to as a way of staying focused. I do this when I write devotionals; I try to keep readers in mind because I want to say something they will want to read and that will help them on their spiritual journey.

I doubt that the "devotional writer" David, whose psalms we turn to for comfort and encouragement, had "readers" in mind. The only audience he had in mind was God.

Whether our "deeds," mentioned in Matthew 6, are works of art or acts of service, we should keep in mind that they're really between us and God. Whether or not anyone else sees does not matter. He is our audience. 🌿 *JULIE ACKERMAN LINK*

That my ways might show forth Your glory,
That You, dear Lord, greatly deserve!
With Your precious blood You've redeemed me—
In all my days, You I would serve! SOMERVILLE

Serve for an audience of one.

Words That Help and Heal

On **November 19, 1863,** two well-known men gave speeches at the dedication of the Soldiers' National Cemetery in Gettysburg, Pennsylvania. The featured speaker, Edward Everett, was a former congressman, governor, and president of Harvard University. Considered one of the greatest orators of his day, Mr. Everett delivered a formal address lasting 2 hours. He was followed by President Abraham Lincoln, whose speech lasted 2 minutes.

TODAY'S READING
Matthew 6:5-15

Our Father in heaven, hallowed be Your name. v. 9

Today, Lincoln's speech, the Gettysburg Address, is widely known and quoted, while Everett's words have almost been forgotten. It is not just Lincoln's eloquent brevity that accounts for this. On that occasion, his words touched the wounded spirit of a nation fractured by civil war, offering hope for the days to come.

Words do not have to be many to be meaningful. What we call the Lord's Prayer is among the shortest and most memorable of all the teachings of Jesus. It brings help and healing as it reminds us that God is our heavenly Father whose power is at work on earth, just as it is in heaven (MATT. 6:9-10). He provides food, forgiveness, and fortitude for each day (VV. 11-13). And all honor and glory belong to Him (V. 13). There is nothing in our past, present, and future that is not included in our Lord's brief words that help and heal. ❀ *DAVID MCCASLAND*

How easy it is to use many words
And give little thought to the things you say;
So willingly yield your lips to the Lord
And hearts will be blest by them every day. D. DEHAAN

Kind words smooth, and quiet, and comfort the hearer. BLAISE PASCAL

The Hidden Life

Some years ago, I came across a poem by George MacDonald titled "The Hidden Life." It tells the story of an intellectually gifted young Scot who turned his back on a prestigious academic career to return to his aging father and to the family farm. There he engaged in what MacDonald called "ordinary deeds" and "simple forms of human helpfulness." His friends lamented what they saw as a waste of his talents.

> **TODAY'S READING**
> **Colossians 3:12-17**
>
> **Whatever you do in word or deed, do all in the name of the Lord Jesus.** v. 17

Perhaps you too serve in some unnoticed place, doing nothing more than ordinary deeds. Others might think that's a waste. But God wastes nothing. Every act of love rendered for His sake is noted and has eternal rewards. Every place, no matter how small, is holy ground. Influence is more than lofty acts and words. It can be a simple matter of human helpfulness: being present, listening, understanding the need, loving, and praying. This is what turns daily duty into worship and service.

The apostle Paul challenged the Colossians: "Whatever you do in word or deed, do all in the name of the Lord Jesus," and "do it heartily, as to the Lord and not to men, knowing that from the Lord you will receive the reward of the inheritance" (COL. 3:17,23-24). God takes notice and delights in using us. ❧

DAVID ROPER

Dear Lord, may I be willing to be hidden and unknown
today, yet ready to speak a word to those who are weary.
May Your Spirit touch my words and make them Your
words that enrich and refresh others.

The way to accomplish much for Christ is to serve Him in any way we can.

As Below, So Above

The **Roman paganism** of Jesus' day taught that the actions of gods in the heavens above affected the earth below. If Zeus got angry, thunderbolts shot out. "As above, so below," went the ancient formula.

Jesus, though, sometimes inverted that. He taught: As below, so above. A believer prays, and heaven responds. A sinner repents, and the angels rejoice. A mission succeeds, and God is glorified. A believer rebels, and the Holy Spirit is grieved.

I believe these things, yet somehow I keep forgetting them. I forget that my prayers matter to God. I forget that the choices I make today bring

> **TODAY'S READING**
> **Luke 24:44-53**
>
> **Tarry in the city of Jerusalem until you are endued with power from on high.** v. 49

delight or grief to the Lord of the universe. I forget that I am helping my neighbors to their eternal destinations.

The good-news message of God's love that Jesus brought to this earth we can now bring to others. That was the challenge He gave His disciples before ascending to His Father (SEE MATT. 28:18-20). We who follow Jesus serve as an extension of His incarnation and ministry. It is why He came to earth. Before He left, He told His disciples that He would send His Spirit from above to them below (LUKE 24:48). He did not leave us alone. He fills us with His power that we might touch lives here below to affect eternity. 🌿

PHILIP YANCEY

Thank You, O my Father,
For giving us Your Son,
And leaving Your Spirit
Till the work on earth is done. GREEN

*You ascended before our eyes, and we turned back grieving,
only to find You in our hearts.* AUGUSTINE

For the Long Run

A **2006 survey** of more than 1,000 adults discovered that most people take an average of 17 minutes to lose their patience while waiting in line. Also, most people lose their patience in only 9 minutes while on hold on the phone. Impatience is a common trait.

James wrote to a group of believers who were struggling with being patient for Jesus' return (JAMES 5:7). They were living under exploitation and distressing times, and James encouraged them to "set the timer of their temper" for the long run. Challenging these believers to persevere under suffering, he tried to

TODAY'S READING
James 5:7-11

Therefore be patient, brethren, until the coming of the Lord. v. 7

stimulate them to stand firm and to live sacrificially until the Lord returned to right every wrong. He wrote: "Establish your hearts, for the coming of the Lord is at hand" (V. 8).

James called them to be like the farmer who waits patiently for the rain and the harvest (V. 7) and like the prophets and the patriarch Job who demonstrated perseverance in difficulties (VV. 10-11). The finish line was just ahead and James encouraged the believers not to give up.

When we are being tried in a crucible of distress, God desires to help us continue living by faith and trusting in His compassion and mercy (V. 11). ❧ *MARVIN WILLIAMS*

FOR FURTHER THOUGHT
What is most difficult about being patient during stressful times? Ask God for the grace to help you live by faith and to live for the long run.

The way to great patience is through great trials.

The Journey Begins

More than 80 years ago, a 9-year-old boy prayed to ask Jesus to be the Savior of his life. His mother wrote these words in a memory book: "Clair made a start today."

Clair—my dad—refers to the day when he made his decision to follow Christ as the *beginning* of his journey. Growing spiritually is a lifelong process—not a one-time event. So how does a new believer feed his faith and continue to grow? These are some things I observed in my dad's life over the years.

He read the Scriptures regularly to increase his understanding of God and made prayer a daily part of his life (1 CHRON. 16:11; 1 THESS. 5:17). Bible reading and prayer help us grow closer to God and withstand temptation (PS. 119:11; MATT. 26:41; EPH. 6:11; 2 TIM. 3:16-17; 1 PETER 2:2). The Holy Spirit began to develop the "fruit of the Spirit" in him as he surrendered his life in faith and obedience (GAL. 5:22-23). We display God's love through our witness and service.

Our spiritual journey is a process. What a privilege to have a relationship in which we can "grow in the grace and knowledge of our Lord and Savior Jesus Christ"! (2 PETER 3:18). 🌱

CINDY HESS KASPER

> **TODAY'S READING**
> **2 Peter 1:5-11**
>
> **If anyone is in Christ, he is a new creation; old things have passed away.**
> 2 Corinthians 5:17

I want my heart to be in tune with God,
In every stage of life may it ring true;
I want my thoughts and words to honor Him,
To lift Him up in everything I do. HESS

Salvation is the miracle of a moment; growth is the labor of a lifetime.

A Neighbor on the Fence

The fence around the side yard of our home was showing some wear and tear, and my husband, Carl, and I decided we needed to take it down before it fell down. It was pretty easy to disassemble, so we removed it quickly one afternoon. A few weeks later when Carl was raking the yard, a woman who was walking her dog stopped to give her opinion: "Your yard looks so much better without the fence. Besides, I don't believe in fences." She explained that she liked "community" and no barriers between people.

TODAY'S READING
Acts 2:41-47

All who believed were together. v. 44

While there are some good reasons to have physical fences, isolating us from our neighbors is not one of them. So I understood our neighbor's desire for the feeling of community. The church I attend has community groups that meet once a week to build relationships and to encourage one another in our journey with God. The early church gathered together daily in the temple (ACTS 2:44,46). They became one in purpose and heart as they fellowshiped and prayed. If they struggled, they would have companions to lift them up (SEE ECCL. 4:10).

Connection to a community of believers is vital in our Christian walk. One way that God chooses to show His love to us is through relationships. 🌿 *ANNE CETAS*

Blest be the tie that binds
Our hearts in Christian love!
The fellowship of kindred minds
Is like to that above. FAWCETT

We all need Christian fellowship to build us up and hold us up.

Much More Than Survival

I n **April 1937,** Mussolini's invading armies forced all the missionaries serving in the Wallamo region to flee Ethiopia. They left behind just 48 Christian converts, who had little more than the gospel of Mark to feed their growth. Few even knew how to read. But when the missionaries returned 4 years later, the church had not just survived; it numbered 10,000!

When the apostle Paul was forced to leave Thessalonica (SEE ACTS 17:1-10), he yearned to learn about the survival of the small band of Christians he left behind (1 THESS. 2:17). But when Timothy visited the Thessalonian church later, he brought word to Paul in Athens about their "faith and love" (3:6). They had become "examples" to the believers in the surrounding regions in Macedonia and Achaia (1:8).

> TODAY'S READING
> **1 Thess. 2:17–3:7**
>
> **Timothy has come to us from you, and brought us good news of your faith and love.** 3:6

Paul never claimed credit for any numerical increase in his ministry. Nor did he attribute it to anyone else. Rather, he gave credit to God. He wrote, "I planted, Apollos watered, but God gave the increase" (1 COR. 3:6).

Difficult circumstances may thwart even our best intentions, separating friends from each other for a season. But God is growing His church through every difficulty. We need only be faithful and leave the results to Him. ❦ *C. P. HIA*

Lord, we are so prone to be fearful when we face opposition, yet so often we want to take credit for every little success. Help us see that You are the One who blesses and builds Your church.

I will build My church, and the gates of Hades shall not prevail against it. JESUS (MATTHEW 16:18)

Sweet Rest

Try as we might—tossing, turning, fluffing the pillow, pounding the pillow—sometimes we just can't fall asleep. After offering some good suggestions on how to get a better night's sleep, a news article concluded that there really is no "right way" to sleep.

There are numerous reasons why sleep eludes us, many of which we can't do much about. But sometimes unwanted wakefulness is caused by anxious thoughts, worry, or guilt. It's then that the example of David in Psalm 4 can help. He called out to God, asking for mercy and for God to hear his prayer (V. 1). He also reminded himself that the Lord *does* hear him when he calls on Him (V.3).

TODAY'S READING
Psalm 4

You have put gladness in my heart. v. 7

David encourages us: "Meditate within your heart on your bed, and be still" (V. 4). Focusing our minds on the goodness, mercy, and love of God for His world, our loved ones, and ourselves can aid us in trusting the Lord (V. 5).

The Lord desires to help us set aside our worries about finding solutions to our problems and place our trust in Him to work things out. He can "put gladness" in our hearts (V.7), so that we might "lie down in peace, and sleep; for You alone, O Lord, make [us] dwell in safety" (V. 8). 🌀   *DAVE EGNER*

Give me a spirit of peace, dear Lord,
Midst the storms and the tempests that roll,
That I may find rest and quiet within,
A calm buried deep in my soul. DAWE

Even when we cannot sleep, God can give us rest.

Food in the Cupboard

My friend Marcia, the director of the Jamaica Christian School for the Deaf, recently illustrated an important way to look at things. In a newsletter article she titled "A Blessed Start," she pointed out that for the first time in 7 years the school began the new year with a surplus. And what was that surplus? A thousand dollars in the bank? No. Enough school supplies for the year? No. It was simply this: A month's supply of food in the cupboard.

When you're in charge of feeding 30 hungry kids on a shoestring budget, that's big! She accompanied her note with this verse from 1 Chronicles 16:34, "Oh, give thanks to the LORD, for He is good! For His mercy endures forever."

> **TODAY'S READING**
> **Matthew 6:25-34**
>
> **Do not worry about your life, what you will eat or what you will drink; nor about . . . what you will put on.** v. 25

Year after year Marcia trusts God to provide for the children and staff at her school. She never has much—whether it's water or food or school supplies. Yet she is always grateful for what God sends, and she is faithful to believe that He will continue to provide.

As we begin a new year, do we have faith in God's provision? To do so is to take our Savior at His word when He said, "Do not worry about your life . . . . Do not worry about tomorrow" (MATT. 6:25,34). ❧

DAVE BRANON

I don't worry o'er the future,
For I know what Jesus said,
And today I'll walk beside Him,
For He knows what is ahead. STANPHILL

***Worry does not empty tomorrow of its sorrow;
it empties today of its strength.*** CORRIE TEN BOOM

The Little Tent

During evangelist **Billy Graham's** historic 1949 Los Angeles campaign, the big tent that held over 6,000 people was filled to overflowing every night for 8 weeks. Close by was a smaller tent set aside for counseling and prayer. Cliff Barrows, longtime music director and close friend and associate of Graham, has often said that the real work of the gospel took place in "the little tent," where people gathered on their knees to pray before and during every evangelistic service. A local Los Angeles woman, Pearl Goode, was the heart of those prayer meetings and many that followed.

> TODAY'S READING
> **Col. 1:1-12; 4:12**
>
> **For it pleased the Father that in Him all the fullness should dwell.** Col. 1:19

In the apostle Paul's letter to the followers of Christ in Colosse, he assured them that he and his colleagues were praying always for them (COL. 1:3,9). In closing he mentioned Epaphras, a founder of the Colossian church, who is "always laboring fervently for you in prayers, that you may stand perfect and complete in all the will of God" (4:12).

Some people are given the high visibility task of preaching the gospel in "the big tent." But God has extended to us all, just as He did to Epaphras and Pearl Goode, the great privilege of kneeling in "the little tent" and bringing others before the throne of God. 🌱 *DAVID MCCASLAND*

They labor well who intercede
For others with a pressing need;
It's on their knees they often work
And from its rigor will not shirk. D. DEHAAN

Prayer is not preparation for the work, it is the work. OSWALD CHAMBERS

Heavenly Perspective

anny Crosby lost her sight as an infant. Yet, amazingly, she went on to become one of the most well-known lyricists of Christian hymns. During her long life, she wrote over 9,000 hymns. Among them are such enduring favorites as "Blessed Assurance" and "To God Be the Glory."

Some people felt sorry for Fanny. A well-intentioned preacher told her, "I think it is a great pity that the Master did not give you sight when He showered so many other gifts upon you." It sounds hard to believe, but she replied: "Do you know that if at birth I had been able to make one petition, it would have been that I was born blind?... Because when I get to heaven, the first face that shall ever gladden my sight will be that of my Savior."

> TODAY'S READING
> **2 Cor. 4:16-18**
>
> **The things which are seen are temporary, but the things which are not seen are eternal.** v. 18

Fanny saw life with an eternal perspective. Our problems look different in light of eternity: "For our light affliction, which is but for a moment, is working for us a far more exceeding and eternal weight of glory, while we do not look at the things which are seen, but at the things which are not seen. For the things which are seen are temporary, but the things which are not seen are eternal" (2 COR. 4:17-18).

All our trials dim when we remember that one glorious day we will see Jesus! 🌿   *DENNIS FISHER*

Dear God, please help us to see this life from a heavenly perspective. Remind us that our trials, however difficult, will one day fade from view when we see You face to face.

The way we view eternity will affect the way we live in time.

True Greatness

Some people feel like a small pebble lost in the immensity of a canyon. But no matter how insignificant we judge ourselves to be, we can be greatly used by God.

In a sermon early in 1968, Martin Luther King Jr. quoted Jesus' words from Mark 10 about servanthood. Then he said, "Everybody can be great, because everybody can serve. You don't have to have a college degree to serve. You don't have to make your subject and your verb agree to serve. You don't have to know about Plato and Aristotle to serve. . . . You only need a heart full of grace, a soul generated by love."

TODAY'S READING
Mark 10:35-45

Whoever desires to become great among you shall be your servant. v. 43

When Jesus' disciples quarreled about who would get the places of honor in heaven, He told them: "Whoever desires to become great among you shall be your servant. And whoever of you desires to be first shall be slave of all. For even the Son of Man did not come to be served, but to serve, and to give His life a ransom for many" (MARK 10:43-45).

I wonder about us. Is that our understanding of greatness? Are we gladly serving, doing tasks that may be unnoticed? Is the purpose of our serving to please our Lord rather than to gain applause? If we are willing to be a servant, our lives will point to the One who is truly great. 🌱 *VERNON GROUNDS*

> No service in itself is small,
> None great, though earth it fill;
> But that is small that seeks its own,
> And great that does God's will. ANON.

Little things done in Christ's name are great things.

Two Men

Two men were killed in our city on the same day. The first, a police officer, was shot down while trying to help a family. The other was a homeless man who was shot while drinking with friends early that day.

The whole city grieved for the police officer. He was a fine young man who cared for others and was loved by the neighborhood he served. A few homeless people grieved for the friend they loved and lost.

TODAY'S READING
John 11:30-37

He groaned in the spirit and was troubled. . . . Jesus wept. vv. 33,35

I think the Lord grieved with them all.

When Jesus saw Mary and Martha and their friends weeping over the death of Lazarus, "He groaned in the spirit and was troubled" (JOHN 11:33). He loved Lazarus and his sisters. Even though He knew that He would soon be raising Lazarus from the dead, He wept with them (V. 35). Some Bible scholars think that part of Jesus' weeping also may have been over death itself and the pain and sadness it causes in people's hearts.

Loss is a part of life. But because Jesus is "the resurrection and the life" (V. 25), those who believe in Him will one day experience an end of all death and sorrow. In the meantime, He weeps with us over our losses and asks us to "weep with those who weep" (ROM. 12:15). ✿ *ANNE CETAS*

Give me a heart sympathetic and tender;
Jesus, like Thine, Jesus, like Thine,
Touched by the needs that are surging around me,
And filled with compassion divine. ANON.

Compassion helps to heal the hurts of others.

All Spruced Up

Getting our children to look good for church was always a challenge. Ten minutes after arriving at church all spruced up, our little Matthew would look like he didn't have parents. I'd see him running down the hall with his shirt half untucked, glasses cockeyed, shoes scuffed up, and cookie crumbs decorating his clothes. Left to himself, he was a mess.

TODAY'S READING
Jude 1:20-25

[Jesus] is able to keep you from stumbling, and to present you faultless. v. 24

I wonder if that is how we look sometimes. After Christ has clothed us in His righteousness, we tend to wander off and live in ways that make us look like we don't belong to God. That's why Jude's promise that Jesus is "able to keep you from stumbling, and to present you faultless" gives me hope (JUDE 1:24).

How can we keep from looking like we don't have a heavenly Father? As we become more yielded to His Spirit and His ways, He will keep us from stumbling. Think of how increasingly righteous our lives would become if we would take time in His Word to be cleansed with "the washing of water by the word" (EPH. 5:26).

What a blessing that Jesus promises to take our stumbling, disheveled lives and present us faultless to the Father! May we increasingly look like children of the King as we reflect His loving care and attention. ❧   *JOE STOWELL*

Lord, thank You for the blessing of being clothed in Your beautiful righteousness and the promise that You will keep me from stumbling and present me faultless before Your Father and my God!

To reflect the presence of the Father, we must rely on the Son.

In Harmony

love playing the 5-string banjo. But it has one drawback. The fifth string will harmonize with only a limited number of simple chords. When other musicians want to play more complicated music, the banjoist has to adapt. He can lend marvelous melodic tones to a jam session only by making the right adjustments.

Just as musicians adjust with their instruments, we as believers also need to make adjustments with our spiritual gifts if we want to harmonize with others to serve God. For instance, those who have the gift of teaching must coordinate with those who have the gift of organizing meetings and with those who make sure meeting rooms are set up and cleaned. All of us have spiritual gifts, and we must work together if God's work is to get done.

> TODAY'S READING
> **1 Peter 4:7-11**
>
> **As each one has received a gift, minister it to one another, as good stewards of the manifold grace of God.** v. 10

The apostle Peter said, "As each one has received a gift, minister it to one another, as good stewards of the manifold grace of God" (1 PETER 4:10). Stewardship requires cooperation. Think about your spiritual gifts (ROM. 12; 1 COR. 12; EPH. 4; 1 PETER 4). Now reflect on how you can dovetail their use with the gifts of other believers. When our talents are used in a complementary way, the result is harmony and glory to God. ❧

DENNIS FISHER

Without a note we sing in tune,
An anthem loud we bring,
When willingly we give our gifts
Of labor to our King. BRANON

Keeping in tune with Christ keeps harmony in the church.

Bricks Without Straw

Many of us face the challenge of working with limited resources. Equipped with less money, less time, dwindling energy, and fewer helpers, our workload may remain the same. Sometimes, it even increases. There's a saying that sums up this predicament: "More bricks, less straw."

This phrase refers to the Israelites' hardship as slaves in Egypt. Pharaoh decided to stop supplying them with straw, yet he required them to make the same number of bricks each day. They scoured the land to find supplies, while Pharaoh's overseers beat them and pressured them to work harder (EX. 5:13).

> TODAY'S READING
> **Exodus 6:1-13**
>
> **I will rescue you . . . , and I will redeem you with an outstretched arm.** v. 6

The Israelites became so discouraged that they didn't listen when God said through Moses, "I will rescue you . . . , and I will redeem you with an outstretched arm" (6:6).

Although the Israelites refused to hear God's message, God was still guiding and directing Moses, preparing him to speak to Pharaoh. God remained firmly on Israel's side—at work behind the scenes. Like the Israelites, we can become so downhearted that we ignore encouragement. In dark times, it's comforting to remember that God is our deliverer (PS. 40:17). He is always at work on our behalf, even if we can't see what He is doing. 🌿

JENNIFER BENSON SCHULDT

Lord, please help me to trust You despite my discouragement. I invite You to fill me with hope through the power of Your Holy Spirit. Let my life testify of Your faithfulness.

Times of trouble are times for trust.

Load Line

n the 19th century, ships were often recklessly overloaded, resulting in those ships going down and the crews being lost at sea. In 1875, to remedy this negligent practice, British politician Samuel Plimsoll led the charge for legislation to create a line on the side of a ship to show if it was carrying too much cargo. That "load line" became known as the Plimsoll Line, and it continues to mark the hulls of ships today.

Sometimes, like those ships, our lives can seem overloaded with fears, struggles, and heartaches. We can even feel that we are in danger of going under. In those times, however, it is reassuring to remember that we have a remarkable resource. We have a heavenly Father who stands ready to help us carry that load. The apostle Peter said, "Therefore humble yourselves under the mighty hand of God, that He may exalt you in due time, casting all your care upon Him, for He cares for you" (1 PETER 5:6-7). He is capable of handling the cares that overwhelm us.

> **TODAY'S READING**
> **1 Peter 5:5-9**
>
> Humble yourselves under the mighty hand of God, that He may exalt you in due time, casting all your care upon Him, for He cares for you. vv. 6-7

Though the testings of life may feel like a burden too heavy to bear, we can have full assurance that our heavenly Father loves us deeply and knows our load limits. Whatever we face, He will help us to bear it. ❧

BILL CROWDER

Heavenly Father, I sometimes feel as if I can't go on. I am tired, I am weak, and I am worn. Thank You that You know my limits better than I do. And that, in Your strength, I can find the enablement to endure.

God may lead us into troubled waters to deepen our trust in Him.

Where Have You Been?

Missionary Egerton Ryerson Young served the Salteaux tribe in Canada in the 1700s. The chief of the tribe thanked Young for bringing the good news of Christ to them, noting that he was hearing it for the first time in his old age. Since he knew that God was Young's heavenly Father, the chief asked, "Does that mean He is *my* Father too?" When the missionary answered, "Yes," the crowd that had gathered around burst into cheers.

The chief was not finished, however. "Well," said the chief, "I do not want to be rude, but it does seem to me...that it took a long time for you to ...tell it to your brother in the woods." It was a remark that Young never forgot.

> **TODAY'S READING**
> **Romans 10:11-15**
>
> **How shall they believe in Him of whom they have not heard? And how shall they hear without a preacher?** v. 14

Many times I've been frustrated by the zigs and zags of my life, thinking of the people I could reach *if only*. Then God reminds me to look around right where I am, and I discover many who have never heard of Jesus. In that moment, I'm reminded that I have a story to tell wherever I go, "for the same Lord over all is rich to all who call upon Him. For 'whoever calls on the name of the Lord shall be saved'" (ROM. 10:12-13).

Remember, we don't have just any story to tell—it's the best story that has ever been told. 🌱　　　　　*RANDY KILGORE*

I love to tell the story,
For some have never heard
The message of salvation
From God's own holy Word. HANKEY

Sharing the good news is one beggar telling another beggar where to find bread.

An Ordinary Day

While exploring a museum exhibit titled "A Day in Pompeii," I was struck by the repeated theme that August 24, AD 79 began as an ordinary day. People were going about their daily business in homes, in markets, and at the port of this prosperous Roman town of 20,000 people. At 8 a.m., a series of small emissions were seen coming from nearby Mount Vesuvius, followed by a violent eruption in the afternoon. In less than 24 hours, Pompeii and many of its people lay buried under a thick layer of volcanic ash. Unexpected.

> TODAY'S READING
> **Matthew 24:36-44**
>
> **Watch therefore, for you do not know what hour your Lord is coming.** v. 42

Jesus told His followers that He would return on a day when people were going about their business, sharing meals, and having weddings, with no idea of what was about to happen. "As the days of Noah were, so also will the coming of the Son of Man be" (MATT. 24:37).

The Lord's purpose was to urge the disciples to be watchful and prepared: "Therefore you also be ready, for the Son of Man is coming at an hour you do not expect" (V. 44).

What surprising joy it would be to welcome our Savior on this ordinary day! 🌱

DAVID MCCASLAND

> Faithful and true would He find us here,
> If He should come today?
> Watching in gladness and not in fear,
> If He should come today?
> Watch for the time is drawing nigh,
> What if it were today? MORRIS

Perhaps today!

The Discipline of Waiting

Waiting is hard. We wait in grocery lines, in traffic, in the doctor's office. We twiddle our thumbs, stifle our yawns, and fret inwardly in frustration. On another level, we wait for a letter that doesn't come, for a prodigal child to return, or for a spouse to change. We wait for a child we can hold in our arms. We wait for our heart's desire.

TODAY'S READING
Psalm 40:1-3

I waited patiently for the LORD; and He inclined to me, and heard my cry. v. 1

In Psalm 40, David says, "I waited patiently for the Lord." The original language here suggests that David "waited and waited and waited" for God to answer his prayer. Yet as he looks back at this time of delay, he praises God. As a result, David says, God "put a new song . . . a hymn of praise" in his heart (40:3 NIV).

"What a chapter can be written of God's delays!" said F. B. Meyer. "It is the mystery of educating human spirits to the finest temper of which they are capable." Through the discipline of waiting, we can develop the quieter virtues— submission, humility, patience, joyful endurance, persistence in well-doing—virtues that take the longest to learn.

What do we do when God seems to withhold our heart's desire? He is able to help us to love and trust Him enough to accept the delay with joy and to see it as an opportunity to develop these virtues—and to praise Him. 🌿   *DAVID ROPER*

Have Thine own way, Lord! Have Thine own way!
Thou art the Potter, I am the clay;
Mold me and make me after Thy will,
While I am waiting, yielded and still. POLLARD

Waiting for God is never a waste of time.

The Wonder of the Cross

While visiting Australia, I had the opportunity on a particularly clear night to see the Southern Cross. Located in the Southern Hemisphere, this constellation is one of the most distinctive. Mariners and navigators began relying on it as early as the 15th century for direction and navigation through the seas. Although relatively small, it is visible throughout most of the year. The Southern Cross was so vivid on that dark night that even I could pick it out of the bundle of stars. It was truly a magnificent sight!

TODAY'S READING
Hebrews 12:1-4

[Look] unto Jesus, the author and finisher of our faith, who for the joy that was set before Him endured the cross. v. 2

The Scriptures tell us of an even more magnificent cross—the cross of Christ. When we look at the stars, we see the handiwork of the Creator; but when we look at the cross, we see the Creator dying for His creation. Hebrews 12:2 calls us to "[look] unto Jesus, the author and finisher of our faith, who for the joy that was set before Him endured the cross, despising the shame, and has sat down at the right hand of the throne of God."

The wonder of Calvary's cross is that while we were still in our sins, our Savior died for us (ROM. 5:8). Those who place their trust in Christ are now reconciled to God, and He navigates them through life (2 COR. 1:8-10). Christ's sacrifice on the cross is the greatest of all wonders! 🌱

BILL CROWDER

When I survey the wondrous cross
On which the Prince of glory died,
My richest gain I count but loss,
And pour contempt on all my pride. WATTS

Christ's cross provides the only safe crossing into eternity.

Better Than Planned

nterruptions are nothing new. Rarely does a day go by as planned.

Life is filled with inconveniences. Our plans are constantly thwarted by forces beyond our control. The list is long and ever-changing: Sickness. Conflict. Traffic jams. Forgetfulness. Appliance malfunctions. Rudeness. Laziness. Impatience. Incompetence.

What we cannot see, however, is the other side of inconvenience. We think it has no purpose other than to discourage us, make life more difficult, and thwart our plans. However, inconvenience could be God's way of protect-

TODAY'S READING
Ephesians 5:15-21

Giving thanks always for all things. v. 20

ing us from some unseen danger, or it could be an opportunity to demonstrate God's grace and forgiveness. It might be the start of something even better than we had planned. Or it could be a test to see how we respond to adversity. Whatever it is, even though we may not know God's reason, we can be assured of His motive—to make us more like Jesus and to further His kingdom on earth.

To say that God's followers throughout history have been "inconvenienced" would be an understatement. But God had a purpose. Knowing this, we can thank Him, being confident that He is giving us an opportunity to redeem the time (EPH. 5:16,20). 🌱   *JULIE ACKERMAN LINK*

Lord, so often it's the little things in life that get to me, and there seem to be so many of them. Whenever I'm tempted to lose my temper, blame someone, or just give up, help me see You.

What happens to us is not nearly as important as what God does in us and through us.

Great Expectations

once asked a counselor what the major issues were that brought people to him. Without hesitation he said, "The root of many problems is broken expectations; if not dealt with, they mature into anger and bitterness."

In our best moments, it's easy to expect that we will find ourselves in a good place surrounded by good people who like and affirm us. But life has a way of breaking those expectations. What then?

TODAY'S READING
Phil. 1:12-21

Christ will be magnified in my body, whether by life or by death. v. 20

Stuck in jail and beset by fellow believers in Rome who didn't like him (PHIL. 1:15-16), Paul remained surprisingly upbeat. As he saw it, God had given him a new mission field. While under house arrest, he witnessed to the guards about Christ, which sent the gospel into Caesar's house. And even though those opposing him were preaching the gospel from wrong motives, Christ was being preached, so Paul rejoiced (V. 18).

Paul never expected to be in a great place or to be well liked. His only expectation was that "Christ will be magnified" through him (V. 20). He wasn't disappointed.

If our expectation is to make Christ visible to those around us regardless of where we are or who we are with, we will find those expectations met and even exceeded. Christ will be magnified. 🌱

JOE STOWELL

Lord, forgive me for making my life all about what I expect and not about glorifying You regardless of my circumstances. May Your love, mercy, and justice be magnified through me today.

Make it your only expectation to magnify Christ wherever you are and whoever you are with.

Precious in God's Eyes

n response to the news that a mutual friend of ours had died, a wise brother who knew the Lord sent me these words, "Precious in the sight of the LORD is the death of His saints" (PS. 116:15). Our friend's vibrant faith in Jesus Christ was the dominant characteristic of his life, and we knew he was home with God in heaven.

His family had that assurance as well, but I had been focused only on their sorrow. And it's appropriate to consider others during their grief and loss.

TODAY'S READING
Psalm 116

Precious in the sight of the LORD is the death of His saints. v. 15

But the verse from Psalms turned my thoughts to how the Lord saw the passing of our friend. Something "precious" is something of great value. Yet, there is a larger meaning here. There is something in the death of a saint that transcends our grief over their absence.

"Precious (important and no light matter) in the sight of the Lord is the death of His saints (His loving ones)" (THE AMPLIFIED BIBLE). Another paraphrase says, "His loved ones are very precious to him and he does not lightly let them die" (THE LIVING BIBLE). God is not flippant toward death. The marvel of His grace and power is that, as believers, our loss of life on earth also brings great gain.

Today we have only a glimpse. One day we'll understand it in the fullness of His light. 🌱 *DAVID MCCASLAND*

So when my last breath
Shall rend the veil in twain
By death I shall escape from death
And life eternal gain. MONTGOMERY

Faith builds a bridge across the gulf of death.

Buyer's Remorse

Have you ever experienced buyer's remorse? I have. Just prior to making a purchase, I feel the surge of excitement that comes with getting something new. After buying the item, however, a wave of remorse sometimes crashes over me. Did I really need this? Should I have spent the money?

TODAY'S READING
Genesis 3:1-8

In Genesis 3, we find the first record of a buyer's remorse. The whole thing began with the crafty serpent and his sales pitch. He persuaded Eve to doubt God's Word (v. 1). He then capitalized on her uncertainty by casting doubt on God's character (vv. 4-5). He promised that her eyes would "be opened" and she would become "like God" (v. 5).

> He has clothed me with the garments of salvation, He has covered me with the robe of righteousness. Isa. 61:10

So Eve ate. Adam ate. And sin entered the world. But the first man and woman got more than they bargained for. Their eyes were opened all right, but they didn't become like God. In fact, their first act was to hide from God (vv. 7-8).

Sin has dire consequences. It always keeps us from God's best. But God in His mercy and grace clothed Adam and Eve in garments made from animal skins (v. 21)—foreshadowing what Jesus Christ would do for us by dying on the cross for our sins. His blood was shed so that we might be clothed with His righteousness—with no remorse! 🌿

POH FANG CHIA

Then will I set my heart to find
Inward adornings of the mind:
Knowledge and virtue, truth and grace,
These are the robes of richest dress. WATTS

**The cross, which reveals the righteousness of God,
provides that righteousness for mankind.**

Heard by God

After reading several children's books with my daughter, I told her that I was going to read a grown-up book for a while and then we would look at books together again. I opened the cover and began to read in silence. A few minutes later, she looked at me doubtfully and said, "Mommy, you aren't really reading." She assumed that since I wasn't speaking, I wasn't processing the words.

TODAY'S READING
1 Samuel 1:9-20

Hannah spoke in her heart; . . . her voice was not heard. v. 13

Like reading, prayer can be silent. Hannah, who longed for a child of her own, visited the temple and "spoke in her heart" as she prayed. Her lips were moving, but "her voice was not heard" (1 SAM. 1:13). Eli the priest saw but misunderstood what was happening. She explained, "I . . . have poured out my soul before the LORD" (V. 15). God heard Hannah's silent prayer request and gave her a son (V. 20).

Since God searches our hearts and minds (JER. 17:10), He sees and hears every prayer—even the ones that never escape our lips. His all-knowing nature makes it possible for us to pray with full confidence that He will hear and answer (MATT. 6:8,32). Because of this, we can continually praise God, ask Him for help, and thank Him for blessings—even when no one else can hear us. ❧

JENNIFER BENSON SCHULDT

Sweet hour of prayer! Sweet hour of prayer!
That calls me from a world of care,
And bids me at my Father's throne
Make all my wants and wishes known. WALFORD

God fills our heart with peace when we pour out our heart to Him.

Guidance Needed

St. Nicholas Church in Galway, Ireland, has both a long history and an active present. It's the oldest church in Ireland, and it provides guidance in a very practical way. The church towers over the town, and its steeple is used by ships' captains as a guide for navigating their way safely into Galway Bay. For centuries, this church has reliably pointed the way home for sailors.

TODAY'S READING
James 4:11-17

When He, the Spirit of truth, has come, He will guide you into all truth. John 16:13

We can all certainly identify with the need for guidance. In fact, Jesus addressed this very need during His Upper Room Discourse. He said that after His departure the Holy Spirit would play a crucial role in the lives of believers. As part of that role, Jesus promised, "When He, the Spirit of truth, has come, He will guide you into all truth" (JOHN 16:13).

What a marvelous provision! In a world of confusion and fear, guidance is often needed. We can easily be misdirected by the culture around us or by the brokenness within us (1 JOHN 2:15-17). God's Spirit, however, is here to help, to direct, and to guide. How thankful we can be that the Spirit of truth has come to give us the guidance that we often so desperately need. Set your course by His life, and you will reach safe harbor. 🌱

BILL CROWDER

Guide me, O Thou great Jehovah,
Pilgrim through this barren land.
I am weak, but Thou art mighty;
Hold me with Thy powerful hand. WILLIAMS

The Spirit is a reliable guide in all of life's seas.

Resolve to Resolve

haven't made any New Year's resolutions since 1975. I haven't needed any new ones—I'm still working on old ones like these: write at least a short note in my journal every day; make a strong effort to read my Bible and pray each day; organize my time; try to keep my room clean (this was before I had a whole house to keep clean).

This year, however, I am adding a new resolution that I found in Paul's letter to the Romans: "Let us not judge one another anymore, but rather resolve this, not to put a stumbling block or a cause to fall in our brother's way" (14:13). Although this resolution is old (about 2,000 years), it is one that we should renew annually. Like believers in Rome centuries ago, believers today sometimes make up rules for others to follow and insist on adherence to certain behaviors and beliefs that the Bible says little or nothing about. These "stumbling blocks" make it difficult for followers of Jesus to continue in the way of faith that He came to show us—that salvation is by grace, not works (GAL. 2:16). It requires only that we trust in His death and resurrection for forgiveness.

> TODAY'S READING
> **Romans 14:1-13**
>
> **Resolve this, not to put a stumbling block or a cause to fall in our brother's way.** v. 13

We can celebrate this good news of Christ in the coming year by resolving not to set up hurdles that cause people to stumble. ❧

JULIE ACKERMAN LINK

Thank You, Lord, that You sent the Holy Spirit to do the work of convincing and convicting. May I be content with my own assignment: to do what leads to peace and edification.

*Faith is the hand that receives God's gift,
then faith is the feet that walk with God.*

An Important Command

When asked to identify the most important rule in life, Jesus replied, "You shall love the LORD your God with all your heart, with all your soul, with all your mind, and with all your strength" (MARK 12:30). In those words, Jesus summed up what God most desires from us.

I wonder how I can possibly learn to love God with all my heart, soul, and mind. Neal Plantinga remarks on a subtle change in this commandment as recorded in the New Testament. Deuteronomy charges us to love God with all our heart, soul, and strength (6:5). Jesus added the word *mind*. Plantinga explains, "You shall love God with everything you have and everything you are. Everything."

TODAY'S READING
Mark 12:28-34

Love the LORD your God with all your heart, with all your soul, with all your mind, and with all your strength. v. 30

That helps us change our perspective. As we learn to love God with everything, we begin to see our difficulties as "our light and momentary troubles"—just as the apostle Paul described his grueling ordeals. He had in mind a "far more exceeding and eternal . . . glory" (2 COR. 4:17).

In the advanced school of prayer, where one loves God with the entire soul, doubts and struggles do not disappear, but their effect on us diminishes. "We love Him because He first loved us" (1 JOHN 4:19), and our urgent questions recede as we learn to trust His ultimate goodness. 🌱   *PHILIP YANCEY*

Once earthly joy I craved, sought peace and rest;
Now Thee alone I seek; give what is best.
This all my prayer shall be:
More love, O Christ, to Thee. PRENTISS

*The most treasured gift we can give to God is one that
He can never force us to give—our love.*

The Telltale Heart

Recently I read about a private investigator in the US who would knock on a door, show his badge to whoever answered, and say, "I guess we don't have to tell you why we're here." Many times, the person would look stunned and say, "How did you find out?" then go on to describe an undiscovered criminal act committed long ago. Writing in *Smithsonian* magazine, Ron Rosenbaum described the reaction as "an opening for the primal force of conscience, the telltale heart's internal monologue."

TODAY'S READING
1 John 3:16-24

If our heart condemns us, God is greater than our heart, and knows all things. v. 20

We all know things about ourselves that no one else knows—failures, faults, sins—that although confessed to God and forgiven by Him may come back to accuse us again and again. John, one of Jesus' close followers, wrote about God's love for us and the call to follow His commands, saying: "By this we know that we are of the truth, and shall assure our hearts before Him. For if our heart condemns us, God is greater than our heart, and knows all things" (1 JOHN 3:19-20).

Our confidence toward God grows out of His love and forgiveness in Christ, not our performance in life. "We know that He abides in us, by the Spirit whom He has given us" (V. 24).

God, who knows everything about us, is greater than our self-condemnation. 🌿

DAVID MCCASLAND

No condemnation now I dread,
I am my Lord's and He is mine;
Alive in Him, my living Head,
And clothed in righteousness divine. WESLEY

The one who receives Christ will never receive God's condemnation.

Before *and* After

What changes take place in a life of faith after severe testing? I thought of this as I read the tragic story of a Jamaican dad who accidentally shot and killed his 18-year-old daughter while trying to protect his family from intruders.

News reports said he went to church (as was his habit) the next day—distraught but still seeking God's help. Faith in God guided him before, and he knew God could sustain him after.

I thought about this in regard to my own life—having also lost a teenage daughter. To review how I viewed life and faith before Melissa's death, I dug into my computer archives to read the

TODAY'S READING
Psalm 55:1-8,16-17

Give ear to my prayer, O God . . . . My heart is . . . pained within me, and the terrors of death have fallen upon me. vv. 1,4

last article I had written before we lost her in June 2002. How would what I said then correspond to what I know now? Had severe testing changed my view of faith in God? In May of that year, I had written this: "David was not afraid to go boldly to God and tell Him what was on his heart. . . . We don't have to be afraid to tell God what is on our heart."

Before I went through tough times, I went to God and He listened to me. After, I discovered that He still listens and comforts and sustains. So I continue to pray in faith. Our faith remains intact and is strengthened because He is the God of the before *and* the after. 🌿   DAVE BRANON

God is still on the throne,
He never forsaketh His own;
His promise is true, He will not forget you,
God is still on the throne. SUFFIELD

What we know of God encourages us to trust Him in all we do not know.

Who's That Hero?

Reading the book of Judges, with its battles and mighty warriors, can sometimes feel like reading about comic book superheroes. We have Deborah, Barak, Gideon, and Samson. However, in the line of judges (or deliverers), we also find Othniel.

The account of his life is brief and straightforward (JUDGES 3:7-11). No drama. No display of prowess. But what we do see is what God did through Othniel: "The Lord raised up a deliverer" (V. 9), "the Spirit of the Lord came upon him" (V. 10), and "the Lord delivered Cushan-Rishathaim king of Mesopotamia into his hand" (V. 10).

TODAY'S READING
Judges 3:7-11

Let your light so shine before men, that they may see your good works and glorify your Father in heaven.

Matthew 5:16

The Othniel account helps us focus on what is most important—the activity of God. Interesting stories and fascinating people can obscure that. We end up concentrating on those and fail to see what the Lord is doing.

When I was young, I wished I could be more talented so that I could point more people to Christ. But I was looking at the wrong thing. God often uses ordinary people for His extraordinary work. It is His light shining through our lives that glorifies God and draws others to Him (MATT. 5:16).

When others look at our life, it is more important that they see God—not us. 🌑 *POH FANG CHIA*

> May the Word of God dwell richly
> In my heart from hour to hour,
> So that all may see I triumph
> Only through His power. WILKINSON

Our limited ability highlights God's limitless power.

Unintentional

When I was returning our grandson Alex to his family after a visit, the traffic seemed especially challenging. Fast-maneuvering cars blocked me from the correct toll lane, forcing me to go through a lane where only cars with a prepaid pass are permitted, which I didn't have. Alex told me that my license plate would be photographed and a ticket might be mailed to me. I was frustrated because a penalty would have to be paid even though my infraction was unintentional.

For the ancient Jews, a violation of God's laws committed even in ignorance was taken very seriously. The Old Testament recognized and provided for unintentional sins through appropriate sacrifices: "If a person sins unintentionally against any of the commandments . . . let him offer to the LORD . . . a young bull without blemish as a sin offering" (LEV. 4:2-3).

> TODAY'S READING
> **Leviticus 4:1-3;**
> **Romans 3:21-26**
>
> **If a person sins unintentionally . . . let him offer to the LORD . . . a young bull without blemish.** Lev. 4:2-3

Old Testament sacrifices were more than a reminder that accidental wrongs have consequences. They were given in anticipation that God in His grace would provide atonement even for wrongs we didn't realize we were doing. He did this through the death of Jesus in our place. God's grace is far greater than we could ever imagine! ✿   *DENNIS FISHER*

Grace, grace, God's grace,
Grace that will pardon and cleanse within;
Grace, grace, God's grace,
Grace that is greater than all our sin. JOHNSTON

Grace is getting what we do not deserve.
Mercy is not receiving what we do deserve.

Maintain Unity

A **man stranded by himself** on an island was finally discovered. His rescuers asked him about the three huts they saw there. He pointed and said, "This one is my home and that one is my church." He then pointed to the third hut: "That was my *former* church." Though we may laugh at the silliness of this story, it does highlight a concern about unity among believers.

TODAY'S READING
Ephesians 4:1-6

Endeavoring to keep the unity of the Spirit in the bond of peace. v. 3

The church of Ephesus during the time of the apostle Paul was comprised of both rich and poor, Jews and Gentiles, men and women, masters and slaves. And where differences exist, so does friction. One concern Paul wrote about was the issue of unity. But observe what Paul said about this issue in Ephesians 4:3. He didn't tell them to be "eager to produce or to organize unity." He told them to endeavor "to keep the unity of the Spirit in the bond of peace." Unity already exists because believers share one body, one Spirit, one hope, one Lord, one faith, one baptism, and one God and Father of all (VV. 4-6).

How do we "keep the unity"? By expressing our different opinions and convictions with lowliness, gentleness, and patience (V. 2). The Spirit will give us the power to react in love toward those with whom we disagree. 🌸 *ALBERT LEE*

Lord, may our walk and our service be a picture of the unity of Father, Son, and Spirit in heaven above. Fill us with the fruit of the Spirit that we might love others as You desire.

Unity among believers comes from our union with Christ.

The Power of Music

In Wales, the music of men's chorus groups is deeply engrained in the culture. Prior to World War II, one Welsh glee club had a friendly yet competitive rivalry with a German glee club, but that bond was replaced with animosity during and after the war. The tension was gradually overcome, though, by the message on the trophy shared by the two choruses: "Speak with me, and you're my friend. Sing with me, and you're my brother."

The power of music to heal and help is a gift from God that comforts many. Perhaps that is why the Psalms speak so deeply to us. There we find lyrics that connect with our hearts, allowing us to speak to God from the depth of our spirits. "But I will sing of Your power; yes, I will sing aloud of Your mercy in the morning; for You have been my defense and refuge in the day of my trouble" (PS. 59:16). Amazingly, David wrote this song as he was being hunted down by men seeking to kill him! Despite his circumstances, David remembered God's power and mercy, and singing of them encouraged him to go on.

May our God give us a song today that will remind us of His goodness and greatness, no matter what we may face. ❧

BILL CROWDER

> TODAY'S READING
> **Psalm 59:6-16**
>
> I will sing of Your power; yes, I will sing aloud of Your mercy in the morning; for You have been my defense and refuge in the day of my trouble. v. 16

This is my story, this is my song,
Praising my Savior all the day long;
This is my story, this is my song,
Praising my Savior all the day long. CROSBY

I will make music to the Lord, the God of Israel. JUDGES 5:3 (NLT)

Where Our Fears Live

Twelve years into our marriage, my wife and I were discouraged by the emotional roller-coaster of hopes raised and dashed in attempting to have children. A friend tried to "explain" God's thinking. "Maybe God knows you'd be a bad father," he said. He knew that my mother had struggled with a terrible temper.

Then, Christmas 1988, we learned we were expecting our first child! But now I had this nagging fear of failure.

TODAY'S READING
1 Kings 17:17-24

Whenever I am afraid, I will trust in You. Psalm 56:3

The following August, Kathryn joined our family. As nurses and doctors tended to my wife, Kathryn cried on the warming tray. I offered my hand to comfort her, and her tiny fingers wrapped around my finger. In that instant, the Holy Spirit swept through me, assuring me of what I had only recently doubted—that I would show love to this little one!

The widow of Zarephath also had doubts. Her son had been struck with a lethal illness. In her despair she cried out, "Have you come to me to bring my sin to remembrance, and to kill my son?" (1 KINGS 17:18). But God had other plans!

We serve a God who is mightier than the struggles we inherit and who is full of the desire to forgive, love, and heal the brokenness that rises up between us and Him. God is present in the places where our fears live. 🌱   *RANDY KILGORE*

Father, make Yourself known to us in our weakest moments and in our greatest fears. Teach us to receive Your love in a way that enables us to show it to others, especially those closest to us.

Love swims against the current of life's false fears.

Hyperseeing

Sculptors have a term for the artist's ability to look at a rough piece of stone and see it in its final, perfected form. It is called "hyperseeing."

Gutzon Borglum (1867–1941) is the sculptor who created many well-known public works of art. Probably the most famous is Mt. Rushmore National Memorial in South Dakota. Borglum's housekeeper captured the concept of hyperseeing when she gazed up at the massive faces of the four US presidents on Mt. Rushmore for the first time. "Mr. Borglum," she gasped, "how did you know Mr. Lincoln was in that rock?"

TODAY'S READING
Romans 8:28-30

When He is revealed, we shall be like Him. 1 John 3:2

Hyperseeing is also a good description of our all-seeing God. He sees all that we are and more. He sees what we shall be when He has completed His work and we stand before Him, holy and without blemish: the exact likeness, the very image of Jesus. The God who started this great work in you will keep at it until He completes it on the very day Jesus Christ appears (SEE PHIL. 1:6).

God will not be denied! He has such a longing for our perfection that nothing can or will remain an obstacle until He has finished the work He began so long ago.

If only . . . if only we will put ourselves in the Master Sculptor's hands. ❀

DAVID ROPER

> Doubt whispers, "Thou art such a blot;
> He cannot love poor thee."
> If what I am He lovest not,
> He loves what I shall be. MACDONALD

God works in us to grow us into what He wants us to be.

Character or Reputation?

egendary basketball coach John Wooden (1910–2010) believed that character is far more important than reputation. "Your reputation is what you're perceived to be by others," Coach Wooden often told his players, "but your character is what you really are. You're the only one that knows your character. You can fool others, but you can't fool yourself."

In the book of Revelation, we find the words of the risen Christ to seven churches in Asia. To the church in Sardis, Jesus said, "I know your works, that you have a name [reputation] that you are alive, but you are dead" (REV. 3:1). The Lord knew the truth about them, and no doubt deep down they knew it too. Jesus told them to wake up and strengthen the spiritual life inside them that was about to die (V. 2). He urged them to remember the truth they had received, obey it, then turn around and start moving in a new direction (V. 3).

> **TODAY'S READING**
> **Revelation 3:1-6**
>
> **You have a name that you are alive, but you are dead.** v. 1

When the Lord shows us what's wrong in our lives, He always provides a remedy for change. When we turn from our sins, He forgives and strengthens us to start over.

How liberating to exchange a false spiritual reputation for the true, life-giving character that comes from knowing Christ our Lord! 🌱

DAVID MCCASLAND

Men talk too much of gold and fame,
And not enough about a name;
And yet a good name's better far
Than all earth's glistening jewels are. GUEST

The true test of our character is what we do when no one is watching.

True Love

During the rehearsal for my brother's wedding ceremony, my husband snapped a picture of the bride and groom as they faced each other in front of the pastor. When we looked at the photograph later, we noticed that the camera's flash had illuminated a metal cross in the background, which appeared as a glowing image above the couple.

The photograph reminded me that marriage is a picture of Christ's love for the church as shown on the cross. When the Bible instructs husbands to love their wives (EPH. 5:25), God compares that kind of faithful, selfless affection to Christ's love for His followers. Because Christ sacrificed His life for the sake of love, we are all to love each other (1 JOHN 4:10-11). He died in our place, so that our sin would not keep us separate from God for eternity. He lived out His words to the disciples: "Greater love has no one than this, than to lay down one's life for his friends" (JOHN 15:13).

> TODAY'S READING
> **John 15:9-17**
>
> **Greater love has no one than this, than to lay down one's life for his friends.** v. 13

Many of us suffer from the pain of abandonment, rejection, and betrayal. Despite all of this, through Christ we can understand the sacrificial, compassionate, and enduring nature of true love. Today, remember that you are loved by God. Jesus said so with His life. 🌀 *JENNIFER BENSON SCHULDT*

Love divine, so great and wondrous,
Deep and mighty, pure, sublime!
Coming from the heart of Jesus—
Just the same through tests of time. BLOM

Nothing speaks more clearly of God's love than the cross of Jesus.

The Great Creator-Healer

A **few years ago,** I had a rather serious skiing accident and severely tore the muscles in one of my legs. In fact, my doctor told me that the tear caused excessive bleeding. The healing process was slow, but during that time of waiting I found myself in awe of our great Creator (SEE COL. 1:16).

I've wrinkled a few car fenders in my lifetime and dropped more than one dish. They've always stayed broken. Not so with my leg. As soon as the tearing of my muscles occurred, the internal healing mechanisms that Christ created in my body went to work. Invisibly, down

TODAY'S READING
Psalm 139:1-16

I will praise You, for I am fearfully and wonderfully made. v. 14

deep in my throbbing leg, the medics of His marvelous design were mending the tear. Before long, I was up and running again with a whole new sense of what the psalmist meant when he said that we are "fearfully and wonderfully made," and my heart was filled with praise (PS. 139:14).

Sometimes it takes something like an injury or a sickness to remind us of the masterful design that we carry around in our bodies. So the next time you face an unwanted interruption—no matter its cause—focus your attention on Jesus' wonderful love and let Him lift your heart to grateful worship in the midst of the pain! ❧

JOE STOWELL

Lord, help us to see beyond the moments of our lives
and to delve deeply into Your marvelous handiwork
and perfect design. Forgive us for our short-sightedness
and teach us to see You in every circumstance.

Worship of the masterful Creator begins with a grateful heart.

Why Cause Grief?

Pastors make an easy target for criticism. Every week they are on display, carefully explaining God's Word, challenging us toward Christlike living. But sometimes we look to find things to criticize. It's easy to overlook all the good things a pastor does and focus on our personal opinions.

Like all of us, our pastors are not perfect. So I'm not saying that we should follow them blindly and never confront error through the proper channels. But some words from the writer of Hebrews may help us find the right way of thinking about our leaders

> **TODAY'S READING**
> **Hebrews 13:17-19**
>
> Obey those who rule over you, . . . for they watch out for your souls. v. 17

who are presenting God's truth and modeling servant leadership. The writer says, "Have confidence in your leaders and submit to their authority, because they keep watch over you as those who must give an account" (13:17 NIV).

Think about that. Before God, our pastor is responsible for guiding us spiritually. We should want that burden to be joyous, not grievous. The passage indicates that causing grief for the pastor "would be of no benefit" (V. 17 NIV).

We honor God and make things better for our church when we give honor to those He has appointed as our leaders. 🌱

DAVE BRANON

Our gracious Father, thank You for the person You led to our church as pastor. May we provide encouragement and support, and may You protect our pastor from error in both word and actions.

Pastors who preach God's Word need a good word from God's people.

On Listening

God gave you two ears** and one mouth for a reason," the saying goes. The ability to listen is an essential life skill. Counselors tell us to listen to each other. Spiritual leaders tell us to listen to God. But hardly anyone says, "Listen to yourself." I'm not suggesting that we have an inner voice that always knows the right thing to say. Nor am I saying we should listen to ourselves instead of to God and others. I'm suggesting that we need to listen to ourselves in order to learn how others might be receiving our words.

TODAY'S READING
Exodus 16:1-8

Do not be rash with your mouth, and let not your heart utter anything hastily before God. Eccl. 5:2

The Israelites could have used this advice when Moses was leading them out of Egypt. Within days of their miraculous deliverance, they were complaining (EX. 16:2). Although their need for food was legitimate, their way of expressing the need was not (V. 3).

Whenever we speak out of fear, anger, ignorance, or pride—even if what we say is true—those who listen will hear more than our words. They hear emotion. But they don't know whether the emotion comes from love and concern or disdain and disrespect, so we risk misunderstanding. If we listen to ourselves before speaking out loud, we can judge our hearts before our careless words harm others or sadden our God. 🌿

JULIE ACKERMAN LINK

Lord, help me to think before I speak, to check my heart.
Help me to control my tongue and to express myself clearly
so that I won't cause dissension. Set a guard on my lips.

Words spoken rashly do more harm than good.

Helpers Needed

To some people, the term *helper* carries with it second-class connotations. Classroom helpers assist trained teachers in their classes. Helpers assist trained electricians, plumbers, and lawyers on the job. Because they aren't as skilled in the profession, they might be viewed as having less value. But everyone is needed to accomplish the task.

TODAY'S READING
Romans 16:1-16

The Helper, the Holy Spirit, . . . will teach you all things. John 14:26

The apostle Paul had many helpers in his work of ministry. He listed them in his letter to Rome (CH. 16). He made special reference to Phoebe, who "has been a helper of many and of myself also" (V. 2). Priscilla and Aquila risked their own lives for Paul (VV. 3-4). And Mary, Paul said, "labored much for us" (V. 6).

Helping is a spiritual gift, according to 1 Corinthians 12:28. Paul listed it among the gifts from the Holy Spirit that are given to believers in Christ's body, the church. The gift of "helps" is just as needed as the others that are listed.

Even the Holy Spirit is called a "Helper." Jesus said, "The Helper, the Holy Spirit, . . . will teach you all things, and bring to your remembrance all things that I said to you" (JOHN 14:26).

In whatever ways the Holy Spirit, the Helper, has gifted you, let Him use you for His honor. 🌼

ANNE CETAS

Dear Lord, thank You for the gifts You have
given me so that I might serve the
body of Christ. Help me to be faithful to use
my gifts to bring You glory.

You are a necessary part of the whole.

The Eleventh Hour

World War I has been ranked by many as one of the deadliest conflicts in human history. Millions lost their lives in the first global modern war. On November 11, 1918, a ceasefire was observed on the eleventh hour of the eleventh day of the eleventh month. During that historic moment, millions around the world observed moments of silence while they reflected upon the war's terrible cost—the loss of life and suffering. It was hoped that "the Great War," as it was called, would truly be "the war that would end all wars."

> TODAY'S READING
> **Matthew 24:3-14**
>
> **Nation shall not lift up sword against nation, neither shall they learn war anymore.** Isaiah 2:4

Despite the many deadly military conflicts that have followed, the hope for lasting peace has not faded. And the Bible offers a hopeful and realistic promise that someday wars will finally end. When Christ returns, Isaiah's prophecy will come true: "Nation shall not lift up sword against nation, neither shall they learn war anymore" (ISA. 2:4). Then the eleventh hour will pass and the first hour of lasting peace in a new heaven and new earth will begin.

Until that day comes, those who follow Christ are to be people who represent the Prince of Peace in the way we conduct our lives and in the way we make a difference in our world. 🌿

DENNIS FISHER

Peace, perfect peace, in this dark world of sin?
The blood of Jesus whispers peace within....
Peace, perfect peace, our future all unknown?
Jesus we know, and He is on the throne. BICKERSTETH

Only in Christ can true peace be realized.

Covering Sinkholes

n late May 2010, tropical storm Agatha hit Central America, producing torrential rains and landslides. Once it finished its course, a 200-foot-deep sinkhole opened in downtown Guatemala City. This sinkhole caused the ground to collapse suddenly, sucking land, electrical poles, and a 3-story building into the depths of the earth.

TODAY'S READING
Psalm 32:1-5

Blessed is he whose transgression is forgiven, whose sin is covered. v. 1

Though sinkholes can be devastating, the most universal and damaging sinkhole is the one that happens in the human heart. King David was an example of this.

The surface of David's life looked stable; however, his interior life rested on a fragile foundation. After his sins of adultery and murder, David thought he had successfully hidden his treacherous acts (2 SAM. 11–12). However, God's intense conviction after Nathan's confrontation caused him to realize that denying the presence of sin in his life weakened the foundation of his spiritual life. To prevent this spiritual sinkhole from worsening, David acknowledged his sin to God in repentance (PS. 32:5). As a result, God covered David's sin and gave him the joy of forgiveness.

We too will experience God's grace when we confess our sins to Him. He will completely forgive and cover our spiritual sinkholes. ❧

MARVIN WILLIAMS

THINKING IT OVER

What habitual sins, secret addictions, or hidden vulnerabilities are weakening your interior life? Remember, God longs to give you complete forgiveness.

When we uncover our sins in repentance, God will cover them.

Tell It on the Mountain

was surprised to see a nationally distributed news article commending a group of teenage snowboarders who hold weekly church services on a Colorado ski slope. In the *Summit Daily News*, Kimberly Nicoletti's story captured a wide audience with her account of teens who love to snowboard and to tell how Jesus changed their lives. Undergirding the teenagers is a Christian youth organization equipping them to demonstrate God's love.

TODAY'S READING
Mark 3:1-15

He went up on the mountain and called to Him those He Himself wanted. And they came to Him. v. 13

It's easier to do things yourself than to train others, yet Jesus poured Himself into a dozen disciples through whom His work would reach the world. In the midst of the pressing need of people clamoring to be healed, He climbed a mountain where "He appointed twelve, that they might be with Him and that He might send them out" (MARK 3:14).

One of those snowboarders in Colorado said of her discipleship training: "I've never been able to build relationships with family or friends; I've kept them at arm's length. [The program] showed me God's love. It opened me to reach out to people."

Experiencing Jesus' love and being in company with Him and His followers, we find courage to act and speak in ways that honor our Lord. 🌼

DAVID MCCASLAND

Let us go forth, as called of God,
Redeemed by Jesus' precious blood;
His love to show, His life to live,
His message speak, His mercy give. WHITTLE

Witnessing isn't a job to be done but a life to be lived.

Bolt on Blake

Usain **Bolt** and **Yohan Blake** of Jamaica made history when they finished first and second respectively in both the men's 100-meter and 200-meter race in the 2012 London Olympics. Despite their rivalry on the track, Bolt paid tribute to Blake as a training partner: "Over the years, Yohan has made me a better athlete. He really pushed me and kept me on my toes." It's clear that the two spurred each other on to greatness on the track.

TODAY'S READING
Hebrews 10:19-25

Let us consider one another in order to stir up love and good works. v. 24

As believers in Christ, we have the privilege and responsibility of encouraging one another in our faith. The writer of Hebrews said, "Let us consider one another in order to stir up love and good works" (HEB. 10:24).

The church is not just an institution or a mere social club. It is where we, who have been brought near to God and washed from sin, can help one another grow in Christlikeness. The purpose of meeting together as a corporate body is to exhort and encourage one another (VV. 19-25).

No believer can function alone. To live as our Lord Jesus wants us to, we need the community of believers. As you meet with other believers, think of who you can come alongside and encourage by your words and actions to be more like the Christ we love and serve. ❀

C. P. HIA

Before our Father's throne
We pour our ardent prayers;
Our fears, our hopes, our aims are one,
Our comforts and our cares. FAWCETT

A healthy church is the best witness to a hurting world.

Limitless Love

Recently, a friend sent me the history of a hymn that I often heard in church when I was a boy:

Could we with ink the ocean fill,
And were the skies of parchment made,
Were every stalk on earth a quill,
And every man a scribe by trade;
To write the love of God above
Would drain the ocean dry;
Nor could the scroll contain the whole
Though stretched from sky to sky.

TODAY'S READING
Psalm 36

Your mercy, O LORD, is in the heavens; Your faithfulness reaches to the clouds. v. 5

These words are part of an ancient Jewish poem and were once found on the wall of a patient's room in an insane asylum.

Also, Frederick M. Lehman was so moved by the poem that he desired to expand on it. In 1917, while seated on a lemon box during his lunch break from his job as a laborer, he added the words of the first two stanzas and the chorus, completing the song "The Love of God."

The psalmist describes the comforting assurance of God's love in Psalm 36: "Your steadfast love, O LORD, extends to the heavens" (V. 5 ESV). Regardless of the circumstances of life—whether in a moment of sanity in a mind otherwise muddled with confusion or during a dark time of trial—God's love is a beacon of hope, our ever-present, inexhaustible source of strength and confidence. ❧

JOE STOWELL

Oh love of God, how rich and pure!
How measureless and strong!
It shall forevermore endure,
The saints' and angels' song. LEHMAN

You are loved with everlasting love.

Empty Fort Strategy

In the Chinese historical novel *Romance of the Three Kingdoms*, author Luo Guanzhong describes the "Empty Fort Strategy," a use of reverse psychology to deceive the enemy. When 150,000 troops from the Wei Kingdom reached Xicheng, which had less than 2,500 soldiers, they found the city gate wide open and the famous military tactician Zhuge Liang calmly playing the zither with two children beside him. The Wei general, baffled by the scene and believing it was an ambush, ordered a full retreat.

> **TODAY'S READING**
> **Judges 7:2-8**
>
> **Behold, I am the LORD, the God of all flesh. Is there anything too hard for Me?** Jeremiah 32:27

The Bible offers another example of a bewildering battle strategy. In Judges 7, God had Gideon use 300 men, horns, jars, and blazing torches against armies that were "as numerous as locusts; and their camels were without number" (V. 12).

Could Israel defeat such a formidable foe? It was humanly impossible! They had neither the manpower nor the military hardware. But they had one thing that worked for them and that was all they needed. They had God's promise: "With these 300 men I will rescue you and give you victory" (V. 7 NLT). The result? Victory!

Are you facing a formidable challenge? The Lord has said, "Behold, I am the Lord, the God of all flesh. Is there anything too hard for Me?" (JER. 32:27). 🌿   *POH FANG CHIA*

Be strong in the Lord and be of good courage;
Your mighty Defender is always the same.
Mount up with wings, as the eagle ascending;
Victory is sure when you call on His name. JOHNSON

With God, all things are possible.

"Lie Down"

Our golden retriever can get so overly excited that he will go into a seizure. To prevent that from happening, we try to calm him. We stroke him, speak to him in a soothing voice, and tell him to lie down. But when he hears "lie down," he avoids eye contact with us and starts complaining. Finally, with a dramatic sigh of resignation, he gives in and plops to the floor.

Sometimes we too need to be reminded to lie down. In Psalm 23, we learn that our Good Shepherd makes us "lie down in green pastures" and leads us "beside the still waters." He knows that we need the calm and rest that these provide, even when we don't realize it ourselves.

TODAY'S READING
Exodus 20:8-11

He makes me to lie down in green pastures; He leads me beside the still waters. He restores my soul. Psalm 23:2-3

Our bodies are designed to have regular rest. God Himself rested on the seventh day after His work of creation (GEN. 2:2-3; EX. 20:9-11). Jesus knew there was a time to minister to the crowds and a time to rest. He instructed His disciples to "come aside . . . and rest a while" (MARK 6:31). When we rest, we refocus and are refreshed. When we are filling every hour with activity—even with worthwhile things— God often gets our attention by making us "lie down."

Rest is a gift—a *good* gift from our Creator who knows exactly what we need. Praise Him that He sometimes makes us "lie down in green pastures." ❧

CINDY HESS KASPER

Heavenly Father, thank You for Your care for our well-being in every area of our lives. Help us to be rested and refreshed in You.

If we don't come apart and rest awhile, we may just plain come apart!

HAVNER

The Power of Love

Books on leadership often appear on best-seller lists. Most of them tell how to become a powerful and effective leader. But Henri Nouwen's book *In the Name of Jesus: Reflections on Christian Leadership* is written from a different perspective. The former university professor who spent many years serving in a community of developmentally disabled adults says: "The question is not: How many people take you seriously? How much are you going to accomplish? Can you show some results? But: Are you in love with Jesus? . . . In our world of loneliness and despair, there is an enormous need for men and women who know the heart of God, a heart that forgives, that cares, that reaches out and wants to heal."

> TODAY'S READING
> **1 John 4:7-10**
>
> **In this is love, not that we loved God, but that He loved us and sent His Son to be the [atoning sacrifice] for our sins.** v. 10

John wrote, "In this the love of God was manifested toward us, that God has sent His only begotten Son into the world, that we might live through Him. In this is love, not that we loved God, but that He loved us and sent His Son to be the [atoning sacrifice] for our sins" (1 JOHN 4:9-10).

"The Christian leader of the future," writes Nouwen, "is the one who truly knows the heart of God as it has become flesh . . . in Jesus." In Him, we discover and experience God's unconditional, unlimited love. ❧

DAVID McCASLAND

Father, please show the wonder of Your great love
through me to others today so that they might know
they need not walk through life alone. Let my heart
personally experience and display Your care.

God's love in our heart gives us a heart for others.

Consider the Lilies

enjoy nature and giving praise to its Creator, but I sometimes wrongly feel guilty for admiring it too much. Then I remember that Jesus used nature as a teaching tool. To encourage people not to worry, He used simple wildflowers as an example. "Consider the lilies," He said, and then reminded people that even though flowers do no work at all, God dresses them in splendor. His conclusion? If God clothes something temporary in such glory, He surely will do much more for us (MATT. 6:28-34).

TODAY'S READING
Psalm 19:1-6

The heavens declare the glory of God; and the firmament shows His handiwork. v. 1

Other portions of Scripture indicate that creation is one of the ways God uses to tell us about Himself:

"The heavens declare the glory of God; and the firmament shows His handiwork," wrote David. "Day unto day utters speech, and night unto night reveals knowledge" (PS. 19:1-2).

"Let the heavens declare His righteousness, for God Himself is Judge," Asaph said (50:6).

And Paul wrote, "For since the creation of the world His invisible attributes are clearly seen, being understood by the things that are made, even His eternal power and Godhead, so that they are without excuse" (ROM. 1:20).

God so loves us and wants us to know Him that He put evidence of Himself everywhere we look. 🍃 *JULIE ACKERMAN LINK*

Father, Your love is overwhelmingly evident, yet so often we miss it. Thank You for the unfailing reminders of Your grace, love, and mercy. Give us eyes to see Your beauty in Your creation.

In God's pattern book of nature we can trace many valuable lessons.

Big Spring

n Michigan's Upper Peninsula is a remarkable natural wonder—a pool about 40 feet deep and 300 feet across that
Native Americans called "Kitch-iti-kipi," or "the big cold
water." Today it is known as The Big Spring. It is fed by
underground springs that push more than 10,000 gallons of
water a minute through the rocks below
and up to the surface. Additionally, the
water keeps a constant temperature of
45 degrees Fahrenheit, meaning that
even in the brutally cold winters of the
Upper Peninsula the pool never freezes.
Tourists can enjoy viewing the waters of
Big Spring during any season of the year.

When Jesus encountered a woman
at Jacob's well, He talked to her about
another source of water that would always satisfy. But He did
not speak of a fountain, spring, river, or lake. He said,
"Whoever drinks of the water that I shall give him will never
thirst. But the water that I shall give him will become in him
a fountain of water springing up into everlasting life" (JOHN 4:14).

Far greater than any natural spring is the refreshment
we have been offered in Christ Himself. We can be satisfied,
for Jesus alone, the Water of Life, can quench our thirst.
Praise God, for Jesus is the source that never runs dry. 🌿

TODAY'S READING
John 4:7-14

**The water that I
shall give him will
become in him a
fountain of water
springing up into
everlasting life.** v. 14

BILL CROWDER

Father, it seems that I drink far too often from the waters of
the world that cannot satisfy. Forgive me, and teach me to
find in Christ the water that can quench the thirst of my heart
and draw me ever closer to You.

The only real thirst-quencher is Jesus—the living water.

On Eagles' Wings

saiah's words about patiently waiting for the Lord anticipate the future with confident hope. From our place of
trial, we wait for salvation that is certain to come. Jesus
assured His followers, "Blessed are those who mourn, for
they shall be comforted" (MATT. 5:4).

Knowing that our destiny is glorious, which is the sure hope of heaven,
we're able to pick up our pace here on
earth. Though weary, we can stretch the
wings of our faith and fly! We can walk
the path of obedience and not get tired.
We can move through routine days and
not grow weary. A better world is coming, when our spirits will call us to
action and our bodies will run and leap
and fly! This is our hope.

> TODAY'S READING
> **Isaiah 40:27-31**
>
> **Those who wait
> on the LORD shall
> renew their
> strength; they
> shall mount up
> with wings like
> eagles.** v. 31

In the meantime, what will be true one day can begin to
be true now. We can be steadfast, patient, and joyful in spite
of deep weariness; kind and calm, less focused on our frailty
and fatigue; more concerned about others than we are about
ourselves; ready to speak a loving word to those who are
struggling. We can get ready now for the day our souls will
take flight. 🌱   *DAVID ROPER*

> I am a little weary of my life—
> Not Thy life, blessed Father! Or the blood
> Too slowly laves the coral shores of thought,
> Or I am weary of weariness and strife.
> Open my soul-gates to Thy living flood;
> I ask not larger heart-throbs, vigor-fraught,
> I pray Thy presence, with strong patience rife. MACDONALD

When you're weary in life's struggles, find your rest in the Lord.

THE BIBLE in ONE YEAR
Numbers 23–25 and Mark 7:14-37

Sunrise

There was a magnificent sunrise this morning, but I was too busy to enjoy it. I turned away and became preoccupied with other things. I thought about that sunrise a few moments ago, and I realize I lost an opportunity for worship this morning.

In the midst of the busyness and stresses of our days, there are patches of beauty all around us, glimpses of God's goodness that we catch here and there along the way. These are the places in the walls of the universe where heaven is breaking through—if only we will take the time to stop and to reflect upon God's love for us.

TODAY'S READING
Exodus 3:1-12
Psalm 119:18

Then Moses said, "I will now turn aside and see this great sight." Exodus 3:3

What if Moses had taken only a fleeting glance at the bush that was burning but "was not consumed"? (EX. 3:2). What if he had ignored it and hurried on to other things? (He had those sheep to take care of, you know, and important work to do.) He would have missed an epic, life-changing encounter with the living God (VV. 4-12).

Sometimes in life we must hurry. But overall, life should be less hurrying and more noticing. Life is the present. Life is being aware; it is seeing God's love breaking through. It is turning aside to the miracle of something like a sunrise. Something transitory, yet symbolic of the eternity that awaits us. 🌿

DAVID ROPER

Open my eyes, that I may see
Glimpses of truth Thou hast for me;
Place in my hands the wonderful key
That shall unclasp and set me free. SCOTT

Lord, open our eyes that we may see.

Jesus' Love for All

t was a bit unusual, but three times in one day I heard the same song. In the early afternoon, I attended a hymnsing at a home for the elderly. As part of her prayer at the end of our time together, Willie, one of the residents, said, "Sing with me, 'Jesus Loves Me.'" In the evening, I attended a gathering with young people who sang it while pounding out the beat with their hands and feet. Later that evening, I received a text message on my phone with an audio recording of my 2 1/2-year-old grand-niece with a sweet little voice, singing, "I am weak, but He is strong." People in their nineties, teenagers, and a toddler all sang that song that day.

> **TODAY'S READING**
> **John 19:17-24**
>
> **He, bearing His cross, went out to a place called the Place of a Skull, . . . where they crucified Him.** vv. 17-18

After hearing that simple song three times, I began to think the Lord might be telling me something. Actually, He gave us all this message long ago: "I love you." We read in John 19 that He allowed people to put a crown of thorns on His head, mock Him, strike Him, strip Him, and crucify Him (VV. 1-6). He had the power to stop them, but He said very little (V. 11). He did it all for love's sake to pay for our sins and to rescue us from punishment.

How much does God love us? Jesus spread out His arms and was nailed to the cross. He died for us, then rose again. That's a precious fact for young and old. 🌱   *ANNE CETAS*

> Jesus loves me! This I know,
> For the Bible tells me so;
> Little ones to Him belong;
> They are weak but He is strong. WARNER

The truest measure of God's love is that He loves without measure!

BERNARD OF CLAIRVAUX

Instant Gratification

When the Polaroid SX-70 camera was introduced in 1972, it revolutionized photography. An article by Owen Edward in *Smithsonian* magazine described the camera as "a miracle of physics, optics and electronics." When a photo was snapped, "a blank square would emerge from the front of the camera and develop before our eyes." People were sold on speedy, immediate results.

TODAY'S READING
Psalm 27:4-14

Wait on the LORD; be of good courage, and He shall strengthen your heart. v. 14

Oswald Chambers saw a strong connection between our desire for the immediate and lust: "Lust simply means, 'I must have this at once'; it may be a bodily appetite or a spiritual possession. . . . I cannot wait for God's time, God is too indifferent; that is the way lust works."

In Psalm 27, David wrote of his waiting on God during a time of great trouble when there was no solution in sight. Instead of giving in to despair, he maintained his confidence that he would "see the goodness of the LORD in the land of the living" (V. 13).

We live in a world that worships the immediate. When it seems there is no sign of our deepest longings being fulfilled, the psalmist urges us to cling to the eternal God. "Wait on the LORD; be of good courage, and He shall strengthen your heart; wait, I say, on the LORD!" (V. 14). 🌸   DAVID MCCASLAND

> Help me, O Lord, to be content! My lips to seal,
> To every vain desire, each whim—instead to kneel,
> Acknowledging Thee, Lord and King, and in that place
> To kneel, to pray, to wait until I see Thy face! ADAMS

The answer to our craving for the immediate is to focus on the eternal.

No More Prejudice

A 2010 survey by *Newsweek* contained some startling statistics: 57 percent of hiring managers believe an unattractive (but qualified) job candidate would have a harder time getting hired; 84 percent of managers said their bosses would hesitate before hiring a qualified older candidate; 64 percent of hiring managers said they believe companies should be allowed to hire people based on appearance. All are clear examples of unacceptable prejudice.

> TODAY'S READING
> **James 2:1-10**
>
> **My brethren, do not hold the faith of our Lord Jesus Christ, the Lord of glory, with partiality.** v. 1

Prejudice is not new. It had crept into the early church, and James confronted it head-on. With prophetic grit and a pastor's heart, he wrote: "My brethren, do not hold the faith of our Lord Jesus Christ, the Lord of glory, with partiality" (JAMES 2:1). James gave an example of this type of prejudice—favoring the rich and ignoring the poor (VV. 2-4). This was inconsistent with holding faith in Jesus without partiality (V. 1), betrayed the grace of God (VV. 5-7), violated the law of love (V. 8), and was sinful (V. 9). The answer to partiality is following the example of Jesus: loving your neighbor as yourself.

We fight the sin of prejudice when we let God's love for us find full expression in the way we love and treat each other. 🌠

MARVIN WILLIAMS

THINKING IT OVER
Who helped you determine what is the right way to
treat people? Was it based on external things?
What are some ways you can love people as Jesus did?

Looking up to Jesus prevents us from looking down on others.

Me and Dad

A **friend once spent a day** installing large stone steps in his backyard. When his 5-year-old daughter begged to help, he suggested she just sing to encourage him in his work. She said no. She wanted to *help*. Carefully, when it would not endanger her, he let her place her hands on the rocks as he moved them.

He could have built the steps in less time without her. At the end of the day, though, he not only had new steps but also a daughter bursting with pride. "Me and Dad made steps," she announced at dinner that night.

From the beginning, God has relied on people to advance His work. After equipping Adam to cultivate the land and supervise the animals, God left the work of the garden in his hands (GEN. 2:15-20).

> TODAY'S READING
> **Matthew 9:35–10:1**
>
> **The LORD God took the man and put him in the garden of Eden to tend and keep it.**
>
> Genesis 2:15

The pattern has continued. When God wanted a dwelling place on earth, a tabernacle and temple did not descend from the sky; thousands of artists and craftsmen worked to fashion them (EX. 35–38; 1 KINGS 6). When Jesus proclaimed the new reign of God's kingdom on earth, He invited human beings to help. He told His disciples, "Pray the Lord of the harvest to send out laborers into His harvest" (MATT. 9:38).

As a father does with his children, so does God welcome us as His kingdom partners. 🌸

PHILIP YANCEY

Heavenly Father, thank You that in Your love and wisdom, You invite us to accomplish Your acts of love, service, and kindness here on earth. Thank You for the privilege of "helping" You.

God uses humble servants to accomplish His great work.

Boo!

One of the early games that many parents play with their children involves a fake scare. Dad hides his face behind his hands and suddenly reveals himself while saying, "Boo!" The child giggles at this silliness.

Being frightened is a fun game until the day when the child experiences a real scare. Then it's no laughing matter.

The first real scare often involves separation from a parent. The child wanders away innocently, moving from one attraction to another. But as soon as she realizes she is lost, she panics and lets out a loud cry of alarm. The parent immediately comes running to reassure the child that she is not alone.

> **TODAY'S READING**
> **Isaiah 30:1-5,18-19**
>
> [God] will be very gracious to you at the sound of your cry; when He hears it, He will answer you. v. 19

As we get older, our fake scares become sophisticated—scary books, movies, amusement park rides. Being scared is so invigorating that we may begin taking bigger risks for bigger thrills.

But when a real scare comes, we may realize that we, like the ancient Israelites (ISA. 30), have wandered from the One who loves and cares for us. Recognizing that we are in danger, we panic. Our call for help does not require sophisticated words or a well-reasoned defense, just a desperate cry.

Like a loving parent, God responds quickly for He longs to have us live in the protection of His love where we need never be afraid. ❧

JULIE ACKERMAN LINK

I never walk alone, Christ walks beside me;
He is the dearest Friend I've ever known;
With such a Friend to comfort and to guide me,
I never, no, I never walk alone. ACKLEY

Trusting God's faithfulness helps dispel our fearfulness.

Not Lost in Translation

Over the years, I've had the opportunity to teach the Bible to many people around the world. Because I can speak only English, I often work with interpreters who can take the words of my heart and translate them into the language of the people. Effective communication is directly dependent upon the skill of these translators. Whether it is Inawaty in Indonesia, Annie in Malaysia, or Jean in Brazil, they ensure that the meaning of my words is clearly expressed.

TODAY'S READING
Romans 8:19-27

[The Spirit] makes intercession for the saints according to the will of God. v. 27

This work of translation resembles one facet of the work of the Holy Spirit in the life of God's people. In our times of prayer, we don't always know how we should pray (ROM. 8:26), and verse 27 encourages us, saying, "Now He who searches the hearts knows what the mind of the Spirit is, because He makes intercession for the saints according to the will of God." When we go to our heavenly Father in prayer, the Holy Spirit comes to our aid by translating our prayers according to God's good purposes for our lives.

What a provision! Not only does God desire for us to share our hearts with Him, He even provides us with the greatest interpreter to help us as we pray. We can be sure that our prayers will never get lost in translation. 🌱   *BILL CROWDER*

Thank You, Father, for the provision of Your Spirit.
I'm grateful that when I pray I can rest in Your help to
make my prayers what they need to be. Teach me to
lean on His perfect understanding of Your desires.

*The participation of the Spirit assures that my prayers
line up with God's purposes.*

Transforming Power

Many people love to play games that test their knowledge. Recently, a colleague and I were testing a Bible-knowledge game. Since we were seated in an open area of our office, those nearby could hear our conversation. Soon questions ranging from Noah's ark to the woman at the well were being answered by those within earshot of us. It was a delight to hear various staff members volunteering responses to Bible questions.

TODAY'S READING
Deuteronomy 6:4-9

These words which I command you today shall be in your heart. v. 6

A knowledge of the Bible is important, but God desires us to be saturated with His Word and to internalize it so we can grow in our relationship with Him. The Holy Spirit uses the Word to make us more like Christ (EPH. 4:20-24). Consider these benefits of internalizing the Bible: joy and rejoicing (JER. 15:16); spiritual success (JOSH. 1:8); a tool in spiritual warfare (MATT. 4:1-11); correction (2 TIM. 3:15-16); light for our path (PS. 119:105); wisdom with problem solving (PROV. 1:1-2); and stimulating faith (ROM. 10:17).

Learning about the Bible just to increase our knowledge can lead to spiritual pride (1 COR. 8:1). But allowing the Holy Spirit to transform us by the Word helps us navigate through life's twists and turns and respond in love to God and to each other. 🌿 *DENNIS FISHER*

My hunger for the truth He satisfies;
Upon the Word, the Living Bread, I feed:
No parching thirst I know, because His grace,
A pool of endless depth, supplies my need. SANDERS

Many books can inform, but only the Bible can transform.

Dressed to Deceive

Hiking in the mountains of Utah, Coty Creighton spotted a goat that didn't look like the rest of the herd. A closer look revealed that the unusual animal was actually a man dressed as a goat. When authorities contacted the man, he described his costume as a painter's suit covered in fleece, and he said he was testing his disguise for a hunting trip.

TODAY'S READING
2 Peter 2:1-3,12-19

Beware of false prophets, who come to you in sheep's clothing, but inwardly they are ravenous wolves. Matthew 7:15

The hunter's deception reminds me of Jesus' words: "Beware of false prophets, who come to you in sheep's clothing, but inwardly they are ravenous wolves" (MATT. 7:15). False teachers do not bear the fruit of God's Spirit (GAL. 5:22-23). Rather, they "walk according to the flesh . . . and despise authority" (2 PETER 2:10). They are bold, egotistical, and given to greed (VV. 10,14). Ruled by their own desires, they exploit people by using "deceptive words" (V. 3). The Bible says these wayward spiritual leaders are headed for destruction and will take many unsuspecting and undiscerning people with them (VV. 1-2).

Jesus, the Good Shepherd, rather than pursuing personal gain, laid down His life for His sheep. God does not want anyone to be misled by false teaching. He wants us to be aware of those who deceive, and follow Him instead—the true Shepherd of our souls. 🌱   *JENNIFER BENSON SCHULDT*

At the name of Jesus
Every knee shall bow,
Every tongue confess Him,
King of glory now. NOEL

Substitutes abound, but there is only one Christ.

Make It Personal

During my days as a teacher and coach at a Christian high school, I thoroughly enjoyed interacting with teenagers, trying to guide them to a purposeful, Christlike life—characterized by love for God and love for others. My goal was to prepare them to live for God throughout life. That would happen only as they made their faith a vital part of life through the help of the Holy Spirit. Those who didn't follow Christ floundered after they left the influence of Christian teachers and parents.

> TODAY'S READING
> **2 Chronicles 24:1-2,15-22**
>
> **Walk in the Spirit, and you shall not fulfill the lust of the flesh.** Galatians 5:16

This is demonstrated in the story of King Joash of Judah and his uncle Jehoiada. Jehoiada, a wise counselor, influenced Joash to live a God-honoring life (2 CHRON. 24:11,14).

The problem was that Joash did not embrace an honorable life as his own. After Jehoiada died, King Joash "left the house of the LORD" (V. 18) and began to worship in a pagan way. He turned and became so evil that he had Jehoiada's son murdered (VV. 20-22).

Having someone in our lives to guide us toward faith and Christlikeness can be good and helpful. Even better is getting to know the Lord ourselves and learning to rely on the Holy Spirit to be our guide (GAL. 5:16). That is making our faith personal. 🌱 *DAVE BRANON*

Lord, thank You for the people in my life who influence me
toward following You. Help me not to depend on them
primarily—but to depend on Your Holy Spirit to guide me.

The faith of others encourages; a faith of our own transforms.

The Silent Pen

ormer **US President Harry Truman** had a rule: Any letters written in anger had to sit on his desk for 24 hours before they could be mailed. If at the end of that "cooling off" period, he still felt the same sentiments, he would send the letter. By the end of his life, Truman's unmailed letters filled a large desk drawer.

How often in this age of immediate communication would even 24 minutes of wise restraint spare us embarrassment! In his epistle, James addressed a universal theme in human history when he wrote about the damage an uncontrolled tongue can bring. "No man can tame the tongue," he wrote. "It is an unruly evil, full of deadly poison" (3:8).

TODAY'S READING
James 3:1-12

The fruit of righteousness is sown in peace by those who make peace. 3:18

When we're gossiping or speaking in anger, we find ourselves outside the lines of what God desires. Our tongues, our pens, and even our keyboards should more often fall silent with thanks in our hearts for the restraint God provides. All too often, when we speak we remind everyone of our brokenness as human beings.

When we want to surprise others with the difference Christ makes, we may need to look no further than restraining our tongue. Others can't help but notice when we honor God with what we say—or don't say. ✪   *RANDY KILGORE*

Help me, Lord, to use my words not to tear down others or
build up my own reputation, but to seek the good of others
first, and in so doing to serve You and Your kingdom.

Whoever guards his mouth and tongue keeps his soul from troubles.
PROVERBS 21:23

The Golden Rule

The concept of The Golden Rule—treat others as you would like to be treated—appears in many religions. So what makes Jesus' version of the saying so exceptional?

Its uniqueness lies in a single word, "therefore," that signals the generosity of our heavenly Father. Here is what Jesus said: "If you then, being evil, know how to give good gifts to your children, how much more will your Father who is in heaven give good things to those who ask Him! *Therefore*, whatever you want men to do to you, do also to them" (MATT. 7:11-12 ITALICS ADDED).

> TODAY'S READING
> **Matthew 7:7-12**
>
> **Therefore, whatever you want men to do to them.** v. 12

All of us fall short of what we know to be true: We do not love others the way God loves us. Jesus lived out that admirable ethic with perfect love by living and dying for all our sins.

We have a loving, giving Father who set aside His own self-interest to reveal the full measure of His love through His Son Jesus. God's generosity is the dynamic by which we treat others as we would like to be treated. We love and give to others because He first loved us (1 JOHN 4:19).

Our heavenly Father asks us to live up to His commands, but He also gives us His power and love to carry it out. We need only to ask Him for it. 🍂

DAVID ROPER

Heavenly Father, I know that I lack Your patience and mercy and love. Please show Your perfect love through me in some small way today. In Your Son Jesus' name I pray.

We have committed The Golden Rule to memory; now let us commit it to life. E. MARKHAM

Without Power

I n late October 2012, a hurricane-spawned superstorm struck the heavily populated northeastern US, leaving massive flooding and destruction in its wake. During the storm, more than 8 million customers lost electricity. Power outages alone caused shortages of food, fuel, and water, along with the chaos of gridlocked transportation. The howling winds and surging waters left many neighborhoods crushed, flooded, and choked with mountains of sand. Media coverage of the event reported: "Millions Without Power."

Like a storm of nature, a personal tragedy can often leave us feeling powerless and in the dark. During such times, God's Word assures us of His help: "He gives power to the weak, and to those who have no might He increases strength" (ISA. 40:29).

At our lowest point, drained of emotional resources, we can place our hope in the Lord and find our strength in Him. He promises us that, for each new day, "Those who wait on the LORD shall renew their strength; they shall mount up with wings like eagles, they shall run and not be weary, they shall walk and not faint" (V. 31).

God is our spiritual power source in every storm of life. ❀

DAVID MCCASLAND

O God, our help in ages past,
Our hope for years to come,
Our shelter from the stormy blast,
And our eternal home! WATTS

It takes the storm to prove the real shelter.

Prone to Wander

One of my favorite classic hymns is "Come, Thou Fount of Every Blessing," which was written in 1757 by 22-year-old Robert Robinson. In the hymn's lyrics is a line that always captures my attention and forces me to do some self-evaluation. The line says, "Prone to wander, Lord, I feel it. Prone to leave the God I love." I feel that way sometimes. Too often I find myself distracted and drifting, instead of having my heart and mind focused on the Savior who loves me and gave Himself for me. Robert Robinson and I are not alone in this.

TODAY'S READING
Psalm 119:9-16

With my whole heart I have sought You; oh, let me not wander from Your commandments! v.10

In those seasons of wandering, our heart of hearts doesn't want to drift from God—but, like Paul, we often do what we don't want to do (ROM. 7:19), and we desperately need to turn back to the Shepherd of our heart who can draw us to Himself. David wrote of this struggle in His great anthem to the Scriptures, Psalm 119, saying, "With my whole heart I have sought You; oh, let me not wander from Your commandments!" (V. 10).

Sometimes, even when our hearts long to seek God, the distractions of life can draw us away from Him and His Word. How grateful we can be for a patient, compassionate heavenly Father whose grace is always sufficient—even when we are prone to wander! 🌸

BILL CROWDER

Prone to wander, Lord, I feel it,
Prone to leave the God I love;
Here's my heart, O take and seal it,
Seal it for Thy courts above. ROBINSON

Our tendency to wander is matched by God's willingness to pursue.

Job Titles

When the British Broadcasting Corporation asked for examples of important-sounding, obscure, and even bizarre job titles, one writer offered hers: Underwater Ceramic Technician. She was a dishwasher at a restaurant. Sometimes titles are used to make a job sound more important.

When the apostle Paul listed some of God's gifts to the church in Ephesians 4:11, he did not intend for these to be understood as high-sounding job titles. All the parts of the body are necessary for the body to function properly. No one part is better than another.

What was of primary importance was the purpose of these gifts. They were "for the equipping of the saints for the work of ministry, for the edifying of the body of Christ, till we all come to . . . the stature of the fullness of Christ" (VV. 12-13).

> **TODAY'S READING**
> **Ephesians 4:11-16**
>
> **For the equipping of the saints for the work of ministry, for the edifying of the body of Christ, till we all come to the unity of the faith.**
> vv. 12-13

It matters little what title we hold. What is important is that we strengthen the faith of God's people. When we gauge our effectiveness by the standard that the Bible gives us, it will not matter when we are moved to another role or no longer hold a specific title. Out of love for God, we serve to build up fellow believers, and we let God give His commendation in heaven as He sees fit (MATT. 25:21). 🌀　　　*C. P. HIA*

Lord, please use me as Your instrument to touch others' lives.
Help me not to be concerned about what title I hold but instead
that my life might show others Your grace.

God's gifts to us are not for us but for others.

Heart Food

love food! I love to see it beautifully presented, and I love to savor the taste. If it were up to me, I would eat more often than I should—although it wouldn't help my waistline! So, it's a good thing my wife, Martie, knows when to lovingly remind me to eat healthful foods in the right amount.

Reading Jeremiah's interesting thought—that when he found the words of God (even the words of God's judgment) he "ate them" (JER. 15:16)—makes me wonder if I ingest God's Word as eagerly, as lovingly, and as often.

> **TODAY'S READING**
> **Jeremiah 15:15-21**
>
> **Your words were found, and I ate them.** v. 16

Clearly, Jeremiah did not actually eat God's Word. It was his way of saying that he read and savored it in his innermost being. And that's exactly where God's Word is intended to go. The Word is heart food! When we ingest it, the Holy Spirit provides the power to help us grow to be more like Jesus. His Word transforms how we think about God, money, enemies, careers, and family. In other words, it's really good for us.

So, "eat" God's Word to your heart's content! No doubt you will find yourself agreeing with the prophet Jeremiah when he said: "Your word was to me the joy and rejoicing of my heart" (15:16). ❧

JOE STOWELL

Lord, cultivate in me an appetite for Your Word. Thank You that the Bible is food for my soul. Lead me to read it, to savor it, to ingest it, and to know the strength that Your words can give to my often-failing heart.

The more you feast on God's Word, the healthier you will become.

Perspective from the Clouds

n 1927 the silent film *Wings*, a World War I film about two American aviators, won the first Academy Award for Best Picture. When it was being filmed, production stopped for several days. Frustrated producers asked the director why. He responded: "All we have is blue sky. The conflict in the air will not be as visible without clouds. Clouds bring perspective." He was right. Only by seeing aerial combat with clouds as a backdrop could the viewer see what was really going on.

TODAY'S READING
Job 3:3-5; 42:5-6

I have heard of You . . . but now my eye sees You. 42:5

We often wish for blue skies instead of storm clouds. But cloudy skies may reveal God's faithfulness. We gain perspective on how God has been faithful in our trials as we look back on the clouds.

At the beginning of his terrible suffering, Job lamented: "May the day perish on which I was born . . . . May a cloud settle on it" (JOB 3:3-5). His experience of despair continued for a long time until God spoke. Then Job exclaimed, "I have heard of You . . . but now my eye sees You" (42:5). Job had encountered the sovereign Creator, and that changed his perspective on God's purposes.

Do clouds of trouble fill your skies today? Sooner than you think, God may use these clouds to help you gain perspective on His faithfulness. 🌱

DENNIS FISHER

God, give us wings to rise above
The clouds of trial that block the sun,
To soar above gray skies and see
The love and goodness of Your Son. SPER

Often the clouds of sorrow reveal the sunshine of His face. JASPER

Sweet Fragrance

Some scents are unforgettable. Recently, my husband mentioned he was running low on shaving cream. "I'll pick some up," I offered. "Can you get this kind?" he asked, showing me the can. "I love the smell—it's the kind my dad always used." I smiled, recalling the time I had been momentarily taken back to my childhood when I got a whiff of the same shampoo my mom used to wash my hair. For both Tom and me, the fragrances had brought an emotional response and pleasant memory of people we loved.

TODAY'S READING
2 Cor. 2:12-17

We are to God the fragrance of Christ among those who are being saved and among those who are perishing. v. 15

Oliver Wendell Holmes said, "Memories, imagination, old sentiments, and associations are more readily reached through the sense of smell than through any other channel."

So, what if our lives were a fragrance that attracted people to God? Second Corinthians 2:15 says that "we are to God the fragrance of Christ among those who are being saved and among those who are perishing." Our fragrance is pleasing to God, but it also attracts others to Him or repels them. We who understand the sacrifice of Jesus have the opportunity to be the "fragrance of Christ"—a reminder of Him—to others.

The sweet scent of the likeness of Christ can be an irresistible pull toward the Savior. *CINDY HESS KASPER*

Let my hands perform His bidding,
Let my feet run in His ways,
Let my eyes see Jesus only,
Let my lips speak forth His praise. JAMES

*When we walk with God, we leave behind a sweet fragrance
that can inspire others to follow.*

Heaven Rejoices!

Joann had been raised in a Christian home. But when she went to college, she began to question her beliefs and walked away from God. After graduation, she traveled to a number of countries, always looking for happiness but never feeling satisfied. While experiencing some difficulties, she recognized that God was pursuing her and that she needed Him.

TODAY'S READING
Luke 15:1-10

There is joy in the presence of the angels of God over one sinner who repents. v. 10

From Germany, Joann called her parents in the US and said, "I have given my life to Christ, and He's changing me! I'm sorry for the worry I have caused you." Her parents were so excited that they called her brothers and sisters-in-law to come over immediately. They wanted to tell them the exciting news in person. "Your sister has received Christ!" they said, rejoicing through tears.

The woman in Luke 15 who found her lost coin called her friends and neighbors together to rejoice with her (V.9). Jesus told this story, and others about a lost sheep and a lost son, to the religious people of His day to show how He came to earth to pursue lost sinners. When we accept God's gift of salvation, there is rejoicing both on earth and in heaven. Jesus said, "There is joy in the presence of the angels of God over one sinner who repents" (V. 10). How wonderful that Jesus has reached down to us and heaven rejoices when we respond! 🌱

ANNE CETAS

I was lost but Jesus found me—
Found the sheep that went astray,
Threw His loving arms around me,
Drew me back into His way. ROWLEY

Angels rejoice when we repent.

Determination

During a **television news report** on the plight of refugees displaced from a war-torn country, I was struck by the words of a 10-year-old girl. Despite there being little possibility of returning to their home, she showed a resilient spirit: "When we go back, I'm going to visit my neighbors; I'm going to play with my friends," she said with quiet determination. "My father says we don't have a house. And I said we are going to fix it."

> TODAY'S READING
> **Ruth 1:6,11-18;**
> **Luke 9:51-53**
>
> **Your people shall be my people, and your God, my God.** Ruth 1:16

There is a place for tenacity in life, especially when it is rooted in our faith in God and love for others. The book of Ruth begins with three women bound together by tragedy. After Naomi's husband and two sons died, she decided to return to her home in Bethlehem and urged her widowed daughters-in-law to stay in their country of Moab. Orpah remained but Ruth vowed to go with Naomi, saying, "Your people shall be my people, and your God, my God" (RUTH 1:16). When Naomi saw that Ruth "was determined to go with her" (V. 18), they began their journey together.

Stubbornness is sometimes rooted in pride, but commitment grows from love. When Jesus went to the cross, "He steadfastly set His face to go to Jerusalem" (LUKE 9:51). From His determination to die for us, we find the resolve to live for Him. 🌱   *DAVID MCCASLAND*

My life, my love, I give to Thee,
Thou Lamb of God who died for me;
Oh, may I ever faithful be,
My Savior and my God! HUDSON

Love calls for commitment.

Mistaken Identity

My youngest brother, Scott, was born when I was a senior in high school. This age difference made for an interesting situation when he grew to college age. On his first trip to his college campus, I went along with him and our mom. When we arrived, people thought we were Scott Crowder and his dad and his grandmom. Eventually, we gave up correcting them. No matter what we said or did, our actual relationships were overridden by this humorous case of mistaken identity.

> **TODAY'S READING**
> **Matthew 16:13-20**
>
> He said to them, "But who do you say that I am?" v. 15

Jesus questioned the Pharisees about His identity: "What do you think about the Christ? Whose Son is He?" They replied, "The Son of David" (MATT. 22:42). The identity of Messiah was critical, and their answer was correct but incomplete. The Scriptures had affirmed that Messiah would come and reign on the throne of His father David. But Jesus reminded them that though David would be Christ's ancestor, He would also be more—David referred to Him as "Lord."

Faced with a similar question, Peter rightly answered, "You are the Christ, the Son of the living God" (16:16). Still today, the question of Jesus' identity rises above the rest in significance—and it is eternally important that we make no mistake in understanding who He is. ❧ *BILL CROWDER*

Frail children of dust, and feeble as frail,
In Thee do we trust, nor find Thee to fail;
Thy mercies how tender, how firm to the end,
Our Maker, Defender, Redeemer, and Friend. GRANT

No mistake is more dangerous than mistaking the identity of Jesus.

Coming Soon!

A "COMING SOON!" announcement often precedes future events in entertainment and sports, or the launch of the latest technology. The goal is to create anticipation and excitement for what is going to happen, even though it may be months away.

While reading the book of Revelation, I was impressed with the "coming soon" sense of imme-diacy permeating the entire book. Rather than saying, "Someday, in the far distant future, Jesus Christ is going to return to earth," the text is filled with phrases like "things which must shortly take place" (1:1) and "the time is near" (v. 3). Three times in the final chapter, the Lord says, "I am coming quickly" (REV. 22:7,12,20). Other versions translate this phrase as, "I'm com-ing soon," "I'm coming speedily," and "I'm on My way!"

> TODAY'S READING
> **Revelation 22:7-21**
>
> **Surely I am coming quickly.** v. 20

How can this be—since 2,000 years have elapsed since these words were written? "Quickly" doesn't seem appropri-ate for our experience of time.

Rather than focusing on a date for His return, the Lord is urging us to set our hearts on His promise that will be ful-filled. We are called to live for Him in this present age "look-ing for the blessed hope and glorious appearing of our great God and Savior Jesus Christ" (TITUS 2:13). ❦　　*DAVID MCCASLAND*

Marvelous message we bring,
Glorious carol we sing,
Wonderful word of the King:
Jesus is coming again! PETERSON

Live as if Christ is coming back today.

Promoting Unity

The language of Proverbs **6:16–19** is strong. In the citing of seven things the Lord hates, sowing "discord among brethren" makes the list. The reason for naming this sin is that it spoils the unity that Christ desires for His followers (JOHN 17:21-22).

Those who sow discord may not initially set out to create divisions. They may be preoccupied instead with their personal needs or the interests of a group they belong to (JAMES 4:1-10). Consider how Lot's herdsmen argued with those of Abraham (GEN. 13:1-18);

> **TODAY'S READING**
> **Proverbs 6:16-19**
>
> **The LORD hates
> . . . one who sows
> discord among
> brethren.** vv. 16,19

Christ's disciples argued about personal preeminence (LUKE 9:46); and divisive groups in the church at Corinth elevated party factions above the unity of the Spirit (1 COR. 3:1-7).

So what is the best way to promote unity? It begins with the transformation of the heart. When we adopt the mind of Christ, we develop an attitude of humility and we focus on service toward others (PHIL. 2:5-11). Only in Him can we access the power to "look out not only for [our] own interests, but also for the interests of others" (V. 4). Soon the needs and hopes of others become more important to us than our own.

With growing bonds of love among us, we find discord replaced with joy and unity (SEE PS. 133:1). 🍃   *DENNIS FISHER*

Like a mighty army moves the church of God;
Brothers, we are treading where the saints have trod.
We are not divided, all one body we—
One in hope and doctrine, one in charity. BARING-GOULD

We can accomplish more together than we can alone.

Gentle Witness

Years ago, I was hospitalized following a life-threatening, 38-foot fall from a bridge. While I was there, the wife of the man in the next bed stopped to speak to me. "My husband just told me what happened to you," she said. "We believe God spared your life because He wants to use you. We've been praying for you."

I was stunned. I had grown up going to church, but I had never imagined that God would want to be involved in my life. Her words pointed me to a Savior I had heard of but did not know—and marked the beginning of my coming to Christ. I cherish the memory of those words from a gentle witness who cared enough to say something to a stranger about the God whose love is real. Her words conveyed care and concern, and offered purpose and promise.

> TODAY'S READING
> **Acts 1:1-11**
>
> **You shall be witnesses to Me in Jerusalem, and in all Judea and Samaria, and to the end of the earth.** v. 8

Jesus challenged His disciples—and us—to tell others about the love of God: "You shall receive power when the Holy Spirit has come upon you; and you shall be witnesses to Me in Jerusalem, and in all Judea and Samaria, and to the end of the earth" (ACTS 1:8).

Through the Holy Spirit our words and witness can have the power to make an eternal difference in the lives of others. 🌿 *BILL CROWDER*

> I love to tell the story of unseen things above,
> Of Jesus and His glory, of Jesus and His love,
> I love to tell the story, because I know 'tis true;
> It satisfies my longings as nothing else can do. HANKEY

A caring word can accomplish more than we could ever imagine.

I'm Alive

aura Brooks, a 52-year-old mother of two, didn't know it but she was one of 14,000 people in 2011 whose name was incorrectly entered into the government database as dead. She wondered what was wrong when she stopped receiving disability checks, and her loan payments and her rent checks bounced. She went to the bank to clear up the issue, but the representative told her that her accounts had been closed because she was dead! Obviously, they were mistaken.

TODAY'S READING
Ephesians 2:1-10

You He made alive, who were dead in trespasses and sins. v. 1

The apostle Paul was not mistaken when he said that the Ephesian believers were at one point dead—spiritually dead. They were dead in the sense that they were separated from God, enslaved to sin (EPH. 2:5), and condemned under the wrath of God. What a state of hopelessness!

Yet God in His goodness took action to reverse this condition for them and for us. The living God "who gives life to the dead" (ROM. 4:17) poured out His rich mercy and great love by sending His Son Jesus to this earth. Through Christ's death and resurrection, we are made alive (EPH. 2:4-5).

When we believe in the death and resurrection of Jesus Christ, we go from death to life. Now we live to rejoice in His goodness! 🌱

MARVIN WILLIAMS

I know I'm a sinner and Christ is my need;
His death is my ransom, no merit I plead.
His work is sufficient, on Him I believe;
I have life eternal when Him I receive. ANON.

Accepting Jesus' death gives me life.

The Spotlight

'll never forget the Easter Sunday in 1993 when Bernhard Langer won the Masters golf tournament. As he stepped off the 18th green to receive the green jacket—one of golf's most coveted prizes—a reporter said, "This must be the greatest day of your life!" Without missing a beat, Langer replied: "It's wonderful to win the greatest tournament in the world, but it means more to win on Easter Sunday— to celebrate the resurrection of my Lord and Savior."

> **TODAY'S READING**
> **Romans 5:1-11**
>
> **We also rejoice in God through our Lord Jesus Christ.** v. 11

Langer had an opportunity to boast about himself, but instead he turned the spotlight on Jesus Christ. It's exactly what Paul was talking about when he said, "We also rejoice [boast] in God through our Lord Jesus Christ, through whom we have now received the reconciliation" (ROM. 5:11).

It's easy to look for ways to draw attention to our own accomplishments, making mental lists of things that are "cool" about ourselves. Even Paul admitted that he had a lot to brag about—but he considered all of it "rubbish" for the sake of knowing Christ (PHIL. 3:8). We would do well to follow his example.

So, if you really want something to boast about, boast about Jesus and what He's done for you. Look for opportunities to turn the spotlight on Him. 🌿   *JOE STOWELL*

> Naught have I gotten but what I received,
> Grace hath bestowed it since I have believed;
> Boasting excluded, pride I abase—
> I'm only a sinner saved by grace! GRAY

You can't boast in Jesus while you're preoccupied with yourself.

Easter Every Day

friend of mine, who is a preschool teacher, overheard an animated conversation among her students. Little Maria threw out the question: "Who loves God?" All of them responded, "I do! I do! I do!" Billy said, "I love *Jesus*." Kelly protested, "But He *died*." Billy said, "Yeah, but every Easter He rises from the dead!"

Obviously, young Billy's understanding of the meaning of Easter is still developing. We know that Jesus died *once for all* (ROM. 6:10; HEB. 10:12) and, of course, rose from the dead *once*. Three days after paying the penalty of our sins on the cross, the sinless Jesus conquered death by rising from the grave and breaking the power of sin. It was this final sacrifice of blood that opened the only way for us to have a relationship with God now and a home with Him forevermore.

> **TODAY'S READING**
> **Hebrews 10:11-18**
>
> **He is not here; for He is risen, as He said.** Matthew 28:6

"Christ died for our sins, . . . He was buried, and . . . He rose again the third day" (1 COR. 15:3-4). He has promised that He is preparing a place for us (JOHN 14:1-4), and He will someday return. One day we will be with our risen Savior.

That's why every year at Eastertime—in fact, every day of the year—we have reason to celebrate the resurrection of our Savior. "I will bless the Lord at all times; His praise shall continually be in my mouth" (PS. 34:1). ❧   *CINDY HESS KASPER*

Living, He loved me; dying, He saved me;
Buried, He carried my sins far away;
Rising, He justified freely forever:
One day He's coming—O glorious day! CHAPMAN

Christ's resurrection is cause for our celebration.

Victory over Death!

An ancient painting I saw recently made a deep impression on me. Its title, *Anastasis*, means "resurrection," and it depicts the triumph of Christ's victory over death in a stunning way. The Lord Jesus, newly emerged from the tomb, is pulling Adam and Eve out of their coffins to eternal life. What is so amazing about this artwork is the way it shows how spiritual and physical death, the result of the fall, were dramatically reversed by the risen Christ.

TODAY'S READING
John 5:24-30

The hour is coming in which all who are in the graves will hear His voice and come forth. vv. 28-29

Prior to His death on the cross, the Lord Jesus predicted a future day when He will call believers into a new and glorified existence: "The hour is coming in which all who are in the graves will hear His voice and come forth" (JOHN 5:28-29).

Because of Christ's victory over death, the grave is not final. We naturally will feel sorrow and grief when those we love die and we are separated from them in this life. But the believer does not grieve as one who has no hope (1 THESS. 4:13). The witness of Jesus' resurrection is that all Christians will one day be taken from their graves to be clothed with glorified resurrection bodies (1 COR. 15:42-44). And so "we shall always be with the Lord" (1 THESS. 4:17). 🌿

DENNIS FISHER

Dear Lord, thank You for sacrificing Your life for our sins so that we might live. We're thankful that because You died and rose again, we can have assurance that one day we'll be with You in a place of no more death.

Because Christ is alive, we too shall live.

A Better World

n one of my favorite *Peanuts* cartoons featuring Charlie Brown, the always confident Lucy declares, "How could the world be getting worse with me in it? Ever since I was born the world has shown a distinct improvement!"

Of course, Lucy is displaying an unrealistic and elevated opinion of herself, but she makes an interesting point. What if we were to try to make the world a better place by displaying the love of Christ wherever God has placed us?

When Peter wrote to persecuted believers, he advised them to "[keep] your conduct honorable" (1 PETER 2:12) by doing good deeds that will ultimately bring glory to God. In other words, we can make our world a better place through our actions. Think of the difference that Christlike deeds of love, mercy, forgiveness, justice, and peace would make in our world. I've always thought that if we lived out this verse, people might say, "Our office is a better place because _____ works here." Or, "Our neighborhood is a better neighborhood." Or, "Our school is a better school."

> TODAY'S READING
> **1 Peter 2:9-12**
>
> **[Keep] your conduct honorable among the Gentiles, that . . . they may, by your good works which they observe, glorify God.** v. 12

We can't change the entire world singlehandedly, but by God's grace we can let the difference Christ has made in us make a difference in the world around us. ❀

JOE STOWELL

> Love is giving for the world's needs,
> Love is sharing as the Spirit leads,
> Love is caring when the world cries,
> Love is compassion with Christlike eyes. BRANDT

***Everyone can do something to make the world better—
we can let Christ shine through us.***

Blessed Are the Meek

One of the problems with the English word *meek* is that it rhymes with *weak*, and people have linked the two words together for years. A popular dictionary offers a secondary definition of *meek* as "too submissive; easily imposed on; spineless; spiritless." This causes some people to question why Jesus would say, "Blessed are the meek, for they shall inherit the earth" (MATT. 5:5).

TODAY'S READING
Matthew 5:1-10

Blessed are the meek, for they shall inherit the earth. v. 5

Greek scholar W. E. Vine says that meekness in the Bible is an attitude toward God "in which we accept His dealings with us as good, and therefore without disputing or resisting." We see this in Jesus who found His delight in doing the will of His Father.

Vine goes on to say that "the meekness manifested by the Lord and commended to the believer is the fruit of power. ... The Lord was 'meek' because He had the infinite resources of God at His command." He could have called angels from heaven to prevent His crucifixion.

Jesus told His weary, burdened followers, "Take My yoke upon you and learn from Me, for I am [meek] and lowly in heart, and you will find rest for your souls" (MATT. 11:29). He was the perfect model of meekness.

When we are tired and troubled, Jesus invites us to discover the peace of meekly trusting Him. 🌿 *DAVID MCCASLAND*

Love sent the Savior to die in my stead.
Why should He love me so?
Meekly to Calvary's cross He was led.
Why should He love me so? HARKNESS

***God has two dwellings, one in heaven and the other
in a meek and thankful heart.*** WALTON

Bottled Water Binge

Here in the United States, we've been on a bottled water binge for a number of years. Even though most people have a safe supply of water that is free and readily available from faucets and drinking fountains, they still purchase bottled water. Choosing to pay for something that I can enjoy at no cost doesn't make sense to me, but some people believe that a product they pay for is superior to anything they receive free.

> **TODAY'S READING**
> **Romans 5:12-21**
>
> **Through one Man's righteous act the free gift came to all men.** v. 18

This sometimes carries over into our spiritual lives. Some struggle to accept that salvation is a gift. They want to do something to earn it. The problem is, no one can afford it. The price of salvation is perfection (MATT. 19:21), and Jesus is the only person who could pay the price (ROM. 5:18). To anyone who thirsts, He promises to "give of the fountain of the water of life freely" (REV. 21:6).

Some people try to purchase the living water of salvation with good deeds and charitable donations. Although these are forms of spiritual service valued by God, they are not what God requires for the forgiveness of our sin. Jesus already paid the price by dying in our place, and He offers to quench our spiritual thirst when we drink freely from God's fountain that will never run dry. ❦ *JULIE ACKERMAN LINK*

Jesus is the Living Water—
Just one drink will make you whole;
Drawing daily from that wellspring
Brings refreshment to the soul. D. DEHAAN

Jesus is the only fountain who can satisfy the thirsty soul.

Free Tomatoes

Packing groceries into the trunk of my car, I glanced at the vehicle next to me. Through the back window, I could see baskets full of bright red tomatoes—shiny, plump, and better looking than any I had seen in the store. When the car's owner appeared seconds later, I said, "What great looking tomatoes!" She replied, "I had a good crop this year. Would you like some?" Surprised by her willingness to share, I gladly accepted. She gave me several free tomatoes to take home—they tasted as good as they looked!

TODAY'S READING
Exodus 35:20-29

Everyone whose spirit was willing . . . brought the LORD's offering for the work of the tabernacle. v. 21

We see an even greater spirit of generosity in the Israelites when they gave to build the tabernacle of the Lord. When asked to provide materials for the sanctuary, "everyone whose spirit was willing . . . brought the LORD's offering for the work of the tabernacle" (EX. 35:21). The Israelites eagerly donated their gold jewelry, colored thread, fine linen, silver, bronze, gemstones, and spices. Some also gave their time and talents (VV. 25-26).

If we follow the Israelites' example and willingly donate our resources, we please and honor God with our attitude and offerings. The Lord, who sees and knows our thoughts and hearts, loves cheerful givers. He Himself is the best example of generosity (JOHN 3:16). 🌼

JENNIFER BENSON SCHULDT

Dear Jesus, You gave everything You had for my sake.
Help me to give with a willing heart so that my gifts
will truly honor You.

The state of our heart is more important than the size of our gift.

You've Got a Friend

One of the ironic consequences of the sweeping growth of social media is that we often find ourselves more personally isolated. One online article warns: "Those who oppose leading one's life primarily or exclusively online claim that virtual friends are not adequate substitutes for real-world friends, and … individuals who substitute virtual friends for physical friends become even lonelier and more depressive than before."

TODAY'S READING
Psalm 23

[Jesus said,] "I have called you friends." *John 15:15*

Technology aside, all of us battle with seasons of loneliness, wondering if anyone knows, understands, or cares about the burdens we carry or the struggles we face. But followers of Christ have an assurance that brings comfort to our weary hearts. The comforting presence of the Savior is promised in words that are undeniable, for the psalmist David wrote, "Yea, though I walk through the valley of the shadow of death, I will fear no evil; for You are with me; Your rod and Your staff, they comfort me" (PS. 23:4).

Whether isolated by our own choices, by the cultural trends that surround us, or by the painful losses of life, all who know Christ can rest in the presence of the Shepherd of our hearts. What a friend we have in Jesus! 🌱   *BILL CROWDER*

I've found a Friend; O such a Friend!
He loved me ere I knew Him;
He drew me with the cords of love,
And thus He bound me to Him. SMALL

Those who know Jesus as their Friend are never alone.

What's in a Name?

My friend wrote a letter to his newborn child that he wanted him to read when he was older: "My dear boy, Daddy and Mummy wish that you will find and stay focused on the Light. Your Chinese name is *xin xuan*. *Xin* means faithfulness, contentment, and integrity; *xuan* stands for warmth and light." He and his wife carefully chose a name based on their hopes for their baby boy.

TODAY'S READING
John 1:35-42

You are Peter, and on this rock I will build My church.
Matthew 16:18

When Jesus renamed Simon as Peter/Cephas (JOHN 1:42), it wasn't a random choice. *Peter* means "the rock." But it took a while for him to live up to his new name. The account of his life reveals him as a fisherman known for his rash ways—a shifting-sand kind of guy. Peter disagreed with Jesus (MATT. 16:22-23), struck a man with a sword (JOHN 18:10-11), and even denied knowing Jesus (VV. 15-27). But in Acts, we read that God worked in and through him to establish His church. Peter truly became a rock.

If you, like Peter, are a follower of Jesus, you have a new identity. In Acts 11:26, we read, "The disciples were first called Christians in Antioch." The name "Christians" means "Christ-ones." You now are one of the Christ-ones. This title lifts up who you are and calls you to become what you are not yet. God is faithful, and He will complete His good work in you (PHIL. 1:6). 🌱   POH FANG CHIA

Dear Father, thank You for the incredible privilege of being called Your child. May we understand more fully what it means to be identified with Your Son, Jesus Christ. Work in us and through us.

We honor God's name when we call Him our Father and live like His children.

Check the Oil

When I helped our daughters learn to drive, I included a little instruction on basic auto maintenance. We visited a local service station where they learned to check the oil every time they put fuel in the car. Today, years later, they often remind me of my six-word slogan, "Oil is cheap; engines are expensive." Adding a quart of oil is nothing compared to replacing an engine.

Maintenance is also important in our spiritual lives. Taking time each day to read the Bible, pray, and listen to God is a key element in avoiding a break-down. In Psalm 5, David wrote, "My voice You shall hear in the morning, O LORD; in the morning I will direct it to You" (V. 3). In the following verses he poured out his heart in praise, thanksgiving, and requests to God.

> **TODAY'S READING**
> **Psalm 5**
>
> **My voice You shall hear in the morning, O LORD; in the morning I will direct it to You.** v. 3

Many people find it essential to begin every day with the Lord. Before checking email, catching the news, or eating breakfast, they find some quiet moments alone to read a por-tion of God's Word, praise Him for His greatness, thank Him for His love, and seek His guidance. Others spend time read-ing and praying at different times of the day.

It's not magic—it's maintenance, as we ask the Lord each day to fill our hearts with His presence on the road of life. 🌿

DAVID MCCASLAND

Give me a strong desire, O Lord, to look into Your Word each day.
Help me hide it in my heart so that I might not stray from Your
truth. Feed me and teach me about Yourself and Your will for me.

***The roots of stability come from being grounded
in God's Word and prayer.***

Not Counting

The play *Amadeus* tells of a composer in the 18th century seeking to understand the mind of God. The devout Antonio Salieri has the earnest desire, but not the aptitude, to create immortal music. It infuriates him that God has instead lavished the greatest of musical genius ever known on the impish Wolfgang Amadeus Mozart.

TODAY'S READING
Matthew 20:1-16

The last will be first, and the first last. v. 16

The play poses the same question as the book of Job, only inverted. The author of Job wonders why God would *punish* the most righteous man on the face of the earth; the author of *Amadeus* ponders why God would *reward* someone so undeserving.

Jesus' parable of the workers and their grossly unfair paychecks confronts this scandal head-on. Some people who have been idly standing around are hired by a landowner at "the eleventh hour" (MATT. 20:6-7). The other workers, who have been serving him all day long, are shocked when each receives identical pay. What employer in his right mind would pay the same amount for one hour's work as for 12!

Jesus' story makes no economic sense, and that was His intent. He was giving us a parable about grace, which cannot be calculated like a day's wages. God dispenses gifts, not wages. 🌿

PHILIP YANCEY

Lord, I forget sometimes that my efforts cannot earn Your love or grace or forgiveness. You have lavished grace on me as a gift and not a wage. Thank You.

*In the realm of grace, the word **deserve** does not apply.*

Choose Life

What is God's will for my life? The question haunted me when I was growing up. What if I couldn't find it? What if I didn't recognize it? God's will seemed like a needle in a haystack. Hidden. Obscured by look-alikes. Outnumbered by counterfeits.

But my view of God's will was wrong because my view of God was wrong. God takes no pleasure in seeing us lost, wandering, searching. He wants us to know His will. He makes it clear, and He makes it simple. He doesn't even make it multiple-choice. He gives just two choices: "life and good" or "death and evil" (DEUT. 30:15). In case the best choice isn't obvious, He even says which one to choose: "Choose life" (V. 19). To choose life is to choose God Himself and obey His Word.

> **TODAY'S READING**
> **Deut. 30:11-20**
>
> **Choose life, that both you and your descendants may live; that you may love the LORD your God, that you may obey His voice.**
> vv. 19-20

When Moses addressed the Israelites for the last time, he pleaded with them to make the right choice by observing "all the words of this law.... Because it is your life" (32:46-47). God's will for us is life. His Word is life. And Jesus is the Word. God may not give a prescription for every decision, but He gave us a perfect example to follow—Jesus. The right choice may not be easy, but when the Word is our guide and worship is our goal, God will grant us the wisdom to make life-affirming choices. 🌱

JULIE ACKERMAN LINK

Lord Jesus, we know that true wisdom comes from leaning on You. Help us to trust in You and to seek Your face and Your will that we find in Your life-giving Word.

The evidence of God's guidance can be seen more clearly by looking back than by looking forward.

Strawberry Mess

My husband and I had recently moved into our house when a man dropped off a large box of strawberries on our front sidewalk. He left a note saying he wanted us to share them with our neighbors. He meant well, but some children discovered the box before any adults did and had a strawberry-throwing party at our white house. When we returned home, we saw children we knew watching us from behind a fence. They had "returned to the scene of the crime" to see how we would react to the mess. We could have just cleaned it up ourselves, but to restore our relationship, we felt it was important to talk with them and require their help in cleaning our strawberry-stained house.

TODAY'S READING
Philippians 4:1-5

Be of the same mind in the Lord. v. 2

Life can get messy with relationship struggles. This was the case in the Philippian church. Two faithful servants, Euodia and Syntyche, were in sharp disagreement. The apostle Paul wrote to the church to encourage them to work through their problems (PHIL. 4:2). He also wanted another person to come alongside them with a spirit of gentleness. He wrote, "I urge you also, true companion, help these women who labored with me in the gospel" (V. 3).

Realizing we've all made messes in life, we can trust the Lord to help us deal gently with others. 🌱   *ANNE CETAS*

Dear Lord, please give me discernment and courage in my relationships. Help me by Your power to be gentle and show the same love to others that You have shown to me.

True love both confronts and restores.

Getting Beyond Ourselves

have one of those friends who seems to be better than I am at just about everything. He is smarter; he thinks more deeply; and he knows where to find better books to read. He is even a better golfer. Spending time with him challenges me to become a better, more thoughtful person. His standard of excellence spurs me on to greater things.

TODAY'S READING
2 Cor. 3:7-18

> We all, . . . beholding as in a mirror the glory of the Lord, are being transformed. v. 18

That highlights a spiritual principle: It's crucial for us to spend time in God's Word so we can connect with the person of Christ. Reading about the impact of Jesus' unconditional love for us compels me to love without demand. His mercy and His free distribution of grace to the most undeserving make me ashamed of my tendency to withhold forgiveness and seek revenge.

I find myself becoming a more thankful person when I realize that, despite my shameful fallenness, the Lord has clothed me in the beauty of His perfect righteousness. His amazing ways and unsurpassed wisdom motivate and transform me. It's hard to be content with my life as it is when in His presence I am drawn to become more like Him.

The apostle Paul calls us to the joy of beholding Christ. As we do so, we are "being transformed into the same image from glory to glory" (2 COR. 3:18). 🌿   *JOE STOWELL*

Lord, help us to come into Your presence with eyes and
hearts wide open to all that You are and want us to become.
Thank You for revealing Yourself to us and for the joy of
basking in the greatness of Your glory.

Stay close to God and you will never be the same.

Loved to Love

Dietrich Bonhoeffer's life was at risk every day he stayed in Hitler's Germany, but he stayed nonetheless. I imagine he shared the apostle Paul's view that being in heaven was his heart's desire, but staying where he was needed was God's present purpose (PHIL. 1:21). So stay he did; as a pastor he offered clandestine worship services and resisted the evil regime under Hitler.

Despite the daily danger, Bonhoeffer penned *Life Together*—a book on hospitality as ministry. He put this principle to the test when he lived and worked in a monastic community and when he was imprisoned. Every meal, every task, and every conversation, Bonhoeffer taught, was an opportunity to show Christ to others, even under great stress or strain.

TODAY'S READING
Deut. 10:12-22

Therefore love the stranger, for you were strangers in the land of Egypt. v. 19

We read in Deuteronomy that just as God ministered to the Israelites who were leaving Egypt, He instructed them to imitate Him by loving and hosting strangers and widows (10:18-19; EX. 22:21-22). We too are loved by God and empowered by His Spirit to serve Him by serving others in countless ways each day through kind words and actions.

Who on our daily journey seems lonely or lost? We can trust the Lord to enable us to bring them hope and compassion as we live and labor together for Him. 🌿 *RANDY KILGORE*

That I may serve Him with a full surrender,
My life a crucible, His eye the test,
Each hour a gift from Him, the gracious Sender,
Each day a pledge to give to Christ my best. ANON.

***The more we understand God's love for us
the more love we'll show to others.***

Left Side of the Road

Growing up in the US, I always thought it interesting that in some countries motorists drive on the left side of the road instead of the right. Then, when I was in England, I heard a London tour guide explain one possible reason for this law: "In the 1800s, pedestrians as well as horse-and-carriages used the same roads. When a carriage was on the right side of the road, a driver's horse whip would sometimes hit a passerby. To remove this hazard, a law was passed requiring all carriages to travel on the left side of the road so the pedestrians could be kept safe."

> TODAY'S READING
> **Galatians 5:1-14**
>
> **For all the law is fulfilled in one word, even in this: "You shall love your neighbor as yourself."** v. 14

Just as the rules of the road are for our benefit and protection, so are God's commands. Because He loves us, He has given them to us for our benefit. Paul writes: "For you, brethren, have been called to liberty; only do not use liberty as an opportunity for the flesh, but through love serve one another. For all the law is fulfilled in one word, even in this: 'You shall love your neighbor as yourself'" (GAL. 5:13-14).

As we apply God's Word to our hearts, let's keep in mind that the God of grace has given us His guidelines to help us grow in our love for Him and our concern for others. ❀

DENNIS FISHER

Thy Word is everlasting truth;
How pure is every page!
That Holy Book shall guide our youth
And well support our age. WATTS

The Bible has treasures of wisdom to mine.

"Isn't God Powerful!"

One day, my 3-year-old granddaughter Katie surprised her mom and dad with a bit of theological expertise. She said to them, "You both had sisters who died. Then God took them up to heaven to be with Him. Isn't God powerful!"

God's immense power is a mystery, yet it is simple enough for a child to understand. In Katie's young way of thinking, she knew that for God to do something so miraculous, it would mean that He is powerful. Without understanding all the details, she knew that God did something wonderful by taking her two aunts to heaven.

> TODAY'S READING
> **Psalm 29**
>
> **Give unto the LORD the glory due to His name.** v. 2

How often do we sit back in our more sophisticated world and marvel: "Isn't God powerful"? Probably not often enough. We can't know how God spun the worlds into existence with His voice (JOB 38-39; PS. 33:9; HEB. 11:3), nor can we know how He maintains control of them (NEH. 9:6). We can't know how He planned and fulfilled the incarnation of Jesus, nor can we understand how He can make Christ's sacrifice sufficient for our salvation. But we know these things are true.

The power of God: immeasurable in its wonder yet clear enough for us to understand. It's yet another reason to praise Him. 🍂

DAVE BRANON

> Our God is an awesome God!
> He reigns from heaven above
> With wisdom, power, and love—
> Our God is an awesome God! MULLINS

Everything God does is marked with simplicity and power. TERTULLIAN

New Beginnings

New beginnings are possible. Just ask Brayan, a young man who joined a gang in elementary school. Brayan ran away when he was 12 years old and for 3 years was lost in gang and drug life. Although he left the gang and returned home, it was difficult for him, as he had been expelled from school for selling drugs. When he enrolled in a new high school, however, a teacher inspired and encouraged him to write about his experiences rather than repeat them. He embraced the challenge and is now experiencing a fresh start.

> **TODAY'S READING**
> **Isaiah 43:14-21**
>
> Behold, I will do a new thing, now it shall spring forth; shall you not know it? v. 19

God, through the prophet Isaiah, encouraged Jewish exiles to think about a new beginning as well. God said, "Do not remember the former things, nor consider the things of old" (ISA. 43:18). He told them to stop dwelling on their punishment and even on His display of power through the original exodus from Egypt. He wanted their attention to be focused on God who would give them a new beginning by bringing them home from Babylon through a new exodus (V. 19).

With God, new beginnings are possible in our hearts. He can help us to let go of the past and start clinging to Him. Relationship with Him provides a new hope for all who will trust Him. 🌱

MARVIN WILLIAMS

Lord, we need Your touch on our lives. Work in our hearts in whatever areas need a fresh start. Help us to do our part and to trust You to do what only You can do.

God gives fresh starts from the inside out.

Misplaced Love

Martin Lindstrom, an author and speaker, thinks that cellphones have become akin to a best friend for many owners. Lindstrom's experiment using an MRI helped him discover why. When the subjects saw or heard their phone ringing, their brains fired off neurons in the area associated with feelings of love and compassion. Lindstrom said, "It was as if they were in the presence of a girl-friend, boyfriend, or family member."

> **TODAY'S READING**
> **Psalm 115**
>
> **Their idols are silver and gold, the work of men's hands.** v. 4

Many things vie for our affection and time and attention, and it seems we're always needing to evaluate where we're focusing our lives. Joshua told the people of Israel that they were to give their affection and worship to God alone (JOSH. 24:14). This was significant in contrast to the idols worshiped by the nations around them. These idols were made of metal and were only the work of men's hands (PS. 115:4). They were totally powerless compared to the Lord. Therefore, God's people were exhorted to find their security in Him and not in other gods (JUDG. 10:13-16). Jesus reiterated this in His discussion of the commandments: "Love the LORD your God with all your heart, with all your soul, and with all your mind" (MATT. 22:37).

The Lord alone is our help and shield (PS. 115:9). May we reserve our worship for Him. 🌿

MARVIN WILLIAMS

FOR FURTHER THOUGHT
What do our actions in the last few months reveal about our affections? Is there any indication that we have placed someone or something above God?

God is most worthy of our affections.

Still Working

Vivian and Don are in their mid-90s and have been married more than 70 years. Recently Vivian suffered a setback when she broke her hip. This has been additionally difficult because for several years both Don and Vivian have been saddened by the realization that they are no longer strong enough to be active in the life and work of their church.

However, Vivian and Don are still hard at work for the Lord: They are prayer warriors. While they may not always be physically present and visible in the life of their church, they are faithful "behind the scenes" in their service for Him.

> TODAY'S READING
> **Matthew 25:14-21**
>
> **Well done, good and faithful servant.** 25:23

The parable of the talents in Matthew 25 reminds us that we must use the "talents" God has given us wisely. All of us have God-given skills and abilities at various levels—and we must not bury, unused, what God has given us.

It is not only in our years of strength that God will use us, but also in our youth and age, as well as in our sickness and weakness. Vivian and Don continue to serve by praying. And like them, we honor our Savior by using our skills— "each according to his own ability" (V. 15)—to serve Him who is worthy. 🌱

DAVE BRANON

Lord, You have done so much for me. Please show me what I can do to serve You—to honor You with the abilities You have provided. May my life be a living sacrifice of love and action for Your honor.

God can use you at any age—if you are willing.

Spoonful of Sugar

Where is **Mary Poppins** when you need her? I know this sounds as if I'm longing for the good old days when cheerfully unrealistic movies featured characters like this fictional nanny, but what I'm really longing for are people with a vision for the future that is realistically optimistic. I yearn for joyful, creative people who can show us the positive side of what we consider negative, who can remind us that "just a spoonful of sugar makes the medicine go down."

> **TODAY'S READING**
> **Psalm 19:7-14**
>
> **The judgments of the LORD are true and righteous altogether.... Sweeter also than honey and the honeycomb.** v. 10

David wrote a song that expressed a similar truth. In his words, "the judgments of the LORD" are "sweeter also than ... honey" (PS. 19:9-10). Seldom do we hear that truth is sweet. More often we hear that it is bitter or hard to swallow. But truth is so much more than medicine to treat what's wrong. It's the diet that will prevent disease. It's not an inoculation or an injection. It's a gourmet meal that should be presented as a culinary delight, enticing the hungry to "taste and see that the LORD is good" (34:8).

We sing "Jesus is the sweetest name I know," but some of us present Him as if He's gone sour. Pure truth, untainted by pride, is the sweetest, most refreshing taste of all to those who hunger for spiritual sustenance. And we have the privilege of serving it to a starving world. 🌿   *JULIE ACKERMAN LINK*

Jesus is the sweetest name I know,
And He's just the same as His lovely name,
And that's the reason why I love Him so;
Oh, Jesus is the sweetest name I know. LONG

The truth of the LORD endures forever. PSALM 117:2

Joining the Family

Maurice Griffin was adopted when he was 32 years old. He had lived with Lisa and Charles Godbold 20 years earlier as a foster child. Although Maurice was now a man living on his own, adoption had been what the family and he had always longed for. Once they were reunited and the adoption was official, Maurice commented, "This is probably the happiest moment in my life. . . . I'm happy to be home."

TODAY'S READING
Galatians 3:26–4:7

You are all sons of God through faith in Christ Jesus. v. 26

Those of us who have joined the family of God may refer to that time as the happiest moment in our lives. When we trust Christ for salvation, we become God's children, and He becomes our heavenly Father. The Bible assures us, "You are all sons of God through faith in Christ Jesus" (GAL. 3:26).

As God's adopted children, we acquire spiritual siblings—our brothers and sisters in Christ—and we all share an eternal inheritance (COL. 1:12). In addition, Jesus' Spirit indwells our hearts and enables us to pray using the name Abba, Father (GAL. 4:6)—like a child calling, "Daddy."

To be a child of God is to experience the closeness and security of a Father who loves us, accepts us, and wants to know us. Our adoption into His family is a wonderful homecoming. ❧　　　　　　　　　　　　　　*JENNIFER BENSON SCHULDT*

I once was an outcast stranger on earth,
A sinner by choice, and an alien by birth;
But I've been adopted, my name's written down,
An heir to the mansion, a robe, and a crown.　BUELL

God's arms are always open to welcome anyone home.

All Kinds of Help

n the wake of the shooting at an elementary school in Newtown, Connecticut, many people have felt strongly compelled to help. Some donated blood for the injured, some provided free lunches and coffee at their restaurants for workers. Others wrote letters of comfort or just gave hugs.

Some sent gifts of money and teddy bears for the children; others offered counseling. People found ways to serve according to their personalities, abilities, and resources.

A story in the Bible about Joseph tells how he used his skills to play an important role in helping people survive a 7-year famine (GEN. 41:53-54). In his case, he could prepare beforehand because he knew a difficult time was

TODAY'S READING
Genesis 41:46-57

Pharaoh said to Joseph, "Inasmuch as God has shown you all this, there is no one as discerning and wise as you." 41:39

coming. After Joseph warned Pharaoh, the king of Egypt, that the lean years were coming, Pharaoh put him in charge of the 7-year preparation time. Joseph used wisdom and discernment from God to get his country ready (41:39). Then, when "the famine was over all the face of the earth, . . . Joseph opened all the storehouses" (V. 56). He was even able to help his own family (45:16-18).

These stories show the heart of God for the world. He has prepared us and made us who we are that we might care for others in whatever way He leads us. 🌿 *ANNE CETAS*

Lord, help me feel the hurt that others feel
When life inflicts some bitter pain,
And use me in some loving way to heal
The wounds that may through life remain. D. DEHAAN

Compassion offers whatever is necessary to heal.

Who's at the Center?

R**ecently, I had** what for me was a "Copernican moment": I am not at the center of the universe. The world doesn't revolve around me. It doesn't move at my pace, in my terms, nor in accord with my preferences.

Though we might wish it to be otherwise, life is not all about us. Everything revolves around the Lord. In Psalm 33, we read that all nature revolves around Him and His control (VV. 6-9). He assigned the sea its boundaries and locked the ocean in vast reservoirs. Everything in nature operates in accordance with the laws He has set.

> **TODAY'S READING**
> **Psalm 33:6-19**
>
> **The counsel of the LORD stands forever, the plans of His heart to all generations.** v. 11

The nations also revolve around the Lord (VV. 10-12). No plan or scheme can stand up against God's. Ultimately, it is the Lord's plan that will stand forever. His intentions can never be shaken.

Finally, the lives of all humanity revolve around the Lord (VV. 13-19). God sees the whole human race. He made our hearts, and He understands everything we do. And He has the power to intervene in our lives and deliver us from situations spinning out of control.

Our life is created to be centered on God, not self. How thankful we can be to serve such a powerful God, who has every aspect of our lives under His control. 🌸 *POH FANG CHIA*

Teach me, Lord, to live out the truth of Psalm 33. May I revere You as I should. May I and all the inhabitants of the world stand in awe of You, for Your counsel and plans stand forever.

When we die to all about us, we live to God above us.

Out of Chaos

Everything I observe makes me believe this is true: Order is not natural. When I consider my office, I'm astounded at how quickly it descends into chaos and how long it takes me to restore order. Order requires intervention; it does not happen naturally.

I shouldn't be surprised. God's role in bringing order out of chaos is a prominent biblical theme. He did it when He was creating the nation of Israel (EX. 7–14). When God said it was time to bring the Hebrew people out of Egypt, Pharaoh objected. His nation's economy depended on the Hebrew workers, so Pharaoh didn't want to lose them. To change Pharaoh's mind, God sent 10 plagues to convince him. Pharaoh's magicians were able to duplicate the first two plagues. But they could not reverse the plagues—any of them. They could cause chaos, but they could not restore order. Only God can do that.

> **TODAY'S READING**
> **Exodus 8:1-15**
>
> **Speak evil of no one, . . . be peaceable, gentle, showing all humility to all men.** Titus 3:2

With effort, we can bring order to our living spaces, but none of us can bring order out of the emotional and spiritual chaos of our lives. Only God can do that. He restores order to chaotic situations when we live as God intended—speaking no evil, being peaceable and gentle, and showing humility to all (TITUS 3:2).

JULIE ACKERMAN LINK

Father, our world and our lives do have much chaos and confusion. We need You to restore our souls. Help us to live as You want us to live—loving others.

When we put our problems in God's hands, He puts His peace in our hearts.

The Link to Life

By the time he was 16, Morris Frank (1908–1980) had lost his sight in both eyes. Several years later, he traveled to Switzerland where he met Buddy, the canine who would help to inspire Frank's involvement with the Seeing Eye guide-dog school.

With Buddy leading the way, Frank learned to navigate busy sidewalks and intersections. Describing the freedom his guide provided, Frank said, "It was glorious: just [Buddy] and a leather strap, linking me to life." Buddy gave Morris Frank a new kind of access to the world around him.

God's Holy Spirit gives us access to abundant spiritual life in Christ. When we accept Christ as Lord, God washes our sins away and renews us "by the Holy Spirit, whom He poured out on us generously through Jesus Christ our Savior" (TITUS 3:5-6 NIV). Once we know Christ, the Holy Spirit helps us experience God's love (ROM. 5:5), understand God's Word (JOHN 14:26), pray (ROM. 8:26), and abound in hope (ROM. 15:13).

Today, as you think about your relationship with God, remember that the Spirit is your guide to life in Christ (ROM. 8:14). ❧

JENNIFER BENSON SCHULDT

> TODAY'S READING
> **Titus 3:1-11**
>
> **According to His mercy He saved us, through the washing of regeneration and renewing of the Holy Spirit.** v. 5

Holy Spirit, Light divine,
Shine upon this heart of mine.
Chase the shades of night away;
Turn my darkness into day. REED

The Holy Spirit guides us into knowledge and spiritual growth.

Waiting . . .

Day after day for years Harry shared with the Lord his concern for his son-in-law John who had turned away from God. But then Harry died. A few months later, John turned back to God. When his mother-in-law Marsha told him that Harry had been praying for him every day, John replied, "I waited too long." But Marsha joyfully shared: "The Lord is still answering the prayers Harry prayed during his earthly life."

Harry's story is an encouragement to us who pray and wait. He continued "steadfastly in prayer" and waited patiently (ROM. 12:12).

> **TODAY'S READING**
> **Psalm 130**
>
> **Rejoicing in hope, patient in tribulation, continuing steadfastly in prayer.** Romans 12:12

The author of Psalm 130 experienced waiting in prayer. He said, "I wait for the LORD, my soul waits" (V. 5). He found hope in God because he knew that "with the LORD there is mercy, and with Him is abundant redemption" (V. 7).

Author Samuel Enyia wrote about God's timing: "God does not depend on our time. Our time is chronological and linear but God . . . is timeless. He will act at the fullness of His time. Our prayer . . . may not necessarily rush God into action, but . . . places us before Him in fellowship."

What a privilege we have to fellowship with God in prayer and to wait for the answer in the fullness of His time. 🌱

ANNE CETAS

Pray on! Pray on! Cease not to pray,
And should the answer tarry, wait;
Thy God will come, will surely come,
And He can never come too late. CHISHOLM

God may delay our request, but He will never disappoint our trust.

Acts of Kindness

was traveling with some men when we spotted a family stranded alongside the road. My friends immediately pulled over to help. They got the car running, talked with the father and mother of the family, and gave them some money for gasoline. When the mother thanked them over and over, they replied, "We're glad to help out, and we do it in Jesus' name." As we drove away, I thought how natural it was for these friends to help people in need and acknowledge the Lord as the source of their generosity.

> TODAY'S READING
> **Acts 4:1-13**
>
> **By the name of Jesus . . . this man stands here before you whole.** v. 10

Peter and John exhibited that same joyful generosity when they healed a lame man who was begging outside the temple in Jerusalem (ACTS 3:1-10). This led to their arrest and appearance before the authorities who asked, "By what power or by what name have you done this?" Peter replied, "If we this day are judged for a good deed done to a helpless man . . . let it be known to you all, and to all the people of Israel, that by the name of Jesus Christ of Nazareth, whom you crucified, whom God raised from the dead, by Him this man stands here before you whole" (4:7-10).

Kindness is a fruit of the Spirit (GAL. 5:22) and a powerful context in which to genuinely speak to others about the Lord. 🌺

DAVID MCCASLAND

Lord, help me to love with both words and deeds,
To reach out to others and meet their needs;
Lord, burden my heart for those lost in sin,
With mercy and love that flows from within. FITZHUGH

***One act of kindness may teach more about
the love of God than many sermons.***

Shout Hallelujah!

A **few days ago,** I spied my old friend Bob vigorously pedaling a bike at our neighborhood gym and staring down at a blood pressure monitor on his finger.

"What are you doing?" I asked.

"Looking to see if I'm alive," he grunted.

"What would you do if you saw you were dead?" I countered.

"Shout hallelujah!" he replied with a radiant smile.

Over the years I've caught glimpses of great inner strength in Bob: patient

TODAY'S READING
1 Cor. 15:50-58

O Death, where is your sting? v. 55

endurance in the face of physical decline and discomfort, and faith and hope as he approaches the end of his life journey. Indeed he has found not only hope, but death has lost its power to tyrannize him.

Who can find peace and hope—and even joy—in dying? Only those who are joined by faith to the God of eternity and who know that they have eternal life (1 COR. 15:52,54). For those who have this assurance, like my friend Bob, death has lost its terror. They can speak with colossal joy of seeing Christ face to face!

Why be afraid of death? Why not rejoice? As the poet John Donne (1572–1631) wrote, "One short sleep past, we wake eternally." 🌿

DAVID ROPER

Beyond the sunset, O blissful morning,
When with our Savior heaven is begun,
Earth's toiling ended, O glorious dawning;
Beyond the sunset, when day is done. BROCK

*For the Christian, dying is the last shadow of
Earth's night before heaven's dawn.*

Never Let Down

When I was a child, one of my favorite pastimes was playing on the teeter-totter in the nearby park. A kid would sit on each end of the board and bounce each other up and down. Sometimes the one who was down would stay there and leave his playmate stuck up in the air yelling to be let down. But the cruelest of all tricks was getting off the teeter-totter and running away when your friend was up in the air—he would come crashing down to the ground with a painful bump.

TODAY'S READING
Lam. 3:13-26

[The LORD's] compassions fail not. They are new every morning.
vv. 22-23

Sometimes we may feel that Jesus does that to us. We trust Him to be there with us through the ups and downs of life. However, when life takes a turn and leaves us with bumps and bruises, it may feel as if He has walked away leaving our lives to come painfully crashing down.

But Lamentations 3 reminds us that "the steadfast love of the LORD never ceases; his mercies never come to an end" (v. 22 ESV) and that God is faithful to the end even when everything seems to be falling apart. This means that in the midst of our pain, even though we may be lonely, we are not alone. And though we may not feel His presence, He is there as our trusted companion who will never walk away and let us down! 🌿
JOE STOWELL

Thank You, Lord, that we can trust in Your faithful presence even when we feel alone. Help us to wait patiently for You to manifest Your steadfast loving presence.

When everyone else fails, Jesus is your most trusted friend.

Fearful Fish

Managing a saltwater aquarium, I discovered, is no easy task. I had to run a portable chemical laboratory to monitor nitrate levels and ammonia content. I pumped in vitamins and antibiotics and sulfa drugs and enzymes. I filtered the water through glass fibers and charcoal.

TODAY'S READING
John 1:6-14

The Word became flesh and dwelt among us, and we beheld His glory. v. 14

You would think my fish would be grateful. Not so. When my shadow loomed above the tank to feed them, they dove for cover into the nearest shell. I was too large for them; my actions incomprehensible. They did not know that my acts were merciful. To change their perceptions would require a form of incarnation. I would have to become a fish and "speak" to them in a language they could understand, which was impossible for me to do.

According to the Scriptures, God, the Creator of the universe, did something that seems impossible. He came to earth in human form as a baby. "The world was made through Him," says John, "and the world did not know Him" (JOHN 1:10). So God, who created matter, took shape within it, as a playwright might become a character within his own play. God wrote a story, using real characters, on the pages of real history. "The Word became flesh and dwelt among us" (V. 14). 🌿

PHILIP YANCEY

All praise to Thee, eternal Lord,
Clothed in a garb of flesh and blood;
Choosing a manger for a throne,
While worlds on worlds are Thine alone. LUTHER

God entered human history to offer us the gift of eternal life.

Down the Up Staircase

The video starts with a puppy at the top of the stairs afraid to go down. Despite much encouragement from people cheering at the bottom, Daisy can't figure it out. She wants so badly to join them, but fear keeps her pacing the landing. Then a bigger dog comes to help. Simon runs up the steps and then back down, showing Daisy how easy it is. Daisy is not convinced. Simon tries again. This time more slowly. Then he watches Daisy try again. But Daisy still is too scared. Once again Simon goes to the top and demonstrates the technique. Finally Daisy dares to let her back legs follow the front ones. Simon stays beside her. She makes it. Everyone celebrates!

> **TODAY'S READING**
> **2 Chronicles 12:1-8**
>
> If My people . . . will humble themselves, and pray . . . and turn from their wicked ways, then I will hear from heaven, and will forgive their sin. 7:14

What a beautiful picture of discipleship. We spend much of our time trying to teach others to climb up, but the more important, and more difficult, thing to learn is how to "go down." Throughout Scripture we read that God desires humility of us. Because the people of Judah humbled themselves, the Lord said, "Therefore I will not destroy them" (2 CHRON. 12:7).

On numerous occasions, God demonstrated humility by coming down (EX. 3:7-8; 19:10-12; MICAH 1:3). Finally God sent Jesus, who spent His life teaching the technique we are to follow (PHIL. 2:5-11). 🌱

JULIE ACKERMAN LINK

More like the Master I would ever be,
More of His meekness, more humility;
More zeal to labor, more courage to be true,
More consecration for work He bids me do. GABRIEL

No one will learn anything at all unless he first learns humility.

Learning to Love

When Hans Egede went to Greenland as a missionary in 1721, he didn't know the Inuit language. His temperament was often overbearing, and he struggled to be kind to the people.

In 1733, a smallpox epidemic swept through Greenland, wiping out almost two-thirds of the Inuit people—and claiming Egede's wife as well. This shared suffering melted Egede's harsh demeanor, and he began to tirelessly labor to care for the people physically and spiritually.

TODAY'S READING
1 Cor. 13:4-13

Love suffers long and is kind. v. 4

Because his life now better represented the stories he told them of God's love, the Inuits could at last grasp His desire to love them too. Even in suffering, their hearts turned to God.

Perhaps you are like the Inuits in this story, and you are unable to see God in the people around you. Or perhaps you are like Hans Egede, who struggled to express love in a way that taught people about God. Knowing we are weak and needy people, God showed us what love is like. He sent His Son, Jesus Christ, to die for our sins (JOHN 3:16). That's how much God loves you and me.

Jesus is the perfect example of the love that is described in 1 Corinthians 13. As we look to Him, we learn that we are loved and we learn how to love in turn. ❧   *RANDY KILGORE*

Jesus, let me find in You a sense that I am loved. And may my heart not grow cold and cluttered by anger and wounds from the past so that others can see Your reflection in me.

May I never be the barrier that blocks one's view of God.

Probing Questions

While **riding on a train** a few years after the American Civil War, General Lew Wallace of the Union Army encountered a fellow officer, Colonel Robert Ingersoll. Ingersoll was one of the 19th century's leading agnostics, and Wallace was a man of faith. As their conversation turned to their spiritual differences, Wallace realized that he wasn't able to answer the questions and doubts raised by Ingersoll. Embarrassed by his lack of understanding about his own faith, Wallace began searching the Scriptures for answers. The result was his confident declaration of the person of the Savior in his classic historical novel *Ben-Hur: A Tale of the Christ.*

> **TODAY'S READING**
> **1 Peter 3:8-17**
>
> **Always be ready to give a defense to everyone who asks you a reason for the hope that is in you.** v. 15

Probing questions from skeptics don't have to be a threat to our faith. Instead, they can motivate us to seek a deeper understanding and equip us to respond wisely and lovingly to those who might question our faith. The apostle Peter encouraged us to pursue the wisdom of God in the Scriptures when he wrote, "Always be ready to give a defense to everyone who asks you a reason for the hope that is in you, with meekness and fear" (1 PETER 3:15).

We don't have to have an answer for every question, but we need the courage, confidence, and conviction to share our love for Christ and the hope that is in us. ❧ *BILL CROWDER*

My hope is in the Lord who gave Himself for me,
And paid the price of all my sin at Calvary.
For me He died, for me He lives,
And everlasting life and light He freely gives. CLAYTON

Christ is the ultimate answer to life's greatest questions.

Christ in the Storm

At the age of 27, Rembrandt painted the seascape *Christ in the Storm on the Sea of Galilee* based on the story in Mark 4. With its distinctive contrast of light and shadow, Rembrandt's painting shows a small boat threatened with destruction in a furious storm. As the disciples struggle against the wind and waves, Jesus is undisturbed. The most unusual aspect, however, is the presence in the boat of a 13th disciple whom art experts say resembles Rembrandt himself.

TODAY'S READING
Mark 4:33-41

Why are you so fearful? How is it that you have no faith? v. 40

Mark's gospel describes the disciples' vivid lesson about who Jesus is and what He can do. While they were frantically trying to save a sinking boat, Jesus was asleep. Didn't He care that they were all about to die? (V. 38). After Jesus calmed the storm (V. 39), He asked the penetrating question, "Why are you so fearful? How is it that you have no faith?" (V. 40). Then they were even more afraid, exclaiming to each other, "Who can this be, that even the wind and the sea obey Him!" (V. 41).

We could also put ourselves in this story and discover, just as Jesus' disciples did, that to each person who trusts in Jesus Christ, He reveals His presence, compassion, and control in every storm of life. ❦   *DAVID MCCASLAND*

Be still, my heart; for faithful is thy Lord,
And pure and true and tried His holy Word;
Though stormy flood which rageth as the sea,
His promises thy stepping-stones shall be. ANON.

God is a safe dwelling place in life's storms.

Too Late

t happens nearly every semester. I tell my freshman college writing class often that they need to keep up with the numerous writing assignments in order to pass the class. But nearly every semester some don't believe me. They're the ones who send me frantic emails after the last day of class and give me their reasons for not taking care of business. I hate to do it, but I have to tell them, "I'm sorry. It's too late. You have failed the class."

That's bad enough when you're a college freshman and you realize you've just wasted a couple thousand dollars. But there is a far more serious, more permanent finality that comes at the end of life if people haven't taken care of business with God about their sin. In those cases, if people die without having put their faith in Jesus Christ as Savior, they face an eternity without Him.

TODAY'S READING
Hebrews 4:1-11

Therefore, since a promise remains of entering His rest, let us fear lest any of you seem to have come short of it. v. 1

What a terrible moment it would be to stand before the Savior Himself and hear Him say, "I never knew you; depart from Me!" (MATT. 7:23). The author of Hebrews warns us to make sure we don't "come short" (4:1) of the eternal rest offered by God. The good news is that it's not too late. Today Jesus freely offers to us salvation and forgiveness through Him. ✿

DAVE BRANON

If you'd like to know the love of God the Father,
Come to Him through Jesus Christ, His loving Son;
He'll forgive your sins and save your soul forever,
And you'll love forevermore this faithful One. FELTEN

Calvary reveals the seriousness of our sin and the vastness of God's love.

"If You Are Willing"

Molly wanted her dad's help, but she was afraid to ask. She knew that when he was working on his computer, he didn't want to be interrupted. *He might get upset at me*, she thought, so she didn't ask him.

We need not have such fears when we come to Jesus. In Matthew 8:1-4, we read about a leper who didn't hesitate to interrupt Jesus with his needs. His disease made him desperate—he had been ostracized from society and was in emo-

TODAY'S READING
Matthew 8:1-4

Lord, if You are willing, You can make me clean. v. 2

tional distress. Jesus was busy with "great multitudes," but the leper made his way through the crowd to talk with Jesus.

Matthew's gospel says that the leper came and "worshiped Him" (V. 2). He approached Jesus in worship, with trust in His power, and with humility, acknowledging that the choice to help belonged to Jesus. He said, "Lord, if You are willing, You can make me clean" (V. 2). In compassion, Jesus touched him (leprosy had made him "untouchable" by the standards of Jewish law), and he was cleansed immediately.

Like the leper, we don't need to hesitate to approach Jesus with our desire for His help. As we go to Him in humility and worship, we can trust that He will make the best choices for us. 🌿   *ANNE CETAS*

What an example this leper is to me, Lord. Give me a heart
of worship, of confidence in Your power, and of trust that
when I bring my needs to You, You'll make the best choice.
May I surrender to Your will.

Let us come boldly to the throne of grace, that we may obtain mercy.
HEBREWS 4:16

Tree of Rest

The lone tree in the field across from my office remained a mystery. Acres of trees had been cut down so the farmer could grow corn. But one tree remained standing, its branches reaching up and spreading out. The mystery was solved when I learned the tree was spared for a purpose. Farmers long ago traditionally left one tree standing so that they and their animals would have a cool place to rest when the hot summer sun was beating down.

At times we find that we alone have survived something, and we don't know why. Soldiers coming home from combat and patients who've survived a life-threatening illness struggle to know why they survived when others did not.

> TODAY'S READING
> **Ezra 9:5-9**
>
> **There is a remnant according to the election of grace.**
> Romans 11:5

The Old Testament speaks of a remnant of Israelites whom God spared when the nation was sent into exile. The remnant preserved God's law and later rebuilt the temple (EZRA 9:9). The apostle Paul referred to himself as part of the remnant of God (ROM. 11:1,5). He was spared to become God's messenger to Gentiles (V. 13).

If we stand where others have fallen, it's to raise our hands to heaven in praise and to spread our arms as shade for the weary. The Lord enables us to be a tree of rest for others. 🌱

JULIE ACKERMAN LINK

Thank You, Father, that You are my place of rest. And that all You have brought me through can be used by You to encourage others. Bring praise to Yourself through me.

Hope can be ignited by a spark of encouragement.

He Changed My Life

Following the death of computer pioneer Steve Jobs in 2011, more than one million people from around the world posted tributes to him online. The common theme was how Jobs had changed their lives. They said they lived differently because of his creative innovations, and they wanted to express their appreciation and their sorrow. The screen of one tablet computer said in large letters: iSad.

Gratitude fuels expression, which is exactly what Psalm 107 describes: "Let the redeemed of the LORD say so, whom He has redeemed from the hand of the enemy" (V. 2). The theme of this psalm is people in great trouble who were delivered by the Lord. Some were homeless and in need (VV. 4-5); some had rebelled against God's Word (VV. 10-11); others were at their wits' end when they cried out to God (VV. 26-27). All were rescued by God. "Oh, that men would give thanks to the LORD for His goodness, and for His wonderful works to the children of men!" (VV. 8,15,21,31).

> **TODAY'S READING**
> **Psalm 107:1-16**
>
> **Let the redeemed of the LORD say so, whom He has redeemed from the hand of the enemy.** v. 2

When we consider the greatness of God's love, His grace in sending Jesus Christ to die for us and rise again, and what He has delivered us from, we cannot keep from praising Him and wanting to tell others how He changed our lives! 🌿

DAVID MCCASLAND

O God, my heart is filled with praise for all that You have done for me. You have changed the focus and purpose of my life because You sent Your Son. Thank You.

Our gratitude to God for salvation fuels our witness to others.

Tears of Gratitude

At a communion service my wife and I attended, the congregation was invited to come forward to receive the bread and cup from one of the pastors or elders. They told each one personally of Jesus' sacrifice for him or her. It was an especially moving experience during what can often become just routine. After we returned to our seats, I watched as others slowly and quietly filed past. It was striking to see how many had tears in their eyes. For me, and for others I talked with later, they were tears of gratitude.

> TODAY'S READING
> **1 Cor. 11:23-32**
>
> **You proclaim the Lord's death till He comes.** v. 26

The reason for tears of gratitude is seen in the reason for the communion table itself. Paul, after instructing the church at Corinth about the meaning of the memorial supper, punctuated his comments with these powerful words: "For as often as you eat this bread and drink this cup, you proclaim the Lord's death till He comes" (1 COR. 11:26). With the elements of communion pointing directly to the cross and the sacrifice of Christ on our behalf, that service was about so much more than ritual—it was about Christ. His love. His sacrifice. His cross. For us.

How inadequate words are to convey the extraordinary worth of Christ! Sometimes tears of gratitude speak what words can't fully express. 🌿

BILL CROWDER

Were the whole realm of nature mine,
That were a present far too small;
Love so amazing, so divine,
Demands my soul, my life, my all. WATTS

**The love Christ showed for us on the cross
is greater than words could ever express.**

Who Gets the Credit?

Chris Langan has an IQ higher than Albert Einstein's. Moustafa Ismail has 31-inch biceps and can lift 600 pounds. Bill Gates is estimated to be worth billions. Those who have extraordinary abilities or possessions might be tempted to think more highly of themselves than they should. But we don't have to be wildly smart, strong, or wealthy to want to take credit for our achievements. Any size of accomplishment carries with it this question: Who will get the credit?

TODAY'S READING
Jeremiah 9:23-26

Let him who glories glory in this, that he understands and knows Me. v.24

During a time of judgment, God spoke to the Israelites through the prophet Jeremiah. He said: "Let not the wise man glory in his wisdom, let not the mighty man glory in his might, nor let the rich man glory in his riches" (JER. 9:23). Rather, "Let him who glories glory in this, that he understands and knows Me" (V. 24). God wanted His people to prize Him and His excellence above anything else.

If we allow praise to inflate our self-image, we're forgetting that "every good gift . . . comes down from the Father" (JAMES 1:17). It's better to give God the glory—not only because it protects our hearts from pride but also because He rightfully deserves it. He is God, the One "who does great things . . . marvelous things without number" (JOB 5:9).

JENNIFER BENSON SCHULDT

Not I, but Christ, be honored, loved, exalted;
Not I, but Christ, be seen, be known, be heard;
Not I, but Christ, in every look and action;
Not I, but Christ, in every thought and word. WHIDDINGTON

We were created to give God the glory.

Heart Matters

Our hearts pump at a rate of 70-75 beats per minute. Though weighing only 11 ounces on average, a healthy heart pumps 2,000 gallons of blood through 60,000 miles of blood vessels each day. Every day, the heart creates enough energy to drive a truck 20 miles. In a lifetime, that is equivalent to driving to the moon and back.

A healthy heart can do amazing things. Conversely, if our heart malfunctions, our whole body shuts down.

> TODAY'S READING
> **Proverbs 4:20-27**
>
> **Keep your heart with all diligence, for out of it spring the issues of life.** v. 23

The same could be said of our "spiritual heart." In Scripture, the word *heart* represents the center of our emotions, thinking, and reasoning. It is the "command center" of our life.

So when we read, "Keep your heart with all diligence" (PROV. 4:23), it makes a lot of sense. But it's difficult advice to keep. Life will always make demands upon our time and energy that cry out for immediate attention. By comparison, taking time to hear God's Word and to do what it says may not shout quite so loudly. We may not notice the consequences of neglect right away, but over time it may give way to a spiritual heart attack.

I'm thankful God has given us His Word. We need His help not to neglect it, but to use it to align our hearts with His every day. 🍂

POH FANG CHIA

Dear Jesus, take my heart and hand,
And grant me this, I pray:
That I through Your sweet love may grow
More like You day by day. GARRISON

To keep spiritually fit, consult the Great Physician.

My Kind of People

Years ago in a worship service, pastor Ray Stedman stepped to the pulpit and read the text for the day: "Don't fool yourselves. Those who indulge in sexual sin, or who worship idols, or commit adultery, or are male prostitutes or practice homosexuality, or are thieves, or greedy people, or drunkards, or are abusive, or cheat people—none of these will inherit the Kingdom of God. Some of you were once like that" (1 COR. 6:9-11 NLT).

> TODAY'S READING
> 1 Cor. 6:9-11
>
> **Such were some of you. But you . . . were justified in the name of the Lord Jesus.** v. 11

Then he looked up, a bemused smile on his face, and said, "I'm curious: How many of you have one or more of these sins in your background? If so, will you stand?"

There was a young man there who had never been in a church before. He had recently been saved at a Billy Graham crusade and came with fear and trembling to church that Sunday, not knowing what he would find. He later told me that when he heard the pastor's question, he looked around to see if anyone would stand. At first no one did, but then most of the congregation was on their feet. He said to himself, "These are my kind of people!"

We can all find ourselves in Paul's list in 1 Corinthians. But when we confess our sin and accept the gift of eternal life paid for by the death of Jesus, we become a new creation saved by grace (ROM. 6:23; 2 COR. 5:17). 🌿   *DAVID ROPER*

He touched me, oh, He touched me,
And oh, the joy that floods my soul!
Something happened and now I know
He touched me and made me whole. GAITHER

Nothing in my hand I bring, simply to Thy cross I cling.

Mom's Finish Line

When Jeff learned that his mother's health was rapidly declining, he immediately caught a plane to be with her. He sat at her bedside holding her hand, singing hymns, comforting her, and expressing his love for her. She passed away, and at her funeral many told Jeff what a blessing his mother had been. She was gifted in Bible teaching, counseling others, and leading prayer groups. These were vital parts of serving Christ until near the end of her life. She finished strong for Christ.

TODAY'S READING
2 Timothy 4:1-8

I have fought the good fight, I have finished the race, I have kept the faith. v. 7

To honor his mother's life, Jeff participated in a 26.2 mile race. During the race he thanked God for her life and grieved her loss. When he crossed the finish line, Jeff pointed his index finger toward heaven—"Where Mom is," he said. She had honored Christ to the end, which reminded him of the words of the apostle Paul: "I have fought the good fight, I have finished the race, I have kept the faith. Finally, there is laid up for me the crown of righteousness, which the Lord . . . will give to me on that Day" (2 TIM. 4:7-8).

We are involved in a "long-distance race." Let's run in such a way that we may obtain the prize of "an imperishable crown" (1 COR. 9:25). What could be more desirable than to finish strong for Christ and to be with Him forever. ❦ *DENNIS FISHER*

Run the straight race through God's good grace,
Lift up your eyes and seek His face;
Life with its way before us lies,
Christ is the path and Christ the prize. MONSELL

The Christian's race is not a sprint—it's a marathon.

Promises Still Kept

n the ancient Near East, a treaty between a superior (a lord or king) and an inferior (his subjects) was called a suzerain treaty. The ratification ceremony required animals to be sacrificed and cut in half. The animal parts were then arranged in two rows on the ground, forming an aisle between them. As the suzerain walked between the halves, he was publicly declaring he would keep the covenant and would become like the slain animals if he failed to keep his word.

When Abram asked God how he could be sure *His* promises would come to pass, God used the culturally significant symbolism of the suzerain treaty to affirm His promises (GEN. 15). When the burning torch passed through the pieces of the sacrifice, Abram understood that God was declaring it was His job to keep the covenant.

> **TODAY'S READING**
> **Genesis 15:5-21**
>
> **When the sun went down . . . there appeared a smoking oven and a burning torch that passed between those pieces.** v. 17

God's covenant with Abram and His assurance of its completion extends to followers of Christ. That is why Paul repeatedly refers to believers as sons of Abraham in his New Testament writings (ROM. 4:11-18; GAL. 3:29). Once we accept Jesus Christ as Savior, God becomes the keeper in our covenant of faith (SEE JOHN 10:28-29).

Because God is the keeper of our salvation, with renewed confidence in Him we trust Him with our lives. 🍂

RANDY KILGORE

He will never fail us, He will not forsake;
His eternal covenant He will never break.
Onward then, and fear not, children of the day;
For His Word shall never, never pass away. HAVERGAL

Our salvation is secure because God does the holding.

Way Out

While in London recently, I decided to take the underground train to my destination. So I paid my fare and descended into the depths of London to catch my train. But getting out of the station can be a scary experience for someone who is unfamiliar with the system. If you don't find the exit, you can quickly get lost in the tunnels.

Being alone in a sparsely populated underground tunnel is an unsettling feeling, so believe me, you don't want to get lost. Needless to say, I was glad when I spotted the sign that says, "WAY OUT" and followed it to safety.

Paul reminds us that when we are vulnerable to falling into sin, "God is faithful; he will not let you be tempted beyond what you can bear. But when you are tempted, he will also provide a way out" (1 COR. 10:13 NIV). It's easy to assume that God is not with us when we are tempted to sin. But this verse assures us that He is present and not just standing idly by. Rather, He is actively providing a way out so we can endure it.

So, the next time you feel tempted, remember that you are not helpless. There is a divinely provided "way out"! Look for the sign, and follow it to safety. 🌱

JOE STOWELL

> TODAY'S READING
> **1 Cor. 10:1-13**
>
> **God is faithful, who will not allow you to be tempted beyond what you are able, but with the temptation will also make the way of escape.** v. 13

Lord, keep us mindful that Your presence with us in
times of temptation means that we need not fall.
Give us the desire to seek Your way out so we can know
the joy of living a life that is pleasing to You.

God is actively working to keep you from the danger of getting lost in sin.

Talking About Jesus

Former **major league baseball player** Tony Graffanino tells of an ongoing ministry effort in a European country. Each year his organization holds a week-long baseball camp. During this week they also offer a daily Bible study. In past years, the leader tried to find reasoned ways to convince the campers that God exists so they would place their faith in Him. After about 13 years, they had seen only 3 people decide to follow Jesus.

Then they changed their approach, says Graffanino. Instead of "trying to present facts, or winning arguments for a debate," they simply talked about "the amazing life and teachings of Jesus." As a result, more campers came to listen, and more chose to follow Him.

The apostle Paul said that when we tell others about the gospel of Jesus Christ, we should set "forth the truth plainly. . . . We do not preach ourselves," he said, "but Jesus Christ as Lord" (2 COR. 4:2,5 NIV). This was Paul's standard for evangelism: "I determined not to know anything among you except Jesus Christ and Him crucified" (1 COR. 2:2).

We should be knowledgeable about the Bible and about the reasons for our belief, and sometimes we need to explain those reasons. But the most compelling and effective story we can tell puts Christ in the center. 🌱 *DAVE BRANON*

Father God, please use me in the lives of others. Remind me to talk about who Jesus is and about His life and teachings. And not to be dragged into debates, but to share Jesus' amazing life.

The risen Christ is the reason for our witness.

Words to Live By

For many years I've maintained a file folder labeled "Speaking." It has become thick with articles, quotations, and illustrations that might be useful. Recently I went through it to discard things that are out of date. I found it difficult to throw away many of the items, not because I haven't used them in a talk but because I haven't put them into practice. I closed the folder thinking, "These aren't words to talk about; these are words to live by."

> **TODAY'S READING**
> **Deuteronomy 4:1-9**
>
> **Surely I have taught you statutes and judgments . . . that you should act according to them.** v. 5

After 40 years in the desert, Moses addressed the people poised to enter the Promised Land: "Now, O Israel, listen to the statutes and the judgments which I teach you to observe, that you may live, and go in and possess the land which the LORD God of your fathers is giving you" (DEUT. 4:1). Moses' repeated theme (VV. 1,2,5,6,9) is that God's commandments are to be kept. He said it well, "Surely I have taught you statutes and judgments . . . that you should act according to them" (V. 5).

It is so easy to talk about doing more than we actually do and to speak about truth we're not living by. We can become bloated with words, yet starved for reality, forgetting that all of God's commands flow from His heart of love for us. 🌺

DAVID MCCASLAND

Help us, Lord, not to be just hearers of the Word; help us
to be doers as well. Teach us to be honest with ourselves
about who we really are. We want to walk in Your ways
and to guide others to You.

The strength of our actions should match the strength of our words.

New Birth

What is there about babies that makes us smile? Many people will stop everything at the sight or sound of a baby and will flock to gaze at the little one. I noticed this when I visited my dad at a nursing home. Though most of the residents were wheelchair-bound and suffered from dementia, the visit of a family with a baby almost unfailingly brought a spark of joy to their eyes that—tentatively at first but then undoubtedly—became a smile. It was amazing to watch.

> TODAY'S READING
> **Psalm 139:7-16**
>
> **You formed my inward parts; You covered me in my mother's womb.** v. 13

Perhaps babies bring a smile because of the wonder of a new life—so precious, tiny, and full of promise. Seeing a baby can remind us of our awesome God and the great love He has for us. He loved us so much that He gave us life and formed us in our mother's womb. "You formed my inward parts," the psalmist says, "You covered me in my mother's womb" (PS. 139:13).

Not only does He give us physical life but He also offers us spiritual rebirth through Jesus (JOHN 3:3-8). God promises believers new bodies and life eternal when Jesus returns (1 COR. 15:50-52).

Physical life and spiritual rebirth—gifts to celebrate from our Father's hand. 🌱   ALYSON KIEDA, OUR DAILY BREAD STAFF EDITOR

In His own image God created man,
He formed his body from the dust of earth;
But more than that, to all who are in Christ
He gives eternal life by second birth.   HESS

I will praise You ... ; marvelous are Your works. PSALM 139:14

Looking Good

Your hair is really healthy," said my hairdresser after giving me a haircut. "I hope it's because you use our products." "No. I'm sorry," I said. "I just use whatever product is cheap and smells good." But then I added, "I also try to eat well. I think that makes a big difference."

When I think about the things we do to make ourselves look good, I'm reminded of some of the things we do to make ourselves look good spiritually. Jesus addressed this issue with the religious leaders in Jerusalem (MATT. 23). They

TODAY'S READING
Matthew 23:23-31

First cleanse the inside. v. 26

followed an elaborate set of religious rules that went well beyond the ones God had given them. They worked hard to look good to their peers, to prove that they were better than others. But their hard work didn't impress God. Jesus said to them, "You cleanse the outside of the cup and dish, but inside [you] are full of extortion and self-indulgence" (V. 25). What the Pharisees did to make themselves look good to others actually revealed that they were not good at all.

Every culture values different religious behaviors and traditions, but God's values transcend cultures. And what He values isn't measured by what others see. God values a clean heart and pure motives. Spiritual health is expressed from the inside out. 🌱

JULIE ACKERMAN LINK

You know me, Lord, for who I am. My motives and heart are open before You. Cleanse me from the inside out. And help me to live as Jesus did—with pure and true motives.

*We might look good on the outside
without really being good on the inside.*

Slow Healing Process

Just **4 weeks** after our son Mark joined the US Army, he injured his knee seriously in a training exercise. As a result, he was released from the military. So, at age 19, he had to use a cane to get around for a while; and because of the severity of the injury he endured 2 years of recovery, rest, and rehab. Finally, Mark was able to set aside the knee braces he had worn since the accident. Although he still experiences residual pain, the long, slow healing process has brought him back to full use of his leg.

Physical healing is often much slower than we anticipate. This is true of spiritual healing as well. The consequences of unwise choices or the actions of hurtful people can create

TODAY'S READING
Revelation 21:1-8

> **God will wipe away every tear from their eyes. . . . There shall be no more pain, for the former things have passed away.** v. 4

burdens or wounds that endure for a lifetime. But for the child of God, there is hope. Although full restoration is not always experienced in this life, the promise of healing is sure. The apostle John wrote, "God will wipe away every tear from their eyes; there shall be no more death, nor sorrow, nor crying. There shall be no more pain, for the former things have passed away" (REV. 21:4).

In our seasons of pain, it is comforting to know that eventually, in His awesome presence, we will be whole forever. 🌿 *BILL CROWDER*

Father, I thank You that in all of our pains and struggles we can find comfort in You. Help us to bring all our hurts to You—both spiritual and physical—and to trust that You will make us whole.

When we come to Christ in our brokenness, He makes us whole.

Many Advisors

The fifteenth-century theologian Thomas à Kempis said, "Who is so wise as to have perfect knowledge of all things? Therefore, trust not too much to your own opinion, but be ready also to hear the opinions of others. Though your own opinion be good, yet if for the love of God you forego it and follow that of another, you shall the more profit thereby." Thomas recognized the importance of seeking the opinions of trusted advisors when making plans for life.

In order to determine God's course for life, the wise person should open up to several avenues of counsel, through which God will bring His guiding wisdom. When a person seeks the wise counsel of others, he shows his realization that he might be overlooking some important factors in his decisions.

> TODAY'S READING
> **Proverbs 15:16-23**
>
> **Without counsel, plans go awry, but in the multitude of counselors they are established.** v. 22

Solomon, the wisest man in Israel, wrote about how important it is to have counsel from others: "Without counsel, plans go awry, but in the multitude of counselors they are established" (PROV. 15:22).

The Lord is the Wonderful Counselor (ISA. 9:6), and He desires to protect us through wise advisors. Seek them out and thank God for them. Let them help you discover a clearer picture of His plan for your life. ❧   *MARVIN WILLIAMS*

Wonderful, wonderful, Jesus is to me,
Counselor, Prince of Peace, Mighty God is He;
Saving me, keeping me from all sin and shame,
Wonderful is my Redeemer, praise His name! LILLENAS

If you seek wise counsel, you multiply your chances for sound decisions.

Surfacing

Human beings straddle visible and invisible realities—the natural and the supernatural. I thought about these two worlds when I went out in a boat to watch whales off the coast of New Zealand. A whale would rest on the surface for a while, then breathe deeply a few times, his exhalations creating a spectacular spout, before plunging a mile deep to feed on squid.

TODAY'S READING
Colossians 1:15-23

By Him all things were created that are in heaven and that are on earth, visible and invisible. v. 16

Despite having its own lively habitat of marine plants and sea creatures, the whale must surface for oxygen from time to time or it dies. Though it knows little about the world above, it needs vital contact with it to survive.

I sometimes feel like that whale, coming up for spiritual air at regular intervals to stay alive. But there is no neat division between the natural and the supernatural. The world we live in is not an either/or world. What I do as a Christian—praying, worshiping, demonstrating God's love to the sick, needy, and imprisoned—is both supernatural and natural.

The same God who created the world that's visible to us actively sustains it and has made a way for us to approach Him, the invisible. Paul wrote, "You, who once were alienated and enemies in your mind by wicked works, yet now He has reconciled in the body of His flesh through death" (COL. 1:21-22).

All our actions take place in the visible world, which we can touch, smell, and see. Yet the Creator and Sustainer of all things has provided a way for us to breathe the spiritual air we need and crave. 🌿　　　　　　　　　　　　*PHILIP YANCEY*

God's throne is always accessible to His children

A New Bucket List

A **friend told me** he had recently accomplished one of the things on his "bucket list" (a list of things to do before you die) when he took his sister to Europe. Although he had traveled there many times, she had never been there. What struck me was the unselfish nature of having that goal on *his* "bucket list." It caused me to wonder how many of my dreams and goals are focused on others, not on myself.

Romans 12:6-21 speaks of God's gifts to us as members of the body of Christ and how we should use them in everyday life. All of them are outward in focus. Teaching, for example, is not for the teacher's self-fulfillment but for the benefit of others. So too with the other gifts mentioned in verses 6 through 8. Paul summarized this openhanded approach by urging us to "be devoted to one another in brotherly love. Honor one another above yourselves" (V. 10 NIV).

> TODAY'S READING
> **Romans 12:6-21**
>
> **Be kindly affectionate to one another with brotherly love, in honor giving preference to one another.** v. 10

Paul exemplified this attitude by including others in his ministry and investing his life in the next generation of believers. Generosity, hospitality, forgiveness, and compassion guided his behavior.

Our goals in life should include giving away the gifts God has given to us. ❧

DAVID MCCASLAND

Grant us, then, the grace for giving
With a spirit large and free,
That our life and all our living
We may consecrate to Thee. MURRAY

For a healthier spiritual life, exercise humility and care for others.

Interruptions

My sister and I were looking forward to our holiday in Taiwan. We had purchased our plane tickets and booked our hotel rooms. But 2 weeks before the trip, my sister learned she had to stay at home in Singapore to handle an emergency. We were disappointed that our plans were interrupted.

Jesus' disciples were accompanying Him on an urgent mission when their trip was interrupted (MARK 5:21-42). The daughter of Jairus, a ruler of the synagogue, was dying. Time was of the essence, and Jesus was on His way to their home. Then, suddenly, Jesus stopped and said, "Who touched My clothes?" (V. 30).

> **TODAY'S READING**
> **Mark 5:21-34**
>
> **The counsel of the LORD stands forever, the plans of His heart to all generations.**
> Psalm 33:11

The disciples seemed irritated by this and said, "You see the multitude thronging You, and You say, 'Who touched Me?'" (V. 31). But Jesus saw it as an opportunity to minister to a suffering woman. Her illness had made her ceremonially unclean and unable to participate in community life for 12 years! (SEE LEV. 15:25-27).

While Jesus was talking to this woman, Jairus' daughter died. It was too late—or so it seemed. But the delay allowed Jairus to experience an even deeper knowledge of Jesus and His power—even power over death!

Sometimes our disappointment can be God's appointment. ❦

POH FANG CHIA

Disappointment—His appointment
No good thing will He withhold;
From denials oft we gather
Treasures of His love untold. YOUNG

Look for God's purpose in your next interruption.

Once upon a Time

Some people say that the Bible is just a collection of fairy tales. A boy slaying a giant. A man swallowed by a big fish. Noah's boat-building experience. Even some religious people think that these events are just nice stories with a good moral.

Jesus Himself, however, spoke of Jonah and the giant fish and Noah and the flood as actual events: "As the days of Noah were, so also will the coming of the Son of Man be. For as in the days before the flood, they were eating and drinking, marrying and giving in marriage, until the day that Noah entered the ark, and did not know until the flood came and took them all away, so also will the coming of the Son of Man be" (MATT. 24:37-39). His return will happen when we're not expecting it.

> TODAY'S READING
> **Matthew 24:32-44**
>
> **The LORD had prepared a great fish to swallow Jonah. And Jonah was in the belly of the fish three days and three nights.**
> Jonah 1:17

Jesus compared Jonah's 3 days inside the big fish to the 3 days He would experience in the grave before His resurrection (MATT. 12:40). And Peter talked about Noah and the flood when he equated it to a future day when Jesus comes back (2 PETER 2:4-9).

God gave us His Word; it's a book that is filled with truth—not fairy tales. And one day, we will live *happily ever after* with Him when Jesus comes again and receives His children to Himself. 🌿 *CINDY HESS KASPER*

We're waiting for You, Lord, to come
And take us home to be with You;
Your promise to return for us
Gives hope because we know it's true. SPER

We have reason for optimism if we're looking for Christ's return.

Anchors in the Storm

When **Matt and Jessica** tried to navigate their sailboat into a Florida inlet during Hurricane Sandy, the craft ran aground. As the waves crashed around them, they quickly dropped anchor. It held the sailboat in place until they could be rescued. They said that if they had not put down the anchor, "We would have lost our boat for sure." Without the anchor, the relentless waves would have smashed the vessel onto the shore.

TODAY'S READING
Joshua 1:1-9

The LORD your God is with you wherever you go. v. 9

We need anchors that hold us secure in our spiritual lives as well. When God called Joshua to lead His people after Moses' death, He gave him anchors of promise he could rely on in troubled times. The Lord said to him, "I will be with you. I will not leave you nor forsake you. . . . The LORD your God is with you wherever you go" (JOSH. 1:5,9). God also gave Joshua and His people the "Book of the Law" to study and observe (VV. 7-8). That, and God's presence, were anchors the Israelites could rely on as they faced many challenges.

When we're in the middle of suffering or when doubts start threatening our faith, what are our anchors? We could start with Joshua 1:5. Although our faith may feel weak, if it's anchored in God's promises and presence, He will safely hold us. 🌿 ANNE CETAS

We have an anchor that keeps the soul
Steadfast and sure while the billows roll,
Fastened to the Rock which cannot move,
Grounded firm and deep in the Savior's love. OWENS

When we feel the stress of the storm, we learn the strength of the anchor.

Listening

In her book *Listening to Others*, Joyce Huggett writes about the importance of learning to listen and respond effectively to those in difficult situations. As she relates some of her own experiences of listening to suffering people, she mentions that they often thank her for all she's done for them. "On many occasions," she writes, "I have not 'done' anything. I have 'just listened.' I quickly came to the conclusion that 'just listening' was indeed an effective way of helping others."

TODAY'S READING
Job 2:11-13

Oh, that I had one to hear me! 31:35

This was the help Job sought from his friends. While it is true that they sat with him for 7 days in silence, "for they saw that his grief was very great" (2:13), they didn't listen when Job started talking. Instead, they talked and talked but failed to comfort him (16:2). "Oh, that I had one to hear me!" Job cried (31:35).

Listening says, "What matters to you matters to me." Sometimes people do want advice. But often they just want to be listened to by someone who loves and cares about them.

Listening is hard work, and it takes time. It takes time to listen long enough to hear the other person's true heart, so that if we do speak, we speak with gentle wisdom.

Oh, Lord, give us a loving heart and a listening ear. 🌀

DAVID ROPER

I cried, and from His holy hill
He bowed a listening ear;
I called my Father, and my God,
And He subdued my fear. WATTS

***When I'm thinking about an answer while others are talking—
I'm not listening.***

More Than We Deserve

Sometimes when people ask how I'm doing, I reply, "Better than I deserve." I remember a well-meaning person responding, "Oh no, Joe, you deserve a lot," to which I replied, "Not really." I was thinking about what I truly deserve—God's judgment.

We easily forget how sinful we are at the core of our being. Thinking of ourselves more highly than we should diminishes our sense of deep indebtedness to God for His grace. It discounts the price He paid to rescue us.

Time for a reality check! As the psalmist reminds us, God "has not dealt with us according to our sins, nor punished us according to our iniquities" (PS. 103:10). Considering who we are in light of a holy and just God, the only thing we truly deserve is hell. And heaven is an absolute impossibility—except for the gift of Christ's sacrifice on the cross. If God never does anything more than redeem us, He has already done far more than we deserve. No wonder the psalmist says, "As the heavens are high above the earth, so great is His mercy toward those who fear Him" (V. 11).

Knowing ourselves for what we are, we can't help but say, "Amazing grace, how sweet the sound!" He gives us so much more than we deserve. 🌿

JOE STOWELL

> **TODAY'S READING**
> **Psalm 103:6-18**
>
> **He has not dealt with us according to our sins, nor punished us according to our iniquities.** v. 10

Lord, thank You for not dealing with me according to my sins.
I am indebted to You for the love and grace that You
demonstrated on the cross to purchase my pardon and
forgiveness—far beyond what I deserve!

*If God never does anything more than redeem us,
He has already done far more than we deserve.*

An Appropriate Name

The name of the southeastern Asian nation of Indonesia is formed by combining two Greek words which together mean "island." That name is appropriate because Indonesia is made up of more than 17,500 islands spanning nearly 750,000 square miles. Indonesia—an appropriate name for a nation of islands.

In the Bible, we find that people were often given names—sometimes at birth, sometimes later—that made a statement about them or their character. Barnabas, whose name means "son of encouragement," continually encouraged those he encountered. Jacob, whose name means "schemer," repeatedly manipulated people and situations for his own selfish ends.

> **TODAY'S READING**
> **Matthew 1:18-25**
>
> **You shall call His name Jesus.** v. 21

And no one has ever been more appropriately named than Jesus. When the angel of the Lord spoke to Joseph about Mary's soon-to-be-born Son, he told Joseph, "You shall call His name JESUS, for He will save His people from their sins" (MATT. 1:21).

Jesus means "the Lord saves" and defines both who Jesus is and why He came. He was also called Immanuel, which means "God with us" (1:23). His name reveals our eternal hope! 🌿

BILL CROWDER

How sweet the Name of Jesus sounds
In a believer's ear!
It soothes his sorrow, heals his wounds,
And drives away his fear. NEWTON

The name of Jesus is at the heart of our faith and our hope.

Pace Yourself

Not long ago I developed a physical problem. My left shoulder and arm were aching, I had a painful rash on my forearm and thumb, and I struggled daily with fatigue. When I finally went to the doctor, I learned that I had a case of shingles. The doctor put me on antiviral medication and said it would take several weeks for the disease to run its course.

TODAY'S READING
Mark 6:30-36

Come aside by yourselves to a deserted place and rest a while. v. 31

Because of this illness, I had to force myself into a new routine. A short nap in the morning and one in the afternoon were necessary to give me the strength to be productive. Until I recovered, I had to learn to pace myself.

At one point when Jesus sent His representatives out to teach in His name, they were so excited with all they were doing that they neglected to take time to eat and rest properly. When they returned, Christ told them: "Come aside by yourselves to a deserted place and rest a while" (MARK 6:31).

Everyone needs rest, and if we go too long without it, we will suffer physically and emotionally. We also will be unable to carry out our responsibilities as well as we should. Is the Lord encouraging you to "come aside . . . and rest a while"? Sometimes a few more rest stops with Him may be necessary. ❧ *DENNIS FISHER*

I come aside from the world of strife,
With its burdens, trials, and the cares of life
To a beautiful, quiet, restful place
Where I commune with my Jesus face to face. BRANDT

To avoid a breakdown, take a break for rest and prayer.

A Call to Comfort

In their book *Dear Mrs. Kennedy,* Jay Mulvaney and Paul De Angelis note that during the weeks following the assassination of US President John Kennedy, his widow, Jacqueline, received nearly one million letters from people in every part of the world. Some came from heads of state, celebrities, and close friends. Others were sent by ordinary people who addressed them to "Madame Kennedy, Washington" and "Mrs. President, America." All wrote to express their grief and sympathy for her great loss.

When people suffer and we long to help, it's good to recall Paul's word-picture of "the God and Father of our Lord Jesus Christ" as "the Father of mercies and God of all comfort" (2 COR. 1:3). Our heavenly Father is the ultimate source of every tender mercy, kind word, and helpful act that brings encouragement and healing. Bible scholar W. E. Vine says that *paraklesis*—the Greek word translated "comfort"—means "a calling to one's side." The words *comfort* and *consolation* appear repeatedly in today's Bible reading as a reminder that the Lord holds us close and invites us to cling to Him.

As the Lord wraps His loving arms around us, we are able to embrace others "with the comfort with which we ourselves are comforted by God" (V. 4).

DAVID MCCASLAND

> TODAY'S READING
> **2 Cor. 1:3-11**
>
> **Blessed be the God and Father of our Lord Jesus Christ, the Father of mercies and God of all comfort.** v. 3

Father, thank You for letting us share with You our worries and cares. We're grateful that You stand beside us to comfort and guide. Help us to console others as You look out for Your own.

God comforts us so that we can comfort others.

Blessed Forgetfulness

My office is downstairs, but I make frequent trips upstairs to various rooms in my house for one thing or another. Unfortunately, by the time I get upstairs I often forget what I was planning to do when I got there. Researcher Gabriel Radvansky has come up with an explanation for this phenomenon. He proposes that a doorway serves as an "event boundary."

After conducting three different experiments, he theorized that a doorway signals the brain that the information held in memory can be filed away—but it's frustrating when I'm standing there trying to remember why I came upstairs. However, forgetfulness can be a blessing. When I shut the door to our bedroom at night and settle down to sleep, it's a blessing to forget the worries of the day.

> **TODAY'S READING**
> **John 10:1-10**
>
> **I am the door. If anyone enters by Me, he will be saved.** v. 9

When I think of the fact that Jesus called Himself "the door" (JOHN 10:7,9), I gain a new appreciation for this metaphor. When sheep enter the pen, they enter a safe place protected from thieves and predators. For believers, the Great Shepherd is the door between us and our enemies. Once we enter the sheepfold, we can "forget" all dangers and threats. We can enjoy divine forgetfulness and rest in the protection of the Great Shepherd. 🌱

JULIE ACKERMAN LINK

Thank You, Father, for the peace of mind that comes from
knowing You are standing watch over the events of our lives.
Help us to rest securely in Your protection.

Christ is the door that keeps us in and keeps the dangers out.

The Crash

For years after the Great Depression, the stock market struggled to win back investors' confidence. Then, in 1952, Harry Markowitz suggested that investors spread their stock holdings over several companies and industries. He developed a theory for portfolio selection that helped investors in uncertain times. In 1990, Markowitz and two others won the Nobel Memorial Prize in Economic Sciences for their theory.

TODAY'S READING
Micah 7:8-9,18-20

He will bring me forth to the light; I will see His righteousness. v. 9

Like those jittery investors, we followers of Jesus may also find ourselves frozen in fear after a "crash" in our personal lives, unsure how to pick up the pieces and move on. We might even spend our remaining lives waiting for a "Markowitz moment," when one big idea or action can help us recover from a previous failure.

We forget that Jesus has already done that on our behalf. He covered our shame, and He set us free to fellowship with God and serve Him daily. Because He gave His life, and rose from the dead, when we "fall," we can "arise" with Him, for "He delights in mercy" (MICAH 7:8,18).

The moment we find Jesus, our eternity with Him begins. He walks alongside us so He can change us into the people we long to be and were created to be. 🌿

RANDY KILGORE

Father, my actions aren't adequate to fix my failures. Thank You for doing that through Your Son Jesus who gave Himself for us. Help me to look up and walk with You.

Look up from your failure, and you'll find God standing ready to receive you.

Quest for Stolen Treasure

n J. R. R. Tolkien's *The Hobbit*, the dwarves gathered to go up against Smaug, the fierce dragon, to retrieve their stolen treasure. In spite of the dangerously frightening quest, Balin, the second-in-command dwarf, expressed confidence in Thorin: "There is one I could follow. There is one I could call King." His commitment to the mission, as dangerous as it was, was empowered by his confidence in his leader.

TODAY'S READING
Matthew 4:18-22

[Jesus] said to them, "Follow Me, and I will make you fishers of men." v. 19

At the beginning of Jesus' earthly ministry, He gathered a group around Him that would join Him in the kingdom task of rescuing the treasure of lost souls from our enemy, Satan. When He called them, He said, "Follow Me" (MATT. 4:19). For them, following Jesus would mean a radical transition from catching fish to the enterprise of being fishers of men and women who were lost in the grip of sin. But the task would not always be easy; Jesus referred to the quest as taking up our cross to follow Him (SEE MATT. 16:24; MARK 8:34; LUKE 9:23).

How do we stay engaged in the battle to reclaim Christ's lost treasures when it seems intimidating or awkward? By keeping our eye on our Leader. He indeed is worthy—One we can follow, the One we call King! 🌱   *JOE STOWELL*

Lord, in the face of intimidation and fear when seeking to engage others with the gospel, remind me that they are Your lost treasures. I count it a privilege to follow You into others' lives.

Follow your Leader into the lives of those around you.

Jordyn's Journey

ordyn Castor was born blind. But this doesn't hold her back from living a full and productive life. The documentary *Can You See How I See?* tells her story. She excels at school and with a little help she enjoys biking and downhill skiing.

Of her sight, Jordyn says: "If I could give my blindness back, I wouldn't do it. I think God made all of us the way we are for a reason . . . and I think my blindness is part of what I am going to do with my life." She is now a university student majoring in computer technology. Her dream is to assist in developing new computer software that will help the blind.

TODAY'S READING
Philippians 4:10-13

I can do all things through Christ who strengthens me. v. 13

How can Jordyn maintain such a positive outlook on life? As a Christ-follower, she understands that God is in control of the circumstances of life. This gives her confidence to pursue opportunities that others might not have believed possible. Certainly, Jordyn's life illustrates this truth from Philippians: "I can do all things through Christ who strengthens me" (4:13).

No matter what our strengths or weaknesses might be, God's providential hand can give us what we need to make a difference for Him in our world. Rely on His strength to help you as you take a step of faith. 🌱   *DENNIS FISHER*

> "I will strengthen," so take courage,
> Child of God, so weak and frail;
> God has said so, and it must be,
> For His promise cannot fail! ANON.

God's call to a task includes His strength to complete it.

As White as Snow

was driving my son home from school one day when snow began to fall. The cottony fluff came down steadily and quickly. Eventually, we slowed to a stop, boxed in by traffic. From inside our vehicle, we watched a transformation take place. Dark patches of soil turned white. Snow softened the sharp outlines of buildings; it coated the cars around us, and accumulated on every tree in sight.

That snowfall reminded me of a spiritual truth: Just as that snow covered everything in sight, God's grace covers our sin. But grace doesn't just *cover* sin, grace *erases* sin. Through the prophet Isaiah, God appealed to the

> **TODAY'S READING**
> **Isaiah 1:1-4,12-18**
>
> **Your sins . . . shall be as white as snow.** v. 18

Israelites, saying, "Come now, and let us reason together . . . though your sins are like scarlet, they shall be as white as snow" (ISA. 1:18). When God made this promise, His children had a painful problem with sin. God compared them to a physical body plagued with "wounds and welts and open sores, not cleansed or bandaged or soothed with oil" (V.6 NIV).

As bad as their sin was, God was willing to extend His grace to them. As His children today, we have the same assurance. Sin may stain our lives, but when we repent and confess it, we have "the forgiveness of sins, according to the riches of [God's] grace" (EPH. 1:7). 🌿 *JENNIFER BENSON SCHULDT*

Lord, give me courage to confess,
To bare my sinful heart to Thee;
Forgiving love You long to show
And from my sin to set me free. D. DEHAAN

The weight of sin is balanced only by the blood of Christ.

Kangaroos and Emus

Two of Australia's indigenous creatures, kangaroos and emus, have something in common—they seldom move backward. Kangaroos, because of the shape of their body and the length of their strong tail, can bounce along with forward movement, but they cannot shift easily into reverse. Emus can run fast on their strong legs, but the joints in their knees seem to make backward movement difficult. Both animals appear on Australia's coat of arms as a symbol that the nation is to be ever moving forward and making progress.

TODAY'S READING
Philippians 3:12-17

Forgetting those things which are behind . . . I press toward the goal for the prize of the upward call of God in Christ Jesus. vv. 13-14

The apostle Paul called for a similar approach to the life of faith in his letter to the Philippians: "Brethren, I do not count myself to have apprehended; but one thing I do, forgetting those things which are behind and reaching forward to those things which are ahead, I press toward the goal for the prize of the upward call of God in Christ Jesus" (3:13-14).

While it is wise to learn from the past, we shouldn't live in the past. We cannot redo or undo the past, but by God's grace we can press forward and serve God faithfully today and in the future. The life of faith is a journey forward as we become like Christ. ❧

BILL CROWDER

I'm pressing on the upward way,
New heights I'm gaining every day;
Still praying as I'm onward bound,
"Lord, plant my feet on higher ground." OATMAN

I will go anywhere—provided it is forward.

The Careful Walk

One of my favorite places to visit in Jamaica is Ocho Rios, home of Dunn's River Falls—a spectacle that never ceases to amaze. Water cascades down a long series of rocks as it makes its way to the Caribbean Sea. Adventurers can climb the falls, scrambling over rounded rocks on an invigorating trek to the top. The flowing water, the potentially slippery surface, and the steep angles make the going slow and a bit treacherous.

To make it safely to the top, climbers must watch every step. If a person is not careful, he or she could fall on the journey. The keys to a successful climb are concentration and caution.

TODAY'S READING
Ephesians 5:1-17

See then that you walk circumspectly, not as fools but as wise. v. 15

I can't think of a better picture of what Paul is saying in Ephesians 5:15 when he says, "walk circumspectly." We should "be very careful . . . how [we] live" (NIV). Clearly, with all of life's possible dangers coming our way as we climb through life, it is vital that we take each step with Jesus wisely and cautiously. A fool, the passage says, lives carelessly; a wise person watches each step so he does not stumble or fall.

Our goal of being "imitators of God" (V.1) is met, Paul says, as we walk carefully in love (VV. 2,15). Through the Holy Spirit's guidance, we can walk in a way that honors God. 🌿

DAVE BRANON

Consistency! How much we need
To walk a measured pace,
To live the life of which we speak,
Until we see Christ's face. ANON.

As we trust God to rule our hearts our feet can walk His way.

The View from the End

Over the course of one year, Richard LeMieux's lucrative publishing business collapsed. Soon, his wealth disappeared, and he became depressed. Eventually, LeMieux began to abuse alcohol and his family deserted him. At the lowest point in his life, he was homeless, broken, and destitute. However, it was during this time that he turned to God. He later wrote a book about what he learned.

The Israelites learned some valuable spiritual lessons when God allowed them to endure homelessness, uncertainty, and danger. Their hardships humbled them (DEUT. 8:1-18).

TODAY'S READING
Deut. 8:1-3,11-16

All things work together for good to those who love God. Romans 8:28

They learned that God would provide for their needs. When they were hungry, He gave them manna. When they were thirsty, He gave them water from a rock. God taught them that, despite difficult times, He could bless them (V. 1). Finally, the Israelites learned that adversity is not a sign of abandonment. Moses reminded them that God had been leading throughout their 40 years in the wilderness (V. 2).

When we encounter desperate times, we can look for the spiritual lessons embedded in our difficulties—lessons that can help us rely on the One who causes all things to work together for our good and for His glory (ROM. 8:28). 🕊

JENNIFER BENSON SCHULDT

Dear God, please give me the faith to believe that You can bring good out of any situation. Help me to see what You want to show me during adversity.

The clearest view of everything that happens comes from heaven.

Room and Board

On a recent trip to England, my wife and I visited Anne Hathaway's Cottage in Stratford-upon-Avon. The house is more than 400 years old, and it was the child-hood and family home of William Shakespeare's wife.

The tour guide drew our attention to a table made with wide boards. One side was used for eat-ing meals and the other for chopping food. In English life, different expres-sions grew from this usage as the word *board* became associated with food, housing, honesty, and authority. An inn would offer "room and board"—that is, sleeping and eating accommodations. In taverns where customers played cards, they were told to keep their hands "above board" to make sure they weren't cheating. And in the home, the father was given a special chair at the head of the table where he was called "chairman of the board."

> TODAY'S READING
> **John 14:1-11**
>
> **I go to prepare a place for you.** v. 2

As I reflected on this, I thought about how Jesus is our "room and board." He is our source of spiritual nourishment (JOHN 6:35,54); He empowers us to live a life of integrity (14:21); He is our loving Master (PHIL. 2:11); and He is even now preparing our eternal home. He promised: "I go to prepare a place for you" (JOHN 14:2; SEE ALSO 14:1-4,23). His grace has provided our ever-lasting room and board. ❦ *DENNIS FISHER*

Pardon for sin and a peace that endureth,
Thine own dear presence to cheer and to guide,
Strength for today and bright hope for tomorrow—
Blessings all mine, with ten thousand beside. CHISHOLM

Christ meets our needs now and for eternity.

Reframing the Picture

or 3 months I had a ringside seat—or should I say a bird's-eye view—of God's amazing handiwork. Ninety feet above the floor of Norfolk Botanical Garden, workers installed a webcam focused on the nest of a family of bald eagles, and online viewers were allowed to watch.

When the eggs hatched, Mama and Papa Eagle were attentive to their offspring, taking turns hunting for food and guarding the nest. But one day when the eaglets still looked like fuzzballs with beaks, both parents disappeared. I worried that harm had come to them.

> TODAY'S READING
> **Deut. 32:7-12**
>
> **As an eagle stirs up its nest, . . . spreading out its wings, . . . so the Lord alone led [Jacob].** vv. 11-12

My concern was unfounded. The webcam operator enlarged the camera angle, and there was Mama Eagle perched on a nearby branch.

As I pondered this "reframed" picture, I thought of times when I have feared that God had abandoned me. The view in the forest heights of Virginia reminded me that my vision is limited. I see only a small part of the entire scene.

Moses used eagle imagery to describe God. As eagles carry their young, God carries His people (DEUT. 32:11-12). Despite how it may seem, the Lord "is not far from each one of us" (ACTS 17:27). This is true even when we feel abandoned. 🍂

JULIE ACKERMAN LINK

Under His wings I am safely abiding;
Though the night deepens and tempests are wild,
Still I can trust Him—I know He will keep me;
He has redeemed me and I am His child. CUSHING

Because the Lord is watching over us,
we don't have to fear the dangers around us.

D-Day

Recently I asked my older sister, Mary Ann, if she remembered when our family moved into the house where we lived for many years. She replied, "You were about 9 months old, and I remember that Mother and Daddy stayed up all night packing boxes and listening to the radio. It was June 6, 1944, and they were listening to live coverage of the Normandy Invasion."

TODAY'S READING
Joshua 24:2,13-18

Today marks the anniversary of what has become known as D-Day—a military term for the day on which a planned operation will begin. Over the years, D-Day has also come to mean a moment of decision or commitment in our personal lives.

Choose for yourselves this day whom you will serve . . . . But as for me and my house, we will serve the LORD. v. 15

At one point in ancient Israel, their leader Joshua, now an old man, challenged the people to another kind of D-Day. After years of struggle to possess their inheritance in the land God had promised them, Joshua urged them to faithfully serve the One who had been so faithful to them (JOSH. 24). "Choose for yourselves this day whom you will serve," he said. "But as for me and my house, we will serve the LORD" (V. 15).

The day we decide to follow the Savior is the greatest turning point in our life. And each day after, we can joyfully renew our commitment to serve Him. 🌿 *DAVID MCCASLAND*

Lord, what a privilege it is to say "yes" to You each day.
Thank You for loving me and forgiving me. Guide me in all my
choices today and help me to serve You faithfully.

Life's biggest decision is what you do with Jesus.

What Do We Want?

My friend Mary tells me that she doesn't always sing all the words to the hymns and choruses in a church service. She says, "It doesn't seem honest to sing, 'All I want is Jesus' when my heart wants many other things too." I appreciate her honesty.

In verse 25 of Psalm 73, Asaph sounds like a spiritually minded man who wants God only: "There is none upon earth that I desire besides You." But that's not how he began this psalm. Initially, he admitted that he wanted the prosperity that others around him had: "For I was envious of the boastful" (V.3). But when he drew near to God, he recognized that he was foolish to be envious (VV. 21-22,28).

TODAY'S READING
Psalm 73:1-3, 21-28

There is none upon earth that I desire besides You. v. 25

Even when we know God, we are often distracted by the prosperity of others. C. S. Lewis wrote, "It would seem that our Lord finds our desires not too strong, but too weak. . . . We are far too easily pleased" with lesser things than Him.

What do we learn about God in this psalm that might help when our desires distract us from God's best? Well, we see that even though we may be tempted to envy what others have, He is continually guiding us and bringing us back to focus on Him. He "is the strength of my heart and my portion forever" (V. 26). ❧

ANNE CETAS

Lord, we do believe that You are the place where true satisfaction is found. But we're weak and sinful and easily distracted from Your best. Teach us to draw near to You, and may You, in turn, draw near to us.

A daily dose of God's wisdom will heal the heart disease of envy.

Lesson from a Toothache

When I was a child I often had a toothache," wrote C. S. Lewis in his classic book *Mere Christianity*. He continued, "and I knew that if I went to my mother she would give me something that would deaden the pain for that night and let me get to sleep. But I did not go to my mother—at least not till the pain became very bad. . . . I knew she would take me to the dentist the next morning. . . . I wanted immediate relief from pain, but I could not get it without having my teeth set permanently right."

TODAY'S READING
Hebrews 12:3-11

If you endure chastening, God deals with you as with sons. v. 7

Similarly, we might not always want to go to God right away when we have a problem or are struggling in a certain area. We know that He could provide immediate relief from our pain, but He is more concerned with dealing with the root of the problem. We may be afraid that He will reveal issues that we are unprepared or unwilling to deal with.

In times like these, it is helpful to remind ourselves that the Lord "deals with [us] as with sons" (HEB. 12:7). His discipline, though perhaps painful, is wise, and His touch is loving. He loves us too much to let us remain as we are; He wants to conform us to the likeness of His Son, Jesus (ROM. 8:29). God's purposes of love can be trusted more than any of our emotions of fear. 🌿

POH FANG CHIA

Thank You, Lord, for showing me my hidden faults, for You treat me as Your dear child. Help me surrender to Your cleansing work till the beauty of Jesus be seen in me.

God's hand of discipline is a hand of love.

Generous God

When our family lived in Chicago several years ago, we enjoyed many benefits. Near the top of my list were the amazing restaurants that seemed to try to outdo each other, not only in great cuisine but also in portion sizes. At one Italian eatery, my wife and I would order a half portion of our favorite pasta dish and still have enough to bring home for dinner the next night! The generous portions made us feel like we were at Grandma's house when she poured on the love through her cooking.

TODAY'S READING
Ephesians 3:14-21

[God] is able to do exceedingly abundantly above all that we ask or think. v. 20

I also feel an outpouring of love when I read that my heavenly Father has lavished on us the riches of His grace (EPH. 1:7-8) and that He is able to do "exceedingly abundantly above all that we ask or think" (3:20). I'm so grateful that our God is not a stingy God who begrudgingly dishes out His blessings in small portions. Rather, He is the God who pours out forgiveness for the prodigal (LUKE 15), and He daily crowns us "with lovingkindness and tender mercies" (PS. 103:4).

At times we think God hasn't provided for us as we would like. But if He never did anything more than forgive our sins and guarantee heaven for us, He has already been abundantly generous! So today, let's rejoice in our generous God. 🌿

JOE STOWELL

Lord, remind me often that You have been exceedingly generous to me. Help me to extend that generosity of spirit toward those around me, so that they may know who You are and rejoice in You.

Praise God from whom all blessings flow!

Crowns of Honor

The Crown Jewels of the United Kingdom are stored securely and protected within the Tower of London under 24-hour guard. Each year, millions visit the display area to "ooh and aah" over these ornate treasures. The Crown Jewels symbolize the power of the kingdom, as well as the prestige and position of those who use them.

TODAY'S READING
John 19:1-8

Part of the Crown Jewels are the crowns themselves. There are three different types: the coronation crown, which is worn when an individual is crowned monarch; the state crown (or coronet), which is worn for various

The soldiers twisted a crown of thorns and put it on His head. v. 2

functions; and the consort crown worn by the wife of a reigning king. Different crowns serve different purposes.

The King of heaven, who was worthy of the greatest crown and the highest honor, wore a very different crown. In the hours of humiliation and suffering that Christ experienced before He was crucified, "the soldiers twisted a crown of thorns and put it on His head, and they put on Him a purple robe" (JOHN 19:2). That day, the crown, which is normally a symbol of royalty and honor, was turned into a tool of mockery and hate. Yet our Savior willingly wore that crown for us, bearing our sin and shame.

The One who deserved the best of all crowns took the worst for us. 🌱   BILL CROWDER

Crown Him the Lord of life:
Who triumphed o'er the grave;
Who rose victorious in the strife
For those He came to save. BRIDGES/THRING

Without the cross, there could be no crown.

An Honest Heart

came across an epitaph on an old gravestone in a cemetery the other day. It read, "J. Holgate: An honest man."

I know nothing of Holgate's life, but because his marker is unusually ornate, he must have struck it rich. But whatever he accomplished in his lifetime, he's remembered for just one thing: He was "an honest man."

Diogenes, the Greek philosopher, spent a lifetime in search of honesty and finally concluded that an honest man could not be found. Honest people are hard to find in any age, but the trait is one that greatly matters. Honesty is not the best policy; it's the only policy, and one of the marks of a man or woman who lives in God's presence. David writes, "LORD, . . . who may dwell in Your holy hill? He who walks uprightly" (PS. 15:1-2).

TODAY'S READING
Psalm 15

I know also, my God, that You test the heart and have pleasure in uprightness.
1 Chronicles 29:17

I ask myself: Am I trustworthy and honorable in all my affairs? Do my words ring true? Do I speak the truth in love or do I fudge and fade the facts now and then, or exaggerate for emphasis? If so, I may turn to God with complete confidence and ask for forgiveness and for a good and honest heart—to make truthfulness an integral part of my nature. The One who has begun a good work in me is faithful. He will do it. 🌱

DAVID ROPER

Lord, help me to be honest
In all I do and say,
And grant me grace and power
To live for You each day. FITZHUGH

Live in such a way that when people think of honesty and integrity, they will think of you.

Keep Calm and Carry On

Keep calm and call mom." "Keep calm and eat bacon." "Keep calm and put the kettle on." These sayings originate from the phrase: "Keep Calm and Carry On." This message first appeared in Great Britain as World War II began in 1939. British officials printed it on posters designed to offset panic and discouragement during the war.

TODAY'S READING
Ezra 5:7-17

We are the servants of the God of heaven and earth. v. 11

Having returned to the land of Israel after a time of captivity, the Israelites had to overcome their own fear and enemy interference as they began to rebuild the temple (EZRA 3:3). Once they finished the foundation, their opponents "hired counselors against them to frustrate their purpose" (4:5). Israel's enemies also wrote accusing letters to government officials and successfully delayed the project (VV. 6,24). Despite this, King Darius eventually issued a decree that allowed them to complete the temple (6:12-14).

When we are engaged in God's work and we encounter setbacks, we can calmly carry on because, like the Israelites, "We are the servants of the God of heaven and earth" (5:11). Obstacles and delays may discourage us, but we can rest in Jesus' promise: "I will build my church, and all the powers of hell will not conquer it" (MATT. 16:18 NLT). It is God's power that enables His work, not our own. 🕊

JENNIFER BENSON SCHULDT

Thou art our life, by which alone we live,
And all our substance and our strength receive.
Sustain us by Thy faith and by Thy power,
And give us strength in every trying hour. PSALTER

God's Spirit gives the power to our witness.

We're Safe

The **United States** Bullion Depository in Fort Knox, Kentucky, is a fortified building that stores 5,000 tons of gold bullion and other precious items entrusted to the federal government. Fort Knox is protected by a 22-ton door and layers of physical security: alarms, video cameras, minefields, barbed razor wire, electric fences, armed guards, and unmarked Apache helicopters. Based on the level of security, Fort Knox is considered one of the safest places on earth.

TODAY'S READING
1 Peter 1:3-5

[God] has begotten us . . . to an inheritance incorruptible and undefiled and that does not fade away, reserved in heaven for you. vv. 3-4

As safe as Fort Knox is, there's another place that's safer, and it's filled with something more precious than gold: Heaven holds our gift of eternal life. The apostle Peter encouraged believers in Christ to praise God because we have "a living hope"—a confident expectation that grows and gains strength the more we learn about Jesus (1 PETER 1:3). And our hope is based on the resurrected Christ. His gift of eternal life will never come to ruin as a result of hostile forces. It will never lose its glory or freshness, because God has been keeping and will continue to keep it safe in heaven. No matter what harm may come to us in our life on earth, God is guarding our souls. Our inheritance is safe.

Like a safe within a safe, our salvation is protected by God and we're secure. 🌿   *MARVIN WILLIAMS*

FOR FURTHER THOUGHT
What about your salvation brings you the greatest joy? How does it make you feel knowing that your salvation is kept safe with God?

An inheritance in heaven is the safest possible place.

Rock-Solid

I t was a sad day in May 2003 when "The Old Man of the Mountain" broke apart and slid down the mountainside. This 40-foot profile of an old man's face, carved by nature in the White Mountains of New Hampshire, had long been an attraction to tourists, a solid presence for residents, and the official state emblem. It was written about by Nathaniel Hawthorne in his short story *The Great Stone Face*.

Some nearby residents were devastated when The Old Man fell. One woman said, "I grew up thinking that someone was watching over me. I feel a little less watched-over now."

TODAY'S READING
Psalm 34:15-22

The eyes of the LORD are on the righteous, and His ears are open to their cry. v. 15

There are times when a dependable presence disappears. Something or someone we've relied on is gone, and our life is shaken. Maybe it's the loss of a loved one, or a job, or good health. The loss makes us feel off-balance, unstable. We might even think that God is no longer watching over us.

But "the eyes of the LORD are on the righteous, and His ears are open to their cry" (PS. 34:15). He "is near to those who have a broken heart" (V. 18). He is the Rock whose presence we can always depend on (DEUT. 32:4).

God's presence is real. He continually watches over us. He is rock-solid. 🌱

ANNE CETAS

The Rock of Ages stands secure,
He always will be there;
He watches over all His own
To calm their anxious care. KEITH

The question is not where is God, but where isn't He?

Meet Shrek

Shrek was a renegade sheep. He went missing from his flock and remained lost for 6 years. The person who found him living in a cave on a high and rugged place in New Zealand didn't recognize him as a sheep. "He looked like some biblical creature," he said. In a way, he was. Shrek was a picture of what happens to sheep who become separated from their shepherd.

Shrek had to be carried down the mountain because his fleece was so heavy (60 lbs or 27 kg) that he couldn't walk down on his own. To relieve Shrek of the weight of his waywardness, he was turned upside down so that he would remain still and not be harmed when the shearer removed his heavy fleece.

> TODAY'S READING
> **Ezekiel 34:11-16**
>
> **I Myself will search for My sheep and seek them out.** v. 11

Shrek's story illustrates the metaphor Jesus used when He called Himself the Good Shepherd (JOHN 10:11), and when God referred to His people as His flock (EZEK. 34:31). Like Shrek, we do not make good choices when we're on our own, and we become weighed down with the consequences (EZEK. 33:10). To relieve us of the weight, we may have to be on our backs for a time. When we end up in this position, it is good to remain still and trust the Good Shepherd to do His work without hurting us. 🌱

JULIE ACKERMAN LINK

> The King of love my Shepherd is,
> Whose goodness faileth never;
> I nothing lack if I am His,
> And He is mine forever. BAKER

God's training is designed to grow us in faith.

The World's Children

After a group of high schoolers visited an orphanage during a ministry trip, one student was visibly upset. When asked why, he said it reminded him of his own situation 10 years earlier.

This young man had been living in an orphanage in another country. He said he recalled people coming to visit him and his friends—just as these students were doing—and then going away. Occasionally someone would come back and adopt a child. But each time he was left behind he would wonder, *What's wrong with me?*

When the teenagers would visit an orphanage—and then leave—those old feelings came back to him. So the others in the group prayed for him—and

> **TODAY'S READING**
> **James 1:22–2:1**
>
> **Pure and undefiled religion before God and the Father is this: to visit orphans and widows in their trouble.** 1:27

thanked God that one day a woman (his new mother) showed up and chose him as her very own son. It was a celebration of an act of love that gave one boy hope.

Across the world are children who need to know of God's love for them (MATT. 18:4-5; MARK 10:13-16; JAMES 1:27). Clearly, we can't all adopt or visit these children—and indeed we are not expected to. But we can all do something: Support. Encourage. Teach. Pray. When we love the world's children, we honor our Father who adopted us into His family (GAL. 4:4-7). 🌿 *DAVE BRANON*

Father, You made each child in Your image. Help us to convey Your love to them with our hands, our help, and our hearts.

The more Christ's love grows in us, the more His love flows from us.

The Light of the Lamb

For countless generations people have looked to the sun and moon to light the day and the night. Whether illuminating our path or providing the life-giving radiance for fruitful crops and the nutrients our bodies need, the sun and moon are part of God's marvelous provision of light. The book of Genesis tells us that God gave "the greater light to rule the day, and the lesser light to rule the night" (GEN. 1:16).

> **TODAY'S READING**
> **Rev. 21:14-27**
>
> **The city had no need of the sun or of the moon to shine in it, for the glory of God illuminated it. The Lamb is its light.** v. 23

But someday God will provide a different kind of illumination. Of the eternal heavenly city, John writes: "The city had no need of the sun or of the moon to shine in it, for the glory of God illuminated it. The Lamb is its light" (REV. 21:23). Interestingly, the word translated "light" here is more accurately rendered lamp. Christ in His glorified state will be the spiritual lamp that lights up that joyous new world.

The Lord Jesus Christ is "the Lamb of God who takes away the sin of the world" (JOHN 1:29). He is also the source of spiritual illumination that makes those who follow Him "the light of the world" (MATT. 5:14). But in eternity He will be the Lamp that lights our way (REV. 21:23). What a thrill it will be one day to live in the light of the Lamb! 🌿   *DENNIS FISHER*

No darkness have we who in Jesus abide—
The light of the world is Jesus;
We walk in the light when we follow our Guide—
The light of the world is Jesus. BLISS

The Light of the world knows no power failure.

Smile!

A **recent study** I read concluded that smiling can be good for your health. Research shows that smiling slows down the heart and reduces stress.

But smiling isn't just good for *you*; a genuine smile blesses those on the receiving end as well. Without saying a word, it can tell others that you like them and that you are pleased with them. A smile can hug someone with love without giving them even the slightest touch.

TODAY'S READING
Numbers 6:22-27

The LORD make His face shine upon you, and be gracious to you. v. 25

Life does not always give us a reason to smile. But when we see a heartfelt smile on a child's face or through aged wrinkles, our hearts are encouraged.

Smiles are also a hint of the image of God in us. In the ancient blessing recorded in the book of Numbers we get an indication that God "smiles": "The LORD make His face shine upon you, and be gracious to you; the LORD lift up His countenance upon you, and give you peace" (NUM. 6:25-26). Those words are a Hebrew idiom for the favor of God on a person's life, asking God to smile on His children.

So today, remember that you are loved by God, and that He is pleased to be gracious to you and to shine His face upon you. 🌿   *JOE STOWELL*

> Lord, may my life be so pleasing to You that You are pleased
> to have Your face shine on me. And as You graciously smile on
> my life, may I find someone today with whom I can share
> Your love through a smile.

Your smile could be a message of cheer from God to a needy soul.

Teaching by Example

While **waiting** for an eye examination, I was struck by a statement I saw in the optometrist's office: "Eighty percent of everything children learn in their first 12 years is through their eyes." I began thinking of all that children visually process through reading, television, film, events, surroundings, and observing the behavior of others, especially their families.

TODAY'S READING
Ephesians 6:1-11

Fathers can have an especially powerful influence on their children. Paul urged fathers not to frustrate them to the point of anger, but to "bring them up in the training and admonition of the Lord" (EPH. 6:4). Think of the power-

Bring [your children] up in the training and admonition of the Lord. v. 4

ful example of a dad whose behavior and consistency inspire admiration from his children. He's not perfect, but he's moving in the right direction. A great power for good is at work when our actions reflect the character of God, rather than distort it.

That's challenging for any parent, so it's no coincidence that Paul urges us to "be strong in the Lord and in the power of His might" (V. 10). Only through His strength can we reflect the love and patience of our heavenly Father.

We teach our children far more from how we live than by what we say. 🌺

DAVID MCCASLAND

Heavenly Father, I need to know Your love in order to love others.
I want to experience and share Your patience and kindness with
those I care about. Fill me and use me.

We honor fathers who not only gave us life,
but who also show us how to live.

Forgotten Memories

Recently, a friend from my youth emailed me a picture of our junior high track team. The grainy black-and-white snapshot showed a vaguely familiar group of teens with our two coaches. I was instantly swept back in time to happy memories of running the mile and the half-mile in track meets. Yet even as I enjoyed remembering those days, I found myself thinking about how easily I had forgotten them and moved on to other things.

TODAY'S READING
Psalm 103:1-8

Bless the LORD, O my soul, and forget not all His benefits. v. 2

As we make our way on the journey of life, it is easy to forget places, people, and events that have been important to us along the way. Time passes, yesterday fades, and we become obsessed with the concerns of the moment. When this happens, we can also forget just how good God has been to us. Perhaps that is why David remembered as he wrote, "Bless the LORD, O my soul; and all that is within me, bless His holy name! Bless the LORD, O my soul, and forget not all His benefits" (PS. 103:1-2).

Never is this remembrance more needed than when the heartaches of life crowd in on us. When we are feeling overwhelmed and forgotten, it's important to recall all that He has done for us. In remembering, we find the encouragement to trust Him in the present and for the future. 🌱 *BILL CROWDER*

When upon life's billows you are tempest tossed,
When you are discouraged, thinking all is lost,
Count your many blessings, name them one by one,
And it will surprise you what the Lord hath done. OATMAN

Remembering God's faithfulness in the past strengthens us for the future.

World's Fastest Walkers

According to a study measuring the pace of life of cities in 32 countries, people in the biggest hurry live here in Singapore. We walk 60 feet in 10:55 seconds, compared to 12:00 seconds for New Yorkers and 31:60 seconds for those living in the African city of Blantyre, Malawi.

But regardless of where you live, the study shows that walking speeds have increased by an average of 10 percent in the past 20 years. And if walking speed is any indicator for the pace of life, we are certainly much busier than before.

> TODAY'S READING
> **Luke 10:38-42**
>
> **She had a sister called Mary, who also sat at Jesus' feet and heard His word.** v. 39

Are you caught up in the frenzy of a busy life? Pause and consider Jesus' words to Martha: "You are worried and troubled about many things. But one thing is needed, and Mary has chosen that good part, which will not be taken away from her" (LUKE 10:41-42).

Notice Jesus' gentle words. He didn't rebuke Martha for wanting to be a good host but rather reminded her about her priorities. Martha had allowed the necessary to get out of proportion. And, in the process, she was so busy doing good that she didn't take time to sit at Jesus' feet.

In our drive to be productive for the Lord, let's remember the one thing worth being concerned about—enjoying time with our Savior. 🌸   *POH FANG CHIA*

And He walks with me, and He talks with me,
And He tells me I am His own,
And the joy we share as we tarry there,
None other has ever known. MILES

Jesus longs for our fellowship even more than we long for His.

The Day My Dad Met Jesus

My grandfather, my father, and his brothers were all tough men who, understandably, didn't appreciate people who "got up in their faces about faith." When my father, Howard, was diagnosed with a rapid and deadly cancer, I was so concerned that I took every opportunity to talk to him about Jesus' love. Inevitably he would end the discussion with a polite but firm: "I know what I need to know."

I promised not to raise the issue again and gave him a set of cards that shared the forgiveness God offers, which he could read when he wanted. I entrusted Dad to God and prayed. A friend also asked God to keep my dad alive long enough to know Jesus.

One afternoon the call came telling me Dad was gone. When my brother met me at the airport, he said, "Dad told me to tell you he asked Jesus to forgive his sin." "When?" "The morning he passed," Mark replied. God had shown him "mercy" as He had shown us (1 TIM. 1:16).

> **TODAY'S READING**
> **1 Timothy 1:15-17**
>
> **I obtained mercy . . . as a pattern to those who are going to believe on Him for everlasting life.** v. 16

Sometimes we talk about the gospel, other times we share our story, still other times we just show a silent Christlike example, and always we pray. We know that salvation is ultimately a work of God and not something we can do for another. God is a gracious God, and no matter what the outcome of our prayers, He can be trusted. 			*RANDY KILGORE*

Softly and tenderly Jesus is calling—
Calling for you and for me;
Patiently Jesus is waiting and watching—
Watching for you and for me! THOMPSON

We plant and water, but God gives the increase.

Restored by the Master

Over the centuries, many attempts have been made to restore damaged and time-worn masterpieces of art. While some of these efforts have skillfully preserved the original work of artists, others have actually damaged many works of genius, including ancient Greek statues and at least two paintings by da Vinci.

In Paul's letter to the Christians at Colosse, he described a restoration process that is impossible in the world of art. It's a restoration of God's people. Paul wrote, "You have put off the old man with his deeds, and have put on the new man who is renewed in knowledge according to the image of Him who created him" (COL. 3:9-10). This is no attempt at renovating the work of a deceased artist. It is a spiritual renewal from the

> TODAY'S READING
> **Colossians 3:8-17**
>
> [You] have put on the new man who is renewed in knowledge according to the image of Him who created him. v. 10

living God who created us and gave us new life in His Son, Jesus Christ. His forgiveness brightens the colors of our lives while His grace sharpens the lines of His purpose for us.

The canvas of our lives is in the skilled hands of our Lord who knows who and what He designed us to be. No matter how sin-damaged and dirty we may be, there is hope for renewal and restoration. The Master Artist is alive and at work within us. 🌺
DAVID MCCASLAND

Praise, my soul, the King of heaven,
To His feet thy tribute bring;
Ransomed, healed, restored, forgiven,
Evermore His praises sing. LYTE

Jesus specializes in restoration.

Veins of Gold

While visiting the charming Cotswold area of England, I purchased some bone china mugs as souvenirs. I used them carefully, but eventually one fell into the sink and shattered. I thought about that mug recently when I learned about the Japanese art of Kintsugi.

Usually when something breaks we are happy to repair it enough to make it functional again. But several hundred years ago, a Japanese artist decided he would make broken china beautiful. So he started using golden resin to hold the fragments together. Pieces repaired by using his method have intricate veins of gold.

Early in the human story, sin entered the world (GEN. 3). Theologians refer to the

> **TODAY'S READING**
> **Romans 6:1-14**
>
> **If we have been united together in the likeness of His death, certainly we also shall be in the likeness of His resurrection.** v. 5

event as "the fall." The inevitable result is brokenness. Life is painful because we keep getting hurt and hurting others with our sharp, jagged edges. But God doesn't want us to stay broken, and His repair work turns our brokenness into beauty.

Like a Kintsugi artist, God repairs us. But He uses something more precious than gold—the blood of His Son. Instead of having veins of gold, we are united by the very veins of Christ. "We have been united together in the likeness of His death" (ROM. 6:5). Nothing is more beautiful than that. 🌀

JULIE ACKERMAN LINK

He shed His blood, poured out His life;
He gave His all at Calvary;
Oh what can we give in return
For love so rich, so full, so free? ANON.

The price of our freedom from sin was paid by Jesus' blood.

Wisdom from Above

If Kiera Wilmot had performed her experiment during her high school science class, it might have earned her an A. But instead she was charged with causing an explosion. Although she had planned to have her teacher approve the experiment, her classmates persuaded her to perform it outside the classroom. When she mixed chemicals inside a plastic bottle, it exploded and she unintentionally unsettled some fellow students.

> **TODAY'S READING**
> **1 Samuel 24:1-10**
>
> **The wisdom that is from above is first pure, then peaceable.** James 3:17

The Old Testament tells the story of another case of peer pressure. David and his men were hiding from Saul in a cave when Saul entered (1 SAM. 24). David's companions suggested that God had delivered Saul to them, and they urged David to kill him (VV. 4,10). If David killed Saul, they thought they could stop hiding and David could become king. But David refused to harm Saul because he was "the LORD's anointed" (V. 6).

People in our lives may sometimes suggest we do what seems most gratifying or practical in the moment. But there is a difference between worldly and spiritual wisdom (1 COR. 2:6-7). Wisdom from above "is first pure, then peaceable, gentle, willing to yield, full of mercy" (JAMES 3:17). When others are urging us to take a certain course of action, we can invite God to influence our response. 🌿 *JENNIFER BENSON SCHULDT*

Have Thine own way, Lord! Have Thine own way!
Hold o'er my being absolute sway!
Fill with Thy Spirit till all shall see
Christ only, always, living in me. POLLARD

One is truly wise who gains his wisdom from above.

Roadside Assistance

An acquaintance of mine was hunting with friends near Balmoral, the country estate of the queen of England. As they walked, he twisted his ankle so badly that he couldn't go on, so he told his friends to continue and he would wait by the side of the road.

As he sat there, a car came down the road, slowed, and stopped. The woman driving rolled the window down and asked if he was okay. He explained and said he was waiting for his friends to return. She said, "Get in; I'll take you back to where you are staying." He limped to the car and opened the door only to realize that it was Queen Elizabeth!

TODAY'S READING
Psalm 46

God is our refuge and strength, a very present help in trouble. v. 1

As shocking as receiving help from the queen of England may be, we have an offer of help that is even more astounding. The Creator-God of the universe descends into our world, sees our trouble, and offers to marshal His resources to help us. As the psalmist confidently affirms, "God is . . . a very present help in trouble" (PS. 46:1). Our Savior helps by giving us grace to endure, His Word to sustain us, friends to encourage and pray for us, and the confidence that He will ultimately work it all together for our spiritual good.

Next time you feel stranded along life's road, look for your Helper. 🍃

JOE STOWELL

Lord, I'm thankful that when I experience trouble You are waiting and wanting to help. Teach me to look to You and to rest in Your kind and loving care until You deliver me safely home.

Rejoice! Your God is a helping King!

Do No Harm

Many consider the ancient Greek physician Hippocrates as the father of Western medicine. He understood the importance of following moral principles in the practice of medicine, and is credited with writing the Hippocratic Oath, which still serves as an ethical guide for today's medical doctors. One key concept of the oath is "to do no harm." It implies that a physician will do only what he thinks will benefit his patients.

TODAY'S READING
Romans 13:8-10

Love does no harm to a neighbor; therefore love is the fulfillment of the law. v. 10

The principle of doing no harm extends to our relationships with others in everyday life. In fact, benevolence is central to New Testament teaching about loving others. In reflecting on the law of God, Paul sees that love is the intent behind many biblical commands: "Love does no harm to a neighbor; therefore love is the fulfillment of the law" (ROM. 13:10).

Each day as we follow Jesus Christ our Savior, we are faced with choices that will affect the lives of others. When we choose a course of action, we should ask ourselves, "Does this reflect Christ's concern for others, or am I only concerned for myself?" Such a sensitivity demonstrates the love of Christ that seeks to heal the broken and help those in need. 🍂 *DENNIS FISHER*

> Lord, I admit that it is easy to be consumed with my
> own wants and needs. Thank You that You showed us
> how to be concerned for others too. Help me to
> follow Your example in caring for others.

Caring for the burdens of others helps us to forget about our own.

Make It Attractive

The story is told of a young boy who, during a bygone era, was aboard a passenger train attempting to make money selling apples. He made his way through the train car, saying, "Apples! Would you like to buy an apple?" When he got to the rear of the car, he still had a bagful of apples and no money.

A gentleman who noticed his plight took him aside and asked to see one of the apples. He proceeded to go to the front of the train, polish it conspicuously with a napkin, and then walk down the aisle eating the apple and commenting on how delicious and refreshing it was. Then he told the boy to try again.

TODAY'S READING
Colossians 4:2-6

Walk in wisdom toward those who are outside, redeeming the time. v. 5

This time, he sold every apple. The difference? The apples had been made attractive to the potential customers.

This story can remind us of one way we can interest others in the gospel of Jesus Christ: Make it attractive to them—show them the difference it has made in our own lives. That is best done by following the words of Paul in Colossians 4:5. "Be wise," he said, "in the way you act toward outsiders; make the most of every opportunity" (NIV). If we show kindness, love, and compassion to others, those who observe us will wonder why, and that may give us an opening to tell them about the beauty of God's love for them. ❧

DAVE BRANON

Dear God, You have given us so much by providing our salvation. Help us to make the gospel attractive to others by the way we shine Jesus' light on those we encounter each day.

The beauty of a changed life can attract others to the One who makes us beautiful.

Focus on the Process

n William Zinsser's book *On Writing Well*, he says that many writers suffer from "the tyranny of the final product." They are so concerned with selling their article or book, they neglect learning the process of how to think, plan, and organize. A jumbled manuscript, Zinsser believes, is produced when "the writer, his eye on the finish line, never gave enough thought to how to run the race."

Author and minister A. W. Tozer applies that principle to our spiritual lives. In his book *The Root of the Righteous*, Tozer describes our tendency to be "concerned only with the fruit . . . [and] ignore the root out of which the fruit sprang."

The apostle Peter reminded first-century believers that Christlike living and effective service result from a process. He urged them to grow in eight areas of spiritual development: faith, virtue, knowledge, self-control, perseverance, godliness, brotherly kindness, and love (2 PETER 1:5-7). If you possess these qualities in increasing measure, Peter said, "you will be neither barren nor unfruitful in the knowledge of our Lord Jesus Christ" (V. 8).

God calls us to a wonderful process of learning to know Him, with the assurance that it will lead to productive service in His name and for His honor. 🕊 *DAVID MCCASLAND*

TODAY'S READING
2 Peter 1:2-11

If these things are yours and abound, you will be neither barren nor unfruitful in the knowledge of our Lord Jesus Christ. v. 8

Lord, so often we want complete and perfect solutions here and now.
But You work graciously in Your good time. Let Your goodness and
patience and virtue shine through us so that we may bless others.

*The Christian life is a process in which we learn
complete dependence on God.*

The Big Comeback

Chad **Pennington** is a former American football player who has suffered multiple career-threatening injuries. Twice, his injuries forced him to endure surgery, months of physical therapy, and weeks of training to get back onto the field. Yet, both times he not only returned to playing but he also excelled at such a high level that he was named Comeback Player of the Year in the National Football League. For Pennington, his efforts were an expression of his determination to return to football.

Spiritually, when sin and failure break our relationship with God and sideline our service, determination alone is not what restores us to rightness with God and usefulness in His kingdom. When we are sidelined because of sin, the path to a comeback is confession as well. "If we confess our sins, He is faithful and just to forgive us our sins and to cleanse us from all unrighteousness" (1 JOHN 1:9).

> TODAY'S READING
> **1 John 1**
>
> **If we confess our sins, He is faithful and just to forgive us our sins and to cleanse us from all unrighteousness.** v. 9

For us to be able to recover from our spiritual failings, we are absolutely dependent on the One who gave Himself for us. And that gives us hope. Christ, who died for us, loves us with an everlasting love and will respond with grace as we confess our faults to Him. Through confession, we can find His gracious restoration—the greatest of all comebacks. ❧

BILL CROWDER

Just as I am, without one plea,
But that Thy blood was shed for me,
And that Thou bidd'st me come to Thee,
O Lamb of God, I come, I come. ELLIOTT

Confession is the path that leads to restoration.

God Sends His Love

went for a long time, years really, where I couldn't perceive God's love for me. If you have ever wondered, as I have, if God loves you, you know that His love can seem distant and impersonal. We know that somewhere "out there" God loves us, but here and now we struggle to feel God's love for us. We tend to think of God loving "the world" as in John 3:16. By extension, we acknowledge that we are included in that set, though it seems impersonal. We know that Christ died for us, but He died for everyone else too.

I think many people find it easier to gain a mental awareness of God's love than to experience it in their heart. Sometimes people will talk about the 12-inch gap between their head and their heart, meaning that they know something with their head but

God's Word said that He loved me . . . . I was almost challenging God to "prove it."

don't feel the reality in their heart. For many years, that's how I felt about God's love for me. I knew in my head that God loved me, but I wanted to feel the reality of God's love in my heart.

Unfortunately, when I could not perceive God's love for me, I ran away from God for a few years. As God began to restore my relationship with Him, I reached a point of knowing that I had to make a decision about whether I would believe that what God said was true. God's Word said that He loved me, but I couldn't see the evidence in my own life. I was almost challenging God to "prove it." In a way, I needed to know that I could trust Him.

It was one of the hottest summers on record, so I went down to the coolest part of the basement with my Bible and a notebook. I spent the entire weekend looking up every verse on God's love, faithfulness, and other attributes. I learned a lot about God that weekend. What started as a philosophical debate with Him somehow touched my heart enough that I surrendered and made a decision to stop resisting Him.

As I walked with God, I began to grow in my relationship with Him, but I continued to battle chronic depression. A wise Christian woman urged me to begin keeping a gratitude journal. She encouraged me to keep a notebook by my bed and to record three things for which I was thankful before turning out the lights. She said that by dwelling on positive things before bedtime, I would sleep better. She challenged me to do this for 90 days, suggesting that it would give me a more positive outlook on life.

I took the challenge. At first I recorded obvious and generic things such as being thankful for friends and family. Then I began to pay closer attention to things throughout the day, and I discovered many things for which I could be thankful: a compliment from someone that lifted my spirits or a thunderstorm that reminded me of God's awesome power. The exercise forced me to become observant. It increased my awareness of the small ways in which God expresses His love toward us every day.

I maintained the journal for only 3 months, but it changed my outlook forever. I began to look for and find God's overtures of love toward me in a multitude of small ways. Taking notice of small things opened my eyes to bigger things God was doing in my life. I began to feel grateful that He had healed me from chronic depression, and I marveled at how He had changed my attitude toward Him from one of desperate defiance, like a hurt animal, to one of quiet acceptance and eager anticipation. Or, to put it a different way, I went from being desperate for a drop of God's love to swimming in the ocean of God's love. Finally, I was floating with total confidence in God's love rather than fighting it like a drowning person.

We want to experience a dynamic relationship with God on a daily basis.

Keeping a list of things for which I could be thankful seemed like a mental activity, but it changed my heart. The mind and the emotions work together in mysterious ways, but it takes both to have a satisfying and well-balanced relationship with God.

It might seem like self-centered ingratitude to keep a list of what God has done for me lately, but perhaps it expresses the deepest longing of our heart to be in a relationship that is personally relevant and dynamic. We don't want a "once upon a time" story about what God did for us 2,000 years ago; we want to experience a dynamic relationship with God on a daily basis. We want a page-turner that keeps us engaged from beginning to end with love, drama, constant action, and ever-present hope in spite of impossible circumstances. Still, in order for us to experience a dynamic love story today, we must go back 2,000 years to the events of the cross that made our love relationship with God possible.

The cross is where God demonstrated His unfailing love for us. God's love involves withholding from us the punishment that we deserve and extending to us the good that we do not deserve. This doesn't mean that God is soft on sin. Quite the contrary. There is a price to be paid, and He was willing to pay the price personally to rescue us. God's Son took on human form and sacrificed His life to save ours. That's the message of the cross: "But God showed his great love for us by sending Christ to die for us while we were still sinners" (ROM. 5:8 NLT). That's unfailing love.

Even though it's true that the cross is the evidence of God's love for me, sometimes the gift of God's Son seems like getting a vacuum cleaner from your husband for Christmas.

Salvation is a gift to be used here and now, each and every day.

We want something personal from God. For this reason, salvation—like a gift we aren't sure we wanted—can seem like a nice gesture on God's part, but we aren't sure what to do with it. We tend to leave it on a shelf somewhere as a reminder of the gift that God gave us. Then we go on with our lives as usual. However, salvation is a gift to be used here and now, each and every day. Salvation isn't a free ticket to heaven; it's an invitation to a relationship that produces abundant life.

One notable example of God's unfailing love occurs when God laments the unfaithfulness of His people and then promises to restore their relationship. He says, "I will make you my wife forever, showing you righteousness and justice, unfailing love and compassion. I will be faithful to you and make you mine, and you will finally know me as the LORD" (HOS. 2:19-20 NLT).

Clearly, God portrays Himself as a lover. His relationship to His people is described as a wedding vow. Despite the unfaithfulness of His bride, He will remain faithful and extend unfailing love to her. Isn't that the kind of relationship we are looking for with God?

Why is it, then, that the message of the cross is often described in cold and sterile terms? God's sacrificial love for us is often explained in judicial terms: We have violated the law of God, and the devil has brought charges against us. God, the righteous Judge, declares us guilty as charged, and the sentence for our criminal violation is the death penalty. Out of love for us, God announces that His Son, Jesus, will pay our penalty so we can live. Jesus died on the cross, guiltless yet convicted as a criminal, to pay our death penalty.

Although this explanation is true, it does not stir our emotions the way a romantic love story might. When a person loves us enough to commit the rest of his or her life to us, we feel special because that person chose us above all others to be his or her lover. That's the way God relates to us. He chose us to be His lover.

God is not perched up in heaven looking down upon the

world with a generic sort of love for humanity as a whole. God interacts with us in ways that indicate His unique love relationship with each one of us. He loves us personally and intimately, like no other person can love us.

God interacts with us in ways that indicate His unique love relationship with each one of us.

If we begin to pay attention, we will notice God's gestures of love toward us. He showers us with tokens of His love and waits for us to notice. Like a trail of anonymous love notes, God's blessings lead us to Him. God doesn't want to force us to love Him. That wouldn't be love at all. Still, He faithfully demonstrates His love in our lives, and He waits for us to respond to His love by loving Him in return. He hopes to enjoy a love relationship with each one of us.

God sends His love. He sent His love 2,000 years ago by heroically sacrificing His Son's life for ours. He continues to send His love each and every day. God's gestures of love toward us as individuals are intended to get our attention and win our hearts. I hope you begin to anticipate and recognize God's demonstration of love toward you each day. ❧

Excerpted and adapted from *Best Friends with God*. © 2010 by Christy Bower.

Who Is This Man?

When Kelly Steinhaus visited Harvard Square to ask college students what they thought of Jesus, the answers were respectful of Him. One said He was "a person who took care of people." Another said, "He sounds like a cool guy." Others rejected Him outright: "He was just a guy. I don't think He was the Savior." And, "I do not accept any faith system that says, 'I am the only way to God.'" Some people thoughtfully question who Jesus is and some reject Him.

> **TODAY'S READING**
> **Matthew 27:32-44**
>
> **Our Lord . . . was . . . declared to be the Son of God . . . by the resurrection from the dead.**
> Romans 1:3-4

As Jesus faced death 2,000 years ago, many people mocked the idea that He was anyone special. "They put up over His head the accusation written against Him: 'THIS IS JESUS THE KING OF THE JEWS'" (MATT. 27:37). Those who said, "You who destroy the temple and build it in three days, save Yourself!" (V. 40) were doubting His power. The religious people even said, "He saved others; Himself He cannot save" (V. 42).

In His death, Jesus may have seemed powerless. But when we read the whole story, we see that He gave His life willingly. He proved Himself to be the Son of God and limitless in power as He burst forth from the tomb. Grasp the value of His death and behold the power of His resurrection. He's the Savior of the world! ❦

DAVE BRANON

Up from the grave He arose,
With a mighty triumph o'er His foes;
He arose a Victor from the dark domain,
And He lives forever with His saints to reign. LOWRY

Jesus' resurrection spelled the death of death.

A Lesson in Worry

My friend handed me a tall glass of water and told me to hold it. The longer I held it, the heavier it felt. Finally my hand grew tired, and I had to put the glass down. "I've learned that worry can be like holding that glass," she said. "The longer I worry about something, the more my fears weigh me down."

King David knew about fear. His whole life had been turned upside down. His son Absalom had stolen the allegiance of the nation of Israel from him and was attempting to take the throne for himself. David didn't know who was loyal to him and who was

TODAY'S READING
Psalm 3

LORD, how they have increased who trouble me! v. 1

against him. His only option seemed to be to run. He said to his servants, "Make haste to depart, lest [Absalom] overtake us suddenly and bring disaster upon us" (2 SAM. 15:14).

In a psalm that David may have written while he was fleeing for his life, he wrote: "I cried to the LORD with my voice, and He heard me from His holy hill" (PS. 3:4). In the midst of his fear, David looked to the Lord. God showed him grace and restored him to the throne.

There are plenty of worries that can weigh us down. But as we release them into God's strong hands, He will help us through our trials. 🌿 *ANNE CETAS*

Thank You, Lord, that we do not have to be weighed down by worry. Help us to place our concerns in Your care so that we do not fear tomorrow.

Worry is a burden that God never meant for us to bear.

Tender Loving Care

Max runs a small farm as a hobby. Recently when he checked on the cows he is raising, he was surprised to see a newborn calf! When he bought the cattle, he had no idea one was pregnant. Sadly, the mother cow had complications and died shortly after her calf was born. Immediately, Max purchased some powdered milk so he could feed the calf from a bottle. "The calf thinks I'm its mother!" Max said.

The tender story of Max's new role with the calf reminded me of how Paul likened himself to a caring mother in dealing with the believers at Thessalonica: "We were gentle among you," he said, "just as a nursing mother cherishes her own children" (1 THESS. 2:7).

> TODAY'S READING
> **1 Thess. 2:1-7**
>
> **We were gentle among you, just as a nursing mother cherishes her own children.** v. 7

Paul adopted a nurturing attitude when teaching people. He knew believers needed the "milk of the word" for spiritual growth (1 PETER 2:2). But he also gave special attention to the concerns of those he cared for. "We dealt with each of you as a father deals with his own children," Paul said, "encouraging, comforting and urging you to live lives worthy of God" (1 THESS. 2:11-12 NIV).

As we serve each other, may we serve with the tender loving care of our Savior, encouraging each other in our spiritual journey (HEB. 10:24). 🌾   *DENNIS FISHER*

Dear Lord, help me to be sensitive and caring as I serve others.
Help me to love others tenderly as You so tenderly
love and care for me.

God pours His love into our hearts to flow out to others' lives.

Dependence Day

n the US, the Fourth of July is a national holiday when outdoor grills are heated up; beaches are packed; and cities and towns have parades and fireworks displays, picnics, and patriotic celebrations. All of this is in remembrance of July 4, 1776, when the 13 American colonies declared their independence.

Independence appeals to all ages. It means "freedom from the control, influence, support, and aid of others." So it's not surprising that teenagers talk about gaining their independence. Many adults have the goal of being "independently wealthy." And senior citizens want to maintain their independence. Whether anyone is ever truly independent is a discussion for another time and place—but it sounds good.

TODAY'S READING
John 15:1-13

I am the vine, you are the branches. He who abides in Me, and I in him, bears much fruit; for without Me you can do nothing. v. 5

Craving political or personal independence is one thing; daring to pursue spiritual independence is problematic. What we need instead is a recognition and acceptance of our deep spiritual dependence. Jesus said, "I am the vine, you are the branches. He who abides in Me, and I in him, bears much fruit; for without Me you can do nothing" (JOHN 15:5).

Far from being self-reliant, we are totally and eternally dependent on the One who died to set us free. Every day is our "dependence day." ❧ *BILL CROWDER*

I need Thee every hour, most gracious Lord;
No tender voice like Thine can peace afford.
I need Thee, O I need Thee; every hour I need Thee!
O bless me now, my Savior, I come to Thee. HAWKS/LOWRY

Our greatest strength comes from dependence on our strong God.

The Growth Chart

f my family ever moves from the house where we live now, I want to unhinge the pantry door and take it with me! That door is special because it shows how my children have grown over the years. Every few months, my husband and I place our children against the door and pencil a mark just above their heads. According to our growth chart, my daughter shot up 4 inches in just 1 year!

Grow in the grace and knowledge of our Lord and Savior Jesus Christ. v. 18

While my children grow physically as a natural part of life, there's another kind of growth that happens with some effort—our spiritual growth in Christ-likeness. Peter encouraged believers to "grow in the grace and knowledge" of Jesus (2 PETER 3:18). He said that maturing in our faith prepares us for Christ's return. The apostle wanted Jesus to come back and find believers living in peace and righteousness (V. 14). Peter viewed spiritual growth as a defense against teaching that incorrectly interprets God's Word and leads people astray (VV. 16-17).

Even when we feel discouraged and disconnected from God, we can remember that He will help us advance in our faith by making us more like His Son. His Word assures us that "He who has begun a good work in [us] will complete it until the day of Jesus Christ" (PHIL. 1:6). 🖋 *JENNIFER BENSON SCHULDT*

Dear God, I invite Your Holy Spirit to mold me into the person You want me to be. Empower me to keep reaching for the holiness I see in Jesus.

Spiritual growth requires the solid food of God's Word.

Not a Hitching Post

You may have heard the saying, "The past is supposed to be a guidepost, not a hitching post." It's easy to become tied to memories of "the good old days" instead of using our experiences to find direction for the road ahead. We are all susceptible to the paralyzing effects of nostalgia—a longing for what used to be.

Jeremiah was a priest from a small town near Jerusalem when God called him to be "a prophet to the nations" (JER. 1:5). He was given the very difficult job of pronouncing God's judgment primarily on the people of Judah, who had turned away from the Lord. Jeremiah made it clear that he was delivering God's message, not his own (7:1-2).

> **TODAY'S READING**
> **Jeremiah 6:13-20**
>
> **Ask for the old paths, where the good way is, and walk in it; then you will find rest for your souls.** v. 16

The Lord said, "Stand in the ways and see, and ask for the old paths, where the good way is, and walk in it; then you will find rest for your souls. But they said, 'We will not walk in it'" (6:16).

God urged His people to look back so they could move ahead. The purpose of considering the ancient paths was to find "the good way" marked by God's faithfulness, His forgiveness, and His forward call.

God can teach us from our past that the best road is the one we walk with Him. 🌿

DAVID MCCASLAND

Though I know not what awaits me—
What the future has in store,
Yet I know that God is faithful,
For I've proved Him oft before. ANON.

God's guidance in the past gives courage for the future.

The Jaws of Death

Lauren Kornacki is glad she took that summer CPR class, but she probably never thought she would have to use it so soon and on someone she loves. Her father was repairing his car when the jack slipped and the car fell on him. Lauren, a 22-year-old, reportedly heroically lifted the 3,300-pound car enough to pull him from underneath! Then she kept him alive with CPR until the paramedics arrived.

TODAY'S READING
Luke 9:1-6

They departed and went through the towns, preaching the gospel and healing everywhere. v. 6

Far greater than Lauren's rescue of her father from the jaws of death is Jesus' rescue of us from the clutches of sin by His death and resurrection. When Jesus sent the 12 disciples to carry out His work, He gave them the assignment to preach the good news of God's desire to rescue people (LUKE 9:1-6). They would not carry this out in their own strength, but Jesus would lift the heavy burden of people's sin as they taught about Him. Their preaching and healing in Jesus' power and authority proved that Jesus had actually brought God's rule to earth.

Many today are trapped under the weight of sin, but our great God can rescue us from underneath those burdens and then send us into the world to tell others that He can set them free. ❦
MARVIN WILLIAMS

THINKING IT OVER
Do you know someone who is trapped under the burden of sin and needs Jesus' rescue? In what practical ways can you be an active agent of Jesus' love?

Those who've been rescued from sin are best able to help in the rescue of others.

Uncertain Times

During a major economic downturn several years ago, many people lost their jobs. Sadly, my brother-in-law was one of them. Writing to me about their situation, my sister shared that although there were uncertainties, they had peace because they knew that God would care for them.

Believers in Jesus can have peace in the midst of uncertainties because we have the assurance that our heavenly Father loves His children and cares for our needs (MATT. 6:25-34). We can bring all our concerns to Him with an attitude of thankfulness, trusting Him to meet our needs and give us peace (PHIL. 4:6-7).

TODAY'S READING
Philippians 4:6-9

The peace of God, which surpasses all understanding, will guard your hearts and minds through Christ Jesus. v. 7

"The peace of God, which surpasses all understanding," writes the apostle Paul, "will guard your hearts and minds through Christ Jesus" (V. 7). To say the peace of God surpasses all understanding reveals that we can't explain it, but we can experience it as He guards our hearts and minds.

Our peace comes from the confidence that the Lord loves us and He is in control. He alone provides the comfort that settles our nerves, fills our minds with hope, and allows us to relax even in the midst of changes and challenges. 🌱

POH FANG CHIA

Heavenly Father, You are all-wise, all-powerful, and all-loving.
In the midst of uncertainties, help me to rest in the certainty of
who You are. I thank You that Your peace will guard my heart.
I place my trust in You.

You will keep him in perfect peace, whose mind is stayed on You,
because he trusts in You. ISAIAH 26:3

Asking Different Questions

When tragedy strikes, questions follow. Our loss of a loved one may lead us to ask God any number of pointed questions: "Why did You let this happen?" "Whose fault was this?" "Don't You care about my pain?" Believe me, as the grieving father of a teenager who died tragically I have asked these very questions.

The book of Job records the questions Job asks as he sits down with friends to lament his suffering. He had lost his family as well as his health and possessions. At one point, he asks, "Why is light given to him who is in misery, and life to the bitter of soul?" (3:20). Later, he asks, "What strength do I have, that I should hope?" (6:11). And, "Does it seem good to You that You should oppress?" (10:3). Many have stood near a headstone placed too early and asked similar questions.

> **TODAY'S READING**
> **Job 38:1-11**
>
> **Where were you when I laid the foundations of the earth?** v. 4

But when you read all the way to the end of the book, you get a surprise. When God responds to Job (CHS. 38–41), He does it in an unexpected way. He turns the tables and asks Job questions—different questions that show His wisdom and sovereignty. Questions about His magnificent creation—the earth, stars, and sea. And the questions all point to this: God is sovereign. God is all-powerful. God is love. And God knows what He is doing. 🌿 *DAVE BRANON*

> We comprehend Him not,
> Yet earth and heaven tell,
> God sits as sovereign on the throne,
> And ruleth all things well. GERHARDT

Our greatest comfort in sorrow is to know that God is in control.

Look to the Hills

Atop **Corcovado Mountain** overlooking the city of Rio de Janeiro, Brazil, stands *Christ the Redeemer*, one of the tallest statues of Christ in the world. Standing 30 meters tall, with arms spreading 28 meters, this sculpture weighs 635 metric tons. It can be seen day or night from almost anywhere in the city. One look to the hills brings this figure of Christ the Redeemer into view.

The New Testament tells us that Christ is not only the Redeemer, but He is also the Creator of the universe, and that Creator is in view in Psalm 121. There the psalmist challenges us to lift our eyes to the hills to see God, for our "help comes from the LORD, who made heaven and earth" (vv. 1-2). He alone is sufficient to be our strength and to guide our steps as we make our way through a dangerous and troubled world.

TODAY'S READING
Psalm 121

I will lift up my eyes to the hills— from whence comes my help? My help comes from the LORD, who made heaven and earth. vv. 1-2

We lift our eyes to the One who keeps us (v. 3), guards us (vv. 5-6), and overshadows us in the face of all types of danger. He preserves us from evil and keeps us safely in His care for all eternity (vv. 7-8).

In faith, we lift our eyes to the One who is our Redeemer and Creator. He is our help and our hope and our eternal home. 🌸   *BILL CROWDER*

O God, our help in ages past,
Our hope for years to come,
Our shelter from the stormy blast,
And our eternal home! WATTS

Christ was lifted up that He might lift us up.

Paranoia in Reverse

remember watching television news reports in 1991 as the nonviolent revolution took place in the streets of Moscow. Russians who had grown up in totalitarianism suddenly declared, "We will act as if we are free," taking to the streets and staring down tanks. The contrast between the faces of the leaders inside and the masses outside showed who was really afraid, and who was really free.

> TODAY'S READING
> **1 John 4:1-6,17-19**
>
> **There is no fear in love; but perfect love casts out fear, because fear involves torment.** v.18

Watching the newsreels from Red Square on Finnish television, I came up with a new definition of *faith*: paranoia in reverse. A truly paranoid person organizes his or her life around a common perspective of fear. Anything that happens feeds that fear.

Faith works in reverse. A faithful person organizes his or her life around a common perspective of trust, not fear. Despite the apparent chaos of the present moment, God does reign. Regardless of how I may feel, I truly matter to a God of love.

What could happen if we in God's kingdom truly acted as if the words of the apostle John were literally true: "He who is in you is greater than he who is in the world" (1 JOHN 4:4). What if we really started living as if the most-repeated prayer in Christendom has actually been answered—that God's will be done on earth as it is in heaven? ❀

PHILIP YANCEY

> Far, far above thy thought
> His counsel shall appear,
> When fully He the work hath wrought
> That caused thy needless fear. GERHARDT

Feeding your faith helps starve your fears.

The Power of a Name

Nicknames are **often descriptive** of some noticeable aspect of a person's character or physical attributes. Growing up, my elementary school friends brutally called me "liver lips" since at that stage of development my lips seemed disproportionately large. Needless to say, I have always been glad that the name didn't stick.

Unlike my nickname, I love the names of God that describe His magnificent characteristics. God is so wonderfully multifaceted that He has many names that communicate His capabilities and character. To name just a few, He is:

> TODAY'S READING
> **Proverbs 18:1-10**
>
> **The name of the LORD is a strong tower.** v. 10

Elohim, the God above all gods
Jehovah Jireh, the God who provides
El-Shaddai, the almighty God
Jehovah Rapha, our healer God
Jehovah Shalom, our God of peace
Jehovah Shamma, our God who is present
Jehovah Yahweh, our loving, covenant-keeping God

It's no wonder the writer of Proverbs encourages us to remember that "the name of the LORD is a strong tower," that in times of need God-fearing people run to it and "are safe" (PROV. 18:10). When unwelcome circumstances threaten you and you feel vulnerable, reflect on one of God's names. Be assured—He will be faithful to His name. 🌱   *JOE STOWELL*

Lord, remind us that Your names reveal Your character. Help us to remember them in our times of need and distress. Thank You for the assurance that You are faithful to Your name.

**God's names, which describe His character,
can bring comfort when we need it most.**

"No Grace"

have nicknamed our car "No Grace." Sunday mornings are the worst. I load the car with all the stuff I need for church, get myself in my seat, close the door, and Jay starts backing out of the garage. While I am still getting settled, the seat belt warning starts buzzing. "Please," I say to it, "all I need is another minute." The answer, apparently, is no, because it continues buzzing until I am buckled in.

This minor annoyance is a good reminder of what life would be like if indeed there were no grace. Each of us would immediately be called to account for every indiscretion. There would be no time for repentance or change of behavior. There would be no forgiveness. No mercy. No hope.

TODAY'S READING
1 Peter 4:1-11

The discretion of a man makes him slow to anger, and his glory is to overlook a transgression.

Proverbs 19:11

Living in this world sometimes feels like falling into a no-grace sinkhole. When minor flaws are blown up into major indiscretions or when people refuse to overlook the faults and offenses of others, we end up burdened by the weight of guilt that we were never meant to carry. God, in His grace, sent Jesus to carry the burden for us. Those who receive God's gift of grace have the privilege of offering it to others on Christ's behalf: "Above all things have fervent love for one another, for 'love will cover a multitude of sins'" (1 PETER 4:8). 🌿

JULIE ACKERMAN LINK

Father God, the culture around us can seem so harsh and hard on people when they fail. Help me to show grace and patience, because You have been gracious to me and have forgiven my sin.

When we gratefully acknowledge the grace we've received, we joyfully give it to those in need.

Grain on the Mountaintop

'**ve been on a number** of mountaintops in the US in my time, and I can tell you that not much grows up there. The summits of mountains are bare rock and lichen. That's not where you would normally find an abundance of grain.

But Solomon, who wrote Psalm 72, asked God for "an abundance of grain . . . on the top of the mountains," to characterize his reign as king. If grain on the mountain is so unusual, what is Solomon suggesting? That God's power can produce results in even the most unpromising soil?

Perhaps you think of yourself as a little person, with very little to bring to the kingdom. Take courage: God can

> **TODAY'S READING**
> **Psalm 72:12-20**
>
> **There will be an abundance of grain in the earth, on the top of the mountains.** v. 16

produce an abundant harvest through you. This is one of the ironies of faith: God uses the insignificant to accomplish the great. Not many of us are wise or noble; most of us are anonymous and far from extraordinary. Yet all of us can be used. And contrary to what we might think, it is because of our weakness that we can be used by God (1 COR. 1:27-29; 2 COR. 12:10).

It's possible to be too big or proud for God to use, but we can never be too little. "Out of weakness" we are "made strong" (HEB. 11:34). By God's great power, we can do all that He has called us to do. 🌿   *DAVID ROPER*

Lord, You work through such common things—those of us with flaws and weaknesses. We are in awe of Your power and humbled by Your choice of us. Our hearts long to be faithful to You.

To experience God's power, we must first admit that we are weak.

True Loyalty

By one estimate, more than 14 trillion frequent-flyer miles have been accumulated by people worldwide. It all started in the early 1980s, when airlines began the first frequent-flyer programs to encourage repeat business by rewarding customers for their loyalty. Accumulated miles could be redeemed for free travel, goods, and services, so it wasn't long before people began planning their travel based as much on personal reward as on price or schedule.

> **TODAY'S READING**
> **2 Cor. 11:23-31**
>
> **If I must boast, I will boast in the things which concern my infirmity.** v. 30

The apostle Paul was an avid first-century traveler, but he wasn't in it for the "frequent-sailor miles." His goal was to reach as many people as he could with the good news of forgiveness and eternal life through faith in Jesus. When some people in the city of Corinth questioned his authority, he wrote a letter describing the price he had paid to bring the gospel to others: "Three times I was beaten with rods; once I was stoned; three times I was shipwrecked; a night and a day I have been in the deep" (2 COR. 11:25). God gave Paul the grace and endurance to risk his life to tell people about Jesus with no thought of personal gain.

Whether we receive persecution or praise for our service to the Lord, may our focus always be loyalty to Him and gratitude for His sacrifice of love. 🌱 *DAVID MCCASLAND*

I am Yours, Lord, yet teach me all it means,
All it involves of love and loyalty,
Of holy service, full and glad,
In unreserved obedience to Thee! BENNETT

Our loyalty to Jesus grows from His love for us.

Feeling Chained?

Boethius lived in sixth-century Italy and served the royal court as a highly skilled politician. Unfortunately, he fell into disfavor with the king. He was accused of treason and imprisoned. While awaiting execution, he asked for writing materials so he could compose his reflections. Later, these became an enduring spiritual classic on consolation.

As Boethius sat in prison, pondering his bleak prospects, his faith in Christ infused his perspective: "Nothing is miserable but what is thought so, and contrariwise, every estate is happy if he that bears it be content." He understood that our view of changing circumstances and contentment is a personal choice.

> **TODAY'S READING**
> **Psalm 16:1-11**
>
> **I have learned in whatever state I am, to be content.**
> Philippians 4:11

The apostle Paul reinforced the idea that the way we view our circumstances is more important than the circumstances themselves. While he too was in prison, he wrote: "I have learned in whatever state I am, to be content" (PHIL. 4:11). Both men could be content because they drew their ultimate satisfaction from God, who never changes.

Do you feel chained to difficult circumstances? God can give you contentment. Lasting satisfaction can be found only with Him, for in His "presence is fullness of joy; at [His] right hand are pleasures forevermore" (PS. 16:11). 🌸   *DENNIS FISHER*

Lord, lead me today as You see best. Use the gifts You've given me to encourage others on their journey. Help me not to compare myself with others but to be content.

When all you have is God, you have all you need.

Lookin' Good!

After trying on my new sunglasses in the car one day, my daughter handed them back and said, "These are *not* sunglasses, Mom. They're just fashion lenses. Let me guess," she teased, "you bought them because you look cute in them."

Okay, I have to admit—my daughter knows me. I hadn't given a passing thought to UV rays or even whether those glasses would actually block the sun. I just really liked the way they looked on me.

TODAY'S READING
Hebrews 10:19-25

Let us consider one another in order to stir up love and good works. v. 24

Most of us like to look good. We want to appear that we "have it all together"—with no struggles or fears or temptations or heartaches.

Trying to maintain a façade of perfection on our spiritual journey doesn't help us or our fellow travelers. But sharing our lives with others in the body of Christ benefits us as well as others. When we are a bit more transparent, we may find people who are struggling in a similar situation. And as we enjoy a growing fellowship with God and become more aware of our own brokenness and inadequacy, God is able to use us more fully to help others.

Let's allow God to strip away any pretense and "let us consider how we may spur one another on toward love and good deeds" (HEB. 10:24 NIV). 🌿 *CINDY HESS KASPER*

> Wearing a mask that shows everything's fine
> Says that life's struggles are not God's design;
> But when we're open, transparent, and true,
> People will trust God to meet their needs too. SPER

Believers stand strong when they don't stand alone.

Living Bridges

People who live in Cherrapunji, India, have developed a unique way to get across the many rivers and streams in their land. They grow bridges from the roots of rubber trees. These "living bridges" take between 10 to 15 years to mature, but once they are established, they are extremely stable and last for hundreds of years.

The Bible compares a person who trusts in God to "a tree planted by the waters, which spreads out its roots by the river" (JER. 17:8). Because its roots are well-nourished, this tree survives soaring temperatures. And during drought it continues to yield fruit.

TODAY'S READING
Jeremiah 17:5-10

Blessed is the man who trusts in the LORD. v. 7

Like a firmly rooted tree, people who rely on God have a sense of stability and vitality despite the worst circumstances. In contrast, people who place their trust in other humans often live with a sense of instability. The Bible compares them to desert shrubs that are frequently malnourished and stand alone (v. 6). So it is with the spiritual lives of people who forsake God.

Where are our roots? Are we rooted in Jesus? (COL. 2:7). Are we a bridge that leads others to Him? If we know Christ, we can testify to this truth: Blessed are those who trust in the Lord (JER. 17:7). 🌿   *JENNIFER BENSON SCHULDT*

Jesus is all the world to me,
My life, my joy, my all;
He is my strength from day to day,
Without Him I would fall. THOMPSON

Even strong trials cannot blow down a person who is rooted in God.

Whoppers or Adventures?

My grandfather loved to tell stories, and I loved to listen. Papaw had two kinds of tales. "Whoppers" were stories with a whiff of truth, but which changed with each new telling. "Adventures" were stories that really happened, and the facts never changed when retold. One day my grandfather told a story that just seemed too far-fetched to be true. "Whopper," I declared, but my grandfather insisted it was true. Although his telling never varied, I simply couldn't believe it, it was that unusual.

TODAY'S READING
Psalm 102:18-28

But You are the same, and Your years will have no end. v. 27

Then one day, while I was listening to a radio program, I heard the announcer tell a story that confirmed the truth of my grandfather's tale. My grandfather's "whopper" suddenly became an "adventure." It was a moving moment of remembrance that made him even more trustworthy in my eyes.

When the psalmist wrote about the unchanging nature of God (102:27), he was offering this same comfort—the trustworthiness of God—to us. The idea is repeated in Hebrews 13:8 with these words, "Jesus Christ is the same yesterday, today, and forever." This can lift our hearts above our daily trials to remind us that an unchanging, trustworthy God rules over even the chaos of a changing world. ❦ *RANDY KILGORE*

> Our God is God—He does not change;
> His truth, His love remain each day the same,
> He's faithful to His matchless name,
> For God is God—He does not change. D. DEHAAN

***Let the sameness of God waft over your heart
with His peace in your storms.***

Small Ways in Small Places

Often I meet with people who serve in what they think are seemingly small ways in small places. They are frequently discouraged by loneliness, feeling that their acts of service are insignificant. When I hear them speak, I think of one of the angels in C. S. Lewis' book *Out of the Silent Planet*. He said: "My people have a law never to speak of sizes or numbers to you. . . . It makes you do reverence to nothings and pass by what is really great."

TODAY'S READING
Isaiah 49:1-6

For who has despised the day of small things?
Zechariah 4:10

Sometimes culture says bigger is better—that size is the truest measure of success. It takes a strong person to resist that trend, especially if he or she is laboring in a small place. But we must not "pass by what is really great."

It's not that numbers aren't important (after all, the apostles counted their converts; SEE ACTS 2:41). Numbers represent living people with eternal needs. We should all work and pray for large numbers of people to enter the kingdom, but numbers mustn't be the basis for self-esteem.

God doesn't call us to find fulfillment in the amount of work we do for Him, or the number of people who are a part of that work, but in faithfully doing our work for His sake. Serving our great God with His strength in a small way is not a stepping-stone to greatness—it is greatness. ❀   *DAVID ROPER*

> Lord, help me remember that there are no small places or
> small people. All are precious in Your sight. May I see the
> value of my work and cherish it as You do.

Anyone doing God's work in God's way is important in His sight.

Water for the World

Although 70 percent of the world is covered by water, less than 1 percent of it is drinkable by humans. Water conservation and sanitation are crucial matters in many parts of the world, as all life depends on having sanitary water.

Jesus went out of His way to introduce a lost woman to another kind of life-giving water. He deliberately chose to go to a town in Samaria, a place where no respectable rabbi would set foot. There, He told this woman about "living water." Those who drink of it, He said, "will never thirst." It will "become in him a fountain of water springing up into everlasting life" (JOHN 4:14).

> TODAY'S READING
> **John 4:7-15**
>
> **He who believes in Me, as the Scripture has said, out of his heart will flow rivers of living water.** 7:38

The living water is Jesus Himself. Those who receive Him have eternal life (V. 14). But the living water He provides also serves another function. Jesus said of those who receive it: "Out of his heart will flow rivers of living water" (7:38). The living water that refreshes us is to refresh others also.

As fresh-water distribution is uneven in the world, so too is the distribution of living water. Many people do not know followers of Jesus who really care about them. It is our privilege to share Him. Christ is, after all, the living water for whom people are thirsting. ❧ 　　　　　　　　　　　C. P. HIA

Lord Jesus, I want to live for You. May Your life and love flow through me as I go about my duties today so that others may see You through me and be drawn to the living water.

Jesus is a never-ending supply of living water for a parched world.

Lasting Regrets

While I was talking with a gifted pianist, she asked me if I played any musical instruments. When I responded, "I play the radio," she laughed and asked if I had ever wanted to play any instrument. My embarrassed answer was, "I took piano lessons as a boy but gave it up." Now, in my adult years, I regret not continuing with the piano. I love music and wish I could play today. That conversation was a fresh reminder to me that life is often constituted by the choices we make—and some of them produce regret.

> TODAY'S READING
> **Psalm 32:1-7**
>
> **When I kept silent, my bones grew old through my groaning all the day long.** v. 3

Some choices produce much more serious and painful regrets. King David discovered this when he chose to sleep with another man's wife and then killed that man. He described the guilt that filled him as devastating, saying, "When I kept silent, my bones grew old through my groaning all the day long. For day and night Your hand was heavy upon me; my vitality was turned into the drought of summer" (PS. 32:3-4). But David acknowledged and confessed his sin to God and found forgiveness (V. 5).

It is only from God that we can receive the grace of forgiveness when our choices have produced painful regrets. And only in Him do we find the wisdom to make better choices. 🌱

BILL CROWDER

Father of mercies, forgive me for the foolish choices I have made. Please enable me to be wiser in my choices. Teach me the value of resting in Your grace.

God's forgiveness frees us from the chains of regret.

Waving the White Flag

Recently, while watching a video of a church service held in South America, I noticed something I had never seen before in church. As the pastor passionately called his flock to yield their lives to Jesus, one of the parishioners took a white hankie out of his pocket and started waving it in the air. Then another, and another. With tears running down their cheeks, they were expressing full surrender to Christ.

TODAY'S READING
Deuteronomy 6:1-9

Hear, O Israel: The LORD our God, the LORD is one! You shall love the LORD your God. vv. 4-5

But I wonder if there was more to the moment than the flags of surrender. I think they were waving flags of love to God. When God told His people to "love the LORD your God" (DEUT. 6:5), it was in the context of His urging them to surrender their lives to Him.

From God's point of view, life with Him is far more than just trying to be good. It is always about relationship—relationship in which surrender is the way we express our grateful love to Him. Jesus, in amazing love for us, surrendered Himself on the cross to rescue us from our helpless bondage to sin and set us on a journey to all that is good and glorious.

We don't have enough words to tell God how much we love Him! So, let's show Him our love by surrendering our hearts and lives to follow Him. 🍃 *JOE STOWELL*

Lord, take my life and make it wholly Thine;
Fill my poor heart with Thy great love divine.
Take all my will, my passion, self, and pride;
I now surrender, Lord—in me abide. ORR

Surrender is God's love language.

He Calls the Stars by Name

O n a plateau high above the Atacama Desert in Chile, one of the world's largest radio telescopes is giving astronomers a view of the universe never seen before. In an Associated Press article, Luis Andres Henao spoke of scientists from many countries "looking for clues about the dawn of the cosmos—from the coldest gases and dust where galaxies are formed and stars are born to the energy produced by the Big Bang."

TODAY'S READING
Psalm 147:1-9

He counts the number of the stars; He calls them all by name. v. 4

The Bible celebrates the mighty power and infinite understanding of God who "counts the number of the stars" and "calls them all by name" (PS. 147:4). Yet the Creator of the universe is not a remote, uncaring force, but a loving heavenly Father who "heals the brokenhearted and binds up their wounds" (V. 3). "The LORD lifts up the humble" (V. 6) and "takes pleasure in those who fear Him, in those who hope in His mercy" (V. 11).

He loves us so much that "He gave His only begotten Son, that whoever believes in Him should not perish but have everlasting life" (JOHN 3:16).

British author J. B. Phillips called Earth "the visited planet," where the Prince of Glory is still working out His plan.

Our hope for today and forever lies in the loving mercy of God who calls each star by name. 🌸

DAVID MCCASLAND

The God who made the firmament,
Who made the deepest sea,
The God who put the stars in place
Is the God who cares for me. BERG

God, who knows the name of every star, knows all our names as well.

Looking for Zacchaeus

Alf Clark walks the city streets looking for Zacchaeus. Well, not the actual one in the Bible—Jesus already found him. Alf and some friends who serve with an urban ministry do what Jesus did in Luke 19. They go purposefully through town to meet with and help those in need.

Alf walks house to house in his neighborhood, knocking on doors and saying to whoever peeks out, "Hi, I'm Alf. Do you have any needs I can pray for?" It's his way of opening up commu-

> TODAY'S READING
> **Luke 19:1-10**
>
> **Today salvation has come to this house.** v. 9

nication and—like Jesus did with tax-collector Zacchaeus— seeking to supply needed counsel and spiritual life and hope.

Notice what Jesus did. Luke simply says that Jesus "passed through" Jericho (LUKE 19:1). Of course, a crowd gathered, as usually occurred when Jesus came to town. Zacchaeus, being "height challenged," climbed a tree. Jesus, while passing through, walked right over to his tree and told him He had to visit at his house. That day salvation came to Zacchaeus's house. Jesus had "come to seek and to save that which was lost" (V. 10).

Do we look for Zacchaeus? He is everywhere, needing Jesus. In what ways can we share Christ's love with people who need the Savior? ❧

DAVE BRANON

God, guide our steps toward and not away from those who need You. Then guide our words and our actions so that we can be purposeful in our encounters with others.

God's good news is too good to keep to ourselves.

The Work of Our Hands

Spring had just turned into summer and crops were beginning to produce fruit as our train rolled across the fertile landscape of West Michigan's shoreline. Strawberries had ripened, and people were kneeling in the morning dew to pick the sweet fruit. Blueberry bushes were soaking up sunshine from the sky and nutrients from the earth.

After passing field after field of ripening fruit, we came to a rusty pile of abandoned metal. The harsh image of orange scrap metal poking out of the earth was a sharp contrast to the soft greens of growing crops. The metal produces nothing. Fruit, on the other hand, grows, ripens, and nourishes hungry humans.

> **TODAY'S READING**
> **Isaiah 17:7-11**
>
> **Because you have forgotten the God of your salvation, . . . the harvest will be a heap of ruins.** vv. 10-11

The contrast between the fruit and the metal reminds me of God's prophecies against ancient cities like Damascus (ISA. 17:1,11). He says, "Because you have forgotten the God of your salvation, . . . the harvest will be a heap of ruins" (VV. 10-11). This prophecy serves as a contemporary warning about the danger and futility of thinking we can produce anything on our own. Apart from God, the work of our hands will become a pile of ruins. But when we join with God in the work of *His* hands, God multiplies our effort and provides spiritual nourishment for many. 🌿

JULIE ACKERMAN LINK

Lord, I want to be a part of what You are doing in Your world.
Apart from You, my work is nothing. Lead me, fill me, use me.
Nourish others through me.

Without Me you can do nothing. JESUS (JOHN 15:5)

Divine Perspective

Jason took a trip to New York during spring break. One afternoon he and some friends piled into a cab and headed for the Empire State Building. To Jason, the ride on the ground seemed chaotic and dangerous. But when he got to the observation deck of the skyscraper and looked down on the city streets, to his amazement he saw order and design. What a difference a change in perspective made!

Habakkuk learned a similar lesson. When he looked at life from his earthly vantage point, it seemed that God was indifferent to the evil permeating society (HAB. 1:2-4). But God gave him a divine perspective and showed him that life is more than what it seems. The deeds of men cannot thwart the purposes of God (2:3).

> **TODAY'S READING**
> **Habakkuk 2:2-14**
>
> **For the vision is yet for an appointed time; . . . it will surely come.** v. 3

Those who don't show any regard for God may seem to prosper at the moment, but God will ultimately right all wrong. God acts sovereignly in all that comes to pass so that everything works toward His good purpose. God's plan will surely take place and be on schedule (V. 3).

We can't sort out the whole picture from where we are in life; only God can. So let us continue to live by faith and not by sight. From His perspective, all things are working together for the believer's good and for His honor. 🌾   POH FANG CHIA

Sovereign Ruler of the skies,
Ever gracious, ever wise,
All my times are in Your hand,
All events at Your command. RYLAND

Our times are in God's hands; our souls are in His keeping.

Courageous and Consistent

While reading the obituary of Eugene Patterson, Pulitzer Prize-winning editor of the *Atlanta Constitution* from 1960 to 1968, I was struck by two things. First, for many years Patterson was a fearless voice for civil rights during a time when many opposed racial equality. In addition, he wrote a column every day for 8 years. That's 2,922 newspaper columns! Day after day, year after year. Courage and consistency were key factors in the impact of his life.

> **TODAY'S READING**
> **Acts 28:11-16, 30-31**
>
> **When Paul saw them, he thanked God and took courage.** v. 15

We see those same qualities in the apostle Paul. Acts 13–28 records his bravery in one harrowing situation after another. After being shipwrecked on his way to stand trial before Caesar, he landed south of Rome, where many brothers in Christ came to meet him (ACTS 28:11-15). "When Paul saw them," Luke wrote, "he thanked God and took courage" (V. 15). During the next 2 years as a prisoner, Paul was allowed to live in his own rented house where he "received all who came to him, preaching the kingdom of God and teaching the things which concern the Lord Jesus Christ with all confidence" (VV. 30-31).

Every follower of Jesus can be a consistent giver and receiver of courage. The Lord can use us today to encourage and strengthen each other. 🌿

DAVID MCCASLAND

O keep up your courage, each day to the end;
Go forth in the strength of the Lord;
Trust wholly in Jesus, thy Savior and Friend,
And feed on His own blessed Word. MILES

When people share their fears with you, share your courage with them.

Confident Access

Mont **Saint-Michel** is a tidal island located about a half-mile off the coast of Normandy, France. For centuries it has been the site of an abbey and monastery that has attracted religious pilgrims. Until the construction of a causeway, it was notorious for its dangerous access that resulted in the death of some pilgrims. At low tide it is surrounded by sand banks and at high tide by water. Accessing the island was a cause for fear.

> **TODAY'S READING**
> **Hebrews 4:14-16**
>
> **Let us therefore come boldly to the throne of grace, that we may obtain mercy and find grace to help in time of need.** v. 16

Access to God for Old Testament Jews was also a cause for fear. When God thundered on Mt. Sinai, the people feared approaching Him (EX. 19:10-16). And when access to God was granted through the high priest, specific instructions had to be followed (LEV. 16:1-34). Accidentally touching the ark of the covenant, which represented the holy presence of God, would result in death (SEE 2 SAM. 6:7-8).

But because of Jesus' death and resurrection, we can now approach God without fear. God's penalty for sin has been satisfied, and we are invited into God's presence: "Let us therefore come boldly to the throne of grace, that we may obtain mercy and find grace" (HEB. 4:16).

Because of Jesus we can come to God through prayer anywhere, anytime. 🌱   *DENNIS FISHER*

> Then boldly let our faith address
> God's throne of grace and power,
> There to obtain delivering grace
> In every needy hour. WATTS

Through prayer, we have instant access to our Father.

Family Trademarks

The Aran Islands, off the west coast of Ireland, are known for their beautiful sweaters. Patterns are woven into the fabric using sheep's wool to craft the garments. Many of them relate to the culture and folklore of these small islands, but some are more personal. Each family on the islands has its own trademark pattern, which is so distinctive that if a fisherman were to drown it is said that he could be identified simply by examining his sweater for the family trademark.

> **TODAY'S READING**
> **1 John 4:7-16**
>
> **Beloved, let us love one another, for love is of God; and everyone who loves is born of God and knows God.** v. 7

In John's first letter, the apostle describes things that are to be trademarks of those who are members of God's family. In 1 John 3:1, John affirms that we are indeed part of God's family by saying, "Behold what manner of love the Father has bestowed on us, that we should be called children of God!" He then describes the trademarks of those who are the children of God, including, "Beloved, let us love one another, for love is of God; and everyone who loves is born of God and knows God" (4:7).

Because "love is of God," the chief way to reflect the heart of the Father is by displaying the love that characterizes Him. May we allow His love to reach out to others through us—for love is one of our family trademarks. 🌿

BILL CROWDER

Father, teach me to love with the love of Christ that others might see Your love reflected in my care and concern for them. May Your love drive and dominate my responses to life and to others.

Love is the family resemblance the world should see in followers of Christ.

Just As I Am

Good memories flooded my mind as I sat in a concert. The group's leader had just introduced the song they were about to sing: "Just As I Am." I remembered how at the end of his sermons my pastor would ask people to come forward while we sang that song, indicating they would like to receive the forgiveness Christ offers for their sins.

But the leader of the musical group at the concert suggested another occasion when we might sing this song. He commented that he likes to think that when he dies and goes to meet the Lord one day, he will sing in thanks to Him:

> **TODAY'S READING**
> **Isaiah 55:1-7**
>
> **Incline your ear, and come to Me. Hear, and your soul shall live.** v. 3

> *Just as I am, without one plea*
> *But that Thy blood was shed for me,*
> *And that Thou bidd'st me come to Thee,*
> *O Lamb of God, I come!*

Years before writing this song, Charlotte Elliott asked a minister how she might find the Lord. He told her, "Just come to Him as you are." She did, and later during a discouraging time of illness, she wrote this hymn about the day she came to Christ and He forgave her sin.

In His Word, the Lord encourages us to seek Him: "Seek the LORD while He may be found, call upon Him while He is near" (ISA. 55:6). He calls to our hearts: "Ho! Everyone who thirsts, come to the waters . . . . Incline your ear, and come to Me. Hear, and your soul shall live" (VV. 1,3).

Because of Jesus' death and resurrection, we can come to Him right now and will one day go into eternity to be with Him forever. Just as I am . . . I come! ❧   *ANNE CETAS*

Let him who thirsts come. Whoever desires, let him take the water of life freely. REVELATION 22:17

City of Refuge

As we entered a town in Australia, we were greeted by a sign that declared: "We welcome all who are seeking refuge and asylum." This kind of welcome seems to resonate with the Old Testament concept of the cities of refuge. In the Old Testament era, cities of refuge (NUM. 35:6) were established to be a safe haven for people who had accidentally killed someone and were needing protection. God had the people establish such cities to provide that refuge.

This concept, however, was not intended to be simply a practice for ancient Israel. More than that, cities of refuge reflected the heart of God for all people. He Himself longs to be our safe haven and our city of refuge in the failures, heartaches, and losses of life. We read in Psalm 59:16–17, "I will sing of Your power; yes, I will sing aloud of Your mercy in the morning; for You have been my defense and refuge in the day of my trouble. To You, O my Strength, I will sing praises; for God is my defense, my God of mercy."

> **TODAY'S READING**
> **Psalm 59:10-17**
>
> **I will sing of Your power; yes, I will sing aloud of Your mercy in the morning; for You have been my defense and refuge in the day of my trouble.** v. 16

For the hurting heart of every generation, our "city of refuge" is not a place. Our city of refuge is a Person—the God who loves us with an everlasting love. May we find our refuge and rest in Him. ❧

BILL CROWDER

How oft in the conflict, when pressed by the foe,
I have fled to my Refuge and breathed out my woe;
How often, when trials like sea billows roll,
Have I hidden in Thee, O Thou Rock of my soul. CUSHING

Refuge can be found in the Rock of Ages.

Graceland

The Graceland Mansion in Memphis, Tennessee, is one of the most visited homes in the US. It was built in the 1930s and named after the original owner's great aunt, Grace. It later became famous as the home of Elvis Presley.

I love the name *Graceland* because it describes the amazing territory into which God placed me when He forgave me of my sin and made me His own. He took me out of the darkness and brought me into His own "graceland."

TODAY'S READING
Romans 5:15-21

The grace of God ... abounded to many. v. 15

The apostle Paul says that "the grace of God and the gift by the grace of the one Man, Jesus Christ, abounded to many" (ROM. 5:15). I'll be forever thankful that the "many" includes me and that God's love has transferred me into the territory of His marvelous, infinite, matchless grace!

Think of the blessing of being in God's graceland. It is a realm where He has given us entrance into His presence and where that same grace continues to overflow into our lives on a daily basis. Paul tells us that even in times of despair God showers us with sufficient grace to see us through (SEE 2 COR. 12:9).

No matter what life may bring, nothing can remove us from the realm of God's grace. ❧

JOE STOWELL

Lord, for the blessings of Your grace
I am forever grateful! Teach me to accept
Your grace and to live in its power. Help me
to share Your story with others.

Remember where you live and rejoice in His grace.

A Shared Bond

When I needed a locksmith to get into my car, I had a pleasant surprise. After he arrived and began opening my little Ford's door, we began chatting and I recognized his warm, familiar accent.

It turned out that my rescuer was originally from Jamaica—a land I've visited often and have grown to love. This changed a negative event into a positive one. We were in a small way kindred spirits because of our shared love for that beautiful island nation.

TODAY'S READING
Ephesians 2:11-18

You are all one in Christ Jesus.

Galatians 3:28

This struck me as a reminder of an even greater camaraderie—the joy of meeting someone new and discovering that he or she is also a believer in Christ.

In some places, this is not unusual because there are many believers. But in those lands where there are few believers, the joy of meeting someone else who loves Jesus must be even greater. It's thrilling to share together the amazing reality of the freedom from sin we have through Christ!

For all who know Jesus, there is a shared bond, a oneness in Christ (GAL. 3:28), a joy of fellowship that can brighten even the darkest day. Praise God that He brings a bond of unity to all who know Him as Savior. 🌸

DAVE BRANON

What a miracle it is, dear Lord, that You can bring together people of all tribes, tongues, and nations to be like-minded in Christ—to share a bond of love and affection for Jesus.

Christian fellowship builds us up and binds us together.

All We Need to Know

In a **Fernando Ortega** rendition of "Just As I Am," Billy Graham's voice can be heard faintly in the background. Dr. Graham is reminiscing about an illness during which he believed he was dying. As he mused on his past, he realized what a great sinner he was and how much he continues to need God's daily forgiveness.

Billy Graham was putting an end to the notion that apart from God we're okay. We can feel good about ourselves, but that confidence must come from the knowledge that we're greatly loved children of God (JOHN 3:16), not that we're very good children (ROM. 7:18).

TODAY'S READING
Romans 7:18-25

For I know that in me (that is, in my flesh) nothing good dwells. v. 18

The first step in becoming a truly "good" person as a follower of Christ is to stop pretending that we're good on our own and to ask God to make us as good as we can be. We will fail many times, but He will keep growing us and changing us. God is faithful and—in His time and in His way—He'll do it.

In his final years, the writer of "Amazing Grace," John Newton, suffered from dementia and lamented the loss of his memory. Yet he confided, "I do remember two things: I am a great sinner, and Jesus is a great Savior." When it comes to faith, those are the only things anyone needs to know. ❧

DAVID ROPER

The Lord has promised good to me,
His word my hope secures;
He will my shield and portion be
As long as life endures. NEWTON

God's grace accepted is God's peace experienced.

Breaking Free

The elephant is the largest land animal on earth—and one of the most powerful. Yet it takes only a strong rope to restrain one. Here's how it works. When the elephant is young, he is tied to a large tree. For weeks, he will strain and pull, but the rope holds him fast. So eventually he gives up.

Then, when the elephant reaches his full size and strength, he won't struggle to get free, for once he feels resistance, he stops. He still believes he's held captive and can't break free.

Satan can play a similar trick on us to hold us captive. The Bible assures us that there is "no condemnation to those

> TODAY'S READING
> **Romans 8:1-11**
>
> **There is therefore now no condemnation to those who are in Christ Jesus.** v. 1

who are in Christ Jesus, who do not walk according to the flesh, but according to the Spirit" (ROM. 8:1). We have been set "free from the law of sin and death" (V. 2). But the enemy of our soul tries to make us believe we are still dominated by sin.

What shall we do then? Reflect on what Christ has done. He died for our sins and declared an end to sin's control over us (V. 3). He rose from the dead and gave us the Holy Spirit. Now we are empowered to live victoriously in Him because "the Spirit of Him who raised Jesus from the dead dwells in [us]" (V. 11).

In Christ, we are set free. ❁

POH FANG CHIA

He has our salvation wrought,
He our captive souls has bought,
He has reconciled to God,
He has washed us in His blood. WESLEY

***Experience true freedom—
take every thought captive in obedience to Christ.***

Broken but Beautiful

Recently, my daughter showed me her collection of sea glass. Also known as beach glass, the varied bits of colored glass are sometimes pieces of pottery but often they are pieces of shattered glass bottles. Originally the glass had a purpose, but then it was casually thrown away and became broken.

If the discarded glass ends up in an ocean, its journey is just beginning. As it is relentlessly tossed about by currents and tides, its jagged edges are ground down by the sand and waves and eventually are smoothed away and rounded off. The result is something beautiful. The jewel-like sea glass has found new life and is treasured by collectors and artists.

> TODAY'S READING
> **Jeremiah 18:1-6**
>
> [The vessel] was marred . . . ; so he made it again into another vessel, as it seemed good to the potter to make. v. 4

In a similar way, a broken life can be renewed when it is touched by God's love and grace. In the Old Testament, we read that when the prophet Jeremiah watched a potter working, he noticed that if an object was marred the potter simply reshaped it (JER. 18:1-6). God explained that in His hands the people of ancient Israel were like clay, which He would shape as He saw best.

We are never too badly broken for God to reshape. He loves us in spite of our imperfections and past mistakes, and He desires to make us beautiful. 🕊 *CINDY HESS KASPER*

Have Thine own way, Lord! Have Thine own way!
Thou art the Potter, I am the clay;
Mold me and make me after Thy will,
While I am waiting, yielded and still. POLLARD

When melted by trial, we can be fully molded by the Potter.

Difficult People

n the book *God in the Dock*, author C. S. Lewis describes the kind of people we have trouble getting along with. Selfishness, anger, jealousy, or other quirks often sabotage our relationship with them. We sometimes think, *Life would be much easier if we didn't have to contend with such difficult people.*

TODAY'S READING
Ephesians 4:1-12

Walk worthy of the calling with which you were called . . . bearing with one another in love. vv. 1-2

Lewis then turns the tables on us by pointing out that these frustrations are what God has to endure with each of us every day. He writes: "You are just that sort of person. You also have a fatal flaw in your character. All the hopes and plans of others have again and again shipwrecked on your character just as your hopes and plans have shipwrecked on theirs." This self-awareness should motivate us to try to show the same patience and acceptance to others that God shows to us daily.

In Ephesians, Paul exhorts us to arm ourselves relationally "with all lowliness and gentleness, with longsuffering, bearing with one another in love" (4:2). The one who is patient is better able to deal with a difficult person without becoming provoked to anger and retaliation. Instead, he or she is able to endure, exhibiting grace in spite of upsetting behavior.

Are there difficult people in your life? Ask God to show His love through you. 🌿   *DENNIS FISHER*

> Some people can be difficult to love,
> And so we do not even try to care;
> But God says, "Love them just as I've loved you—
> You'll bring Me glory as My love you share." CETAS

See others as God sees you.

The Upright Thumb

According to an African fable, four fingers and a thumb lived together on a hand. They were inseparable friends. One day, they noticed a gold ring lying next to them and conspired to take it. The thumb said it would be wrong to steal the ring, but the four fingers called him a self-righteous coward and refused to be his friend. That was just fine with the thumb; he wanted nothing to do with their mischief. This is why, the legend goes, the thumb still stands separate from the other fingers.

TODAY'S READING
Genesis 6:11-22

Noah found grace in the eyes of the LORD. 6:8

This tale reminds me that at times we may feel we're standing alone when wrongdoing surrounds us. In Noah's day, the earth was filled with violence; every thought in every heart was "evil continually" (GEN. 6:5,11). Yet "Noah found grace in the eyes of the LORD" (V. 8). Fully devoted to God, Noah obeyed Him and built the ark. The Lord, in His grace, spared him and his family.

We too have been shown God's grace through His Son Jesus' life, death, and resurrection. We have every reason to bring Him honor and stand strong for Him in our daily lives. He is always near, even abiding in us, so we never really stand alone. His "ears are open to [our] cry" (PS. 34:15). ❧

JENNIFER BENSON SCHULDT

They show their colors when they stand
For what is true and right;
And those who venture all on God
Are pleasing in His sight. D. DEHAAN

It's easy to stand with a crowd; it takes courage to stand alone.

Finding God's Pathway

The Channel Tunnel opened on May 6, 1994, nearly two centuries after it was first proposed in 1802 by Napoleon's engineer, Albert Mathieu. Today the 31-mile passage beneath the English Channel allows thousands of people, cars, and trucks to travel by train each day between England and France. For centuries, people had sailed across the Channel until this surprising new way to go under it was completed.

> **TODAY'S READING**
> **Psalm 77:10-20**
>
> **Your way was in the sea, Your path in the great waters.** v. 19

God planned an unexpected route for His people too—one we read about in Exodus 14:10-22. Faced with certain death, either from Pharaoh's army or by drowning, the Israelites were near panic. But God parted the Red Sea and they walked through on dry land. Years later, the psalm writer Asaph used this event as evidence of God's mighty power, "Your road led through the sea, your pathway through the mighty waters—a pathway no one knew was there! You led Your people along that road like a flock of sheep, with Moses and Aaron as their shepherds" (PS. 77:19-20 NLT).

God can create roads where we see only obstacles. When the way ahead of us seems uncertain, it's good to remember what God has done in the past. He specializes in pathways in any circumstance—pathways that point us to His love and power. ❀ *DAVID MCCASLAND*

Thank You, God, for the miraculous ways You have worked in the past. Help me to remember Your power and faithfulness when I can see only trouble and difficulty.

The God who created a way for our salvation can certainly see us through our daily trials.

Holy, Holy, Holy

Time flies when you're having fun." This cliché has no basis in fact, but experience makes it seem true.

When life is pleasant, time passes all too quickly. Give me a task that I enjoy, or a person whose company I love, and time seems irrelevant.

My experience of this "reality" has given me a new understanding of the scene described in Revelation 4. In the past, when I considered the four living creatures seated around God's throne who keep repeating the same few words, I thought, *What a boring existence!*

I don't think that anymore. I think about the scenes they have witnessed with their many eyes (V. 8). I consider the view they have from their position around God's throne (V.6). I think of how amazed they are at God's wise and loving involvement with wayward earthlings. Then I think, *What better response could there be? What else is there to say but, "Holy, holy, holy"?*

> TODAY'S READING
> **Revelation 4**
>
> **They do not rest day or night, saying: "Holy, holy, holy, Lord God Almighty, who was and is and is to come!"** v. 8

Is it boring to say the same words over and over? Not when you're in the presence of the one you love. Not when you're doing exactly what you were designed to do.

Like the four creatures, we were designed to glorify God. Our lives will never be boring if we're focusing our attention on Him and fulfilling that purpose. 🌿 *JULIE ACKERMAN LINK*

Holy, holy, holy, Lord God Almighty!
Early in the morning our song shall rise to Thee;
Holy, holy, holy! Merciful and mighty!
God in three Persons, blessed Trinity! HEBER

A heart in tune with God can't help but sing His praise.

Power of Simplicity

ew people take time to study the US Internal Revenue Service income tax regulations—and for good reason. According to *Forbes* magazine, in 2013 tax codes surpassed the four million-word mark. In fact, the tax laws have become so complex that even the experts have a hard time processing all the regulations. It's burdensome in its complexity.

TODAY'S READING
Mark 12:28-34

Then one of the scribes came, and . . . asked Him, "Which is the first commandment of all?" v. 28

The religious leaders in ancient Israel did the same thing in their relationship with God. They made it too complex with laws. The growing burden of religious regulations had increased to the point where even an expert in Moses' law struggled to understand its core. When one such leader asked Jesus what mattered most in the Commandments, Jesus responded, "'You shall love the LORD your God with all your heart, with all your soul, with all your mind, and with all your strength.' This is the first commandment. And the second, like it, is this: 'You shall love your neighbor as yourself.' There is no other commandment greater than these" (MARK 12:30-31).

The law of Moses was burdensome, but faith in Christ is simple and His "burden is light" (MATT. 11:30). It's light because God was willing to forgive us and love us. Now He enables us to love Him and our neighbor. 🌱

BILL CROWDER

I love Thee because Thou hast first loved me,
And purchased my pardon on Calvary's tree;
I love Thee for wearing the thorns on Thy brow;
If ever I loved Thee, my Jesus, 'tis now. FEATHERSTONE

God's love in our heart gives us a heart for Him and others.

Example That Encourages

he story is told that in the late 1800s a group of European pastors attended D. L. Moody's Bible conference in Massachusetts. Following their custom, they put their shoes outside their room before they slept, expecting them to be cleaned by hotel workers. When Moody saw the shoes, he mentioned the need to others because he knew their custom. But he was met with silence. Moody collected all the shoes and cleaned them himself. A friend who made an unexpected visit to his room revealed what Moody had done. The word spread, and the next few nights others took turns doing the cleaning.

> TODAY'S READING
> **2 Timothy 2:1-7**
>
> **I then, your Lord and Teacher, have washed your feet .... I have given you an example, that you should do as I have done to you.** John 13:14-15

Moody's leadership style of humility inspired others to follow his example. The apostle Paul reminded Timothy to "be strong in the grace that is in Christ Jesus. And the things you have heard me say in the presence of many witnesses entrust to reliable men who will also be qualified to teach others" (2 TIM. 2:1-2 NIV). When we remember that our strength is a result of God's grace, that keeps us humble. Then in humility we pass on God's truth by being an example that encourages and inspires others to follow.

Jesus Himself is our example of servanthood. He gave His very life for us. ❂

ALBERT LEE

Lord Jesus, I know little about humility. Show me and teach
me as I read about Your example in Your Word. Give me the
grace to humble myself and serve others.

Humility is the result of knowing God and knowing yourself.

Life-Giving Rain

During the August heat of 1891, R. G. Dyrenforth arrived in Midland, Texas, determined to blast rain from the sky. Known as a "concussionist," he and his team launched and detonated huge balloons filled with explosive gases, fired cannons, and exploded piles of dynamite on the ground—shaking both earth and sky. Some believed he made it rain a little, but most said all he caused was noise. The explosive power was impressive but ineffective.

TODAY'S READING
Acts 6:1-10

They were not able to resist the wisdom and the Spirit by which he spoke. v. 10

When the early church needed overseers, they sought people with a different kind of power. They chose "seven men of good reputation, full of the Holy Spirit and wisdom" (ACTS 6:3) to manage the daily distribution of food. One of those was Stephen, a man "full of faith and power, [who] did great wonders and signs among the people" (V. 8). When disputes arose, those who argued with Stephen "were not able to resist the wisdom and the Spirit by which he spoke" (V. 10).

The Bible makes it clear that Stephen's spiritual effectiveness came from being filled with the Holy Spirit, who gave him the right balance of faith, wisdom, and power.

God's Spirit in our lives today replaces the loud noise of self-interest with His gentle, life-giving rain. 🍂

DAVID MCCASLAND

Holy Spirit, I want my life to be marked by Your power.
May my words and actions give life-giving rain to
encourage others to know You and trust You.

*In our life for Christ we accomplish nothing
without the power of the Spirit.*

The Parable of the Sting

can still see Jay Elliott's shocked face as I burst through his front door almost 50 years ago with a "gang" of bees swirling around me. As I raced out his back door, I realized the bees were gone. Well, sort of—I'd left them in Jay's house! Moments later, he came racing out his back door—chased by the bees I had brought to him.

TODAY'S READING
1 Peter 2:9-12

They may, by your good works which they observe, glorify God in the day of visitation. v. 12

I had more than a dozen stings, with little effect. Jay had a different experience. Though he'd been stung only once or twice by "my" bees, his eyes and throat swelled up in a painful allergic reaction. My actions had caused a lot of pain for my friend.

That's a picture of what's true in our interpersonal relationships too. We hurt others when our actions aren't Christlike. Even after an apology, the "sting" sticks.

People would be right to expect an absence of harshness and an air of patience from those who follow Christ. We forget sometimes that people struggling with faith, or life, or both, watch Christians with expectation. They hope to see less anger and more mercy, less judgment and more compassion, less criticism and more encouragement. Jesus and Peter told us to live good lives so God is given the glory (MATT. 5:16; 1 PETER 2:12). May our actions and reactions point those around us to our loving Father. 🌱

RANDY KILGORE

We have found that it's easy to hurt others with our words or actions. Teach us, Father, to pause and to think before we speak or act. Fill us with kindness and care.

May others see less of me and more of Jesus.

Is There Hope?

sat quietly at the graveside of my father, waiting for the private family burial of my mother to begin. The funeral director carried the urn that held her ashes. My heart felt numb and my head was in a fog. *How can I handle losing them both within just 3 months?* In my grief I felt loss and loneliness and a little hopeless facing a future without them.

TODAY'S READING
Matthew 28:1-10

He is not here; for He is risen, as He said. v. 6

Then the pastor read about another graveside. On the first day of the week, early in the morning, women went to Jesus' tomb, carrying spices for His body (MATT. 28:1; LUKE 24:1). There they were startled to find an open and empty tomb—and an angel. "Do not be afraid," he said to them (MATT. 28:5). They didn't need to be afraid of the empty tomb or of the angel, because he had good news for them.

Hope stirred when I heard the next words: "He is not here; for He is risen, as He said" (v. 6). Because Jesus had come back to life, death had been conquered! Jesus reminded His followers just a few days before His death: "Because I live, you will live also" (JOHN 14:19).

Even though we grieve at the loss of our loved ones, we find hope through the resurrection of Jesus and His promise that there is life after death. 🌿   ANNE CETAS

Thank You, Lord, for comfort and hope. What would we do without You? Your death and resurrection provide all we need for this life and the next.

Because He lives, we live.

Walking Billboards

Pete Peterson's first contact with Vietnam was in the Vietnam War. During a bombing raid in 1966, his plane was shot down and he was taken prisoner. Over 30 years later he returned as US Ambassador to Vietnam. One press article called him "a walking billboard for reconciliation." He realized years ago that God had not saved his life for him to live in anger. Because he believed this, he used the rest of his life and his position to make a difference by pushing for better safety standards for children in Vietnam.

TODAY'S READING
2 Cor. 5:16-21

We are ambassadors for Christ. v. 20

It is a great responsibility and honor to be appointed as a representative of your country to another. As followers of Christ we are "ambassadors for Christ" (2 COR. 5:20). Just as God sent Christ to reconcile us to Himself (V. 18), we now have the ministry of "reconciliation" (V. 19). Our message is that all can be redeemed in Christ because God "made Him who knew no sin to be sin for us, that we might become the righteousness of God in Him" (V. 21).

In response to the reconciling love Jesus offers us, we can share that love with others. Let's take our role seriously. Wherever God places us in this world, He can use us as walking billboards of reconciliation for Jesus Christ. 🌱   *C. P. HIA*

I am a stranger here, within a foreign land;
My home is far away, upon a golden strand,
Ambassador to be of realms beyond the sea,
I'm here on business for the King! CASSEL

Good news kept silent is no news at all.

Is Somebody Singing?

From **200 miles above Earth,** Chris Hadfield, Canadian astronaut and commander of the International Space Station, joined in song with a group of students in a studio on Earth. Together they performed "Is Somebody Singing," co-written by Hadfield and Ed Robertson.

One phrase of the song caught my attention: "You can't make out borders from up here." Although we humans draw many lines to separate ourselves from one another—national, ethnic, ideological—the song reminded me that God doesn't see such distinctions. The important thing to God is that we love Him and each other (MARK 12:30-31).

> **TODAY'S READING**
> **John 17:20-26**
>
> **[Bear] with one another in love, endeavoring to keep the unity of the Spirit in the bond of peace.**
>
> Ephesians 4:2-3

Like a loving father, God wants His family united. We cannot accomplish what God has for us to do if we refuse to be reconciled with one another. In His most impassioned prayer, on the night before He was crucified, Jesus pleaded with God to unite His followers: "That they all may be one, as You, Father, are in Me, and I in You; that they also may be one in Us" (JOHN 17:21).

Singing illustrates unity as we agree on the lyrics, chords, and rhythms. Singing can also promote unity as it binds us together in peace, proclaims God's power through praise, and demonstrates God's glory to the world. ❧ 	*JULIE ACKERMAN LINK*

O for a thousand tongues to sing
My great Redeemer's praise,
The glories of my God and King,
The triumphs of His grace. WESLEY

Singing God's praises will never go out of style.

Believing in Advance

In a German prison camp in World War II, undiscovered by the guards, some Americans built a homemade radio. One day news came that the German high command had surrendered, ending the war. Because of a communications breakdown, however, the guards did not yet know this. As word spread among the prisoners, a loud celebration broke out. For 3 days, they sang, waved at guards, and shared jokes over meals. On the fourth day, they awoke to find that all the Germans had fled. Their waiting had come to an end.

TODAY'S READING
Rev. 22:12-21

Surely I am coming quickly. v. 20

A number of Bible stories center on waiting: Abraham waiting for a child (GEN. 12–21). The Israelites waiting for deliverance from Egypt. Prophets waiting for the fulfillment of their own predictions. The disciples waiting for Jesus to act like the powerful Messiah they anticipated. Jesus' final words at the end of Revelation are "I am coming quickly," followed by an urgent, echoing prayer, "Amen. Even so, come, Lord Jesus!" (22:20). For this, we still wait.

Here's the question I ask myself: As we wait, why are we so often fearful and anxious? We can, like the Allied prisoners, act on the good news we say we believe. What is faith in God, after all, but believing in advance what will only make sense in reverse? 🌱

PHILIP YANCEY

Faith looks beyond the shadow
Of dread and doubt and fear
And finds the Savior waiting
And always standing near. FRENCH

Waiting tries our faith and so we wait in hope.

Following the Master

At a dog show near my home, I watched a Cardigan Welsh corgi named Trevor perform. At his master's command, he ran several yards away and immediately returned, he jumped fences, and he identified objects using his sense of smell. After finishing each exercise, he sat down at his master's feet and waited for more instructions.

Trevor's careful attention to his master's instruction reminded me of the devotion God desired from His people as they followed Him through the wilderness. God led in a unique way. His presence appeared as a cloud. If the cloud ascended, He wanted His people to move to another area. If the cloud descended, they were to stay put. "At the command of the LORD they remained encamped, and at the command of the LORD they journeyed" (NUM. 9:23). The Israelites followed this practice day or night, regardless of how long they had to remain in one place.

> TODAY'S READING
> **Numbers 9:15-23**
>
> **At the command of the LORD they remained encamped, and at the command of the LORD they journeyed.** v. 23

God wasn't simply testing the Israelites; He was leading them to the Promised Land (10:29). He wanted to take them to a better place. So it is with us when God asks us to follow Him. He wants to lead us to a place of closer fellowship with Himself. His Word assures us that He is loving and faithful in leading those who humbly follow Him. ❧   *JENNIFER BENSON SCHULDT*

In fellowship sweet we will sit at His feet,
Or we'll walk by His side in the way;
What He says we will do, where He sends we will go;
Never fear, only trust and obey. SAMMIS

God asks His children to follow the Leader.

Our Foundation

The Bavarian city of **Nördlingen** is unique. It sits in the middle of the Ries Crater, a large circular depression caused by the impact of a huge meteorite a long time ago. The immense pressure of the impact resulted in unusual crystallized rock and millions of microscopic diamonds. In the 13th century, these speckled stones were used to build St. George's Church. Visitors can see the beautiful crystal deposits in its foundation and walls. Some might say it has a heavenly foundation.

> TODAY'S READING
> **1 Cor. 3:1-11**
>
> **For no other foundation can anyone lay than that which is laid, which is Jesus Christ.** v. 11

The Bible talks of a different kind of heavenly foundation. The Lord Jesus came to our world from heaven (JOHN 3:13). When He went back into heaven after His death and resurrection, He left His followers who became the "living temple" of God, of which He is the foundation. The apostle Paul says, "For no other foundation can anyone lay than that which is laid, which is Jesus Christ" (1 COR. 3:11).

The church building in Bavaria is built on a foundation from pieces of rock from the physical heavens. But the spiritual church—all believers in Christ—is founded on the ultimate heavenly foundation, Christ Jesus (ISA. 28:16; 1 COR. 10:3-4). Praise God that because of what Jesus has done our salvation is secure. 🌱

DENNIS FISHER

> On Christ salvation rests secure;
> The Rock of Ages will endure;
> Nor can that faith be overthrown
> Which rests upon the "Living Stone." ANON.

Christ, the Rock, is our sure hope.

A Word for the Struggler

There is an old adage that says, "Don't bite off more than you can chew." It's wise not to take on more responsibilities than we can handle. At some time, however, we will likely feel overwhelmed by the size and difficulty of a task we have agreed to do.

This can happen even in our walk of faith in Christ when our commitment to God seems too much to bear. But the Lord has an encouraging word for us when our confidence wavers.

> **TODAY'S READING**
> **Hebrews 10:32-39**
>
> **Do not cast away your confidence, which has great reward.** v. 35

The writer of Hebrews urged his readers to recall the courage they demonstrated during the early days of their faith (10:32-33). Despite public insults and persecution, they aided believers in prison, and they joyfully accepted the confiscation of their own property (VV. 33-34). With that in mind, he says, "Therefore, do not cast away your confidence, which has great reward. For you have need of endurance, so that after you have done the will of God, you may receive the promise" (VV. 35-36).

Our confidence is not in ourselves but in Jesus and His promise to return at just the right time (V. 37).

It is God's power that enables us to continue in our journey of faith. Recalling the Lord's faithfulness in days past stirs our confidence in Him today. 🍃 *DAVID MCCASLAND*

> When life becomes a heavy load,
> An upward climb, a winding road,
> In daily tasks, Lord, let me see
> That with me You will always be. D. DEHAAN

Trusting God's faithfulness stirs up our confidence.

Live in Love

n the African country where my friend Roxanne lives, water is a precious commodity. People often have to travel long distances to collect water from small, contaminated creeks—leading to sickness and death. It's difficult for organizations like orphanages and churches to serve the people because of a lack of water. But that's beginning to change.

Through Roxanne's leadership and the unselfish gifts of some loving people in established churches, clean water wells are being dug. At least six new wells are now operational, allowing churches to be centers of hope and encouragement. A health center and a home for 700 orphans will also be able to be opened because of access to water.

TODAY'S READING
Psalm 112

Unto the upright there arises light in the darkness; he is gracious, and full of compassion. v. 4

That's the kind of love that can flow from believers in Christ when we have experienced the love and generosity of God. Paul says in 1 Corinthians 13 that if we don't have love, our voices clang on people's ears and our faith means nothing. And the apostle John says that if we have material possessions and see others in need and take action, that's evidence that God's love is abiding in us (1 JOHN 3:16).

God desires that we deal "graciously" (PS. 112:5) with those in need, for His heart is gracious toward us. ❧ *DAVE BRANON*

Be not weary in your serving;
Do your best for those in need;
Kindnesses will be rewarded
By the Lord who prompts the deed. ANON.

Kindness is Christianity with its working clothes on.

Keeping Darkness at Bay

I n J. R. R. Tolkien's book *The Hobbit*, the wizard Gandalf explains why he has selected a small hobbit like Bilbo to accompany the dwarves to fight the enemy. He says, "Saruman believes it is only great power that can hold evil in check, but that is not what I have found. I found it is the small everyday deeds of ordinary folk that keep the darkness at bay. Small acts of kindness and love."

That's what Jesus teaches us as well. Warning us that we would live in dark times, He reminded us that because of Him we are "the light of the world" (MATT. 5:14) and that our good deeds would be the power against the darkness for the glory of God (V. 16). And Peter, writing to believers in Christ who were facing severe persecution, told them to live so that those accusing them would "by [their] good works which they observe, glorify God" (1 PETER 2:12).

> TODAY'S READING
> **Matthew 5:11-16**
>
> **Let your light so shine before men, that they may see your good works and glorify your Father.** v. 16

There is one force that the darkness cannot conquer— the force of loving acts of kindness done in Jesus' name. It is God's people who turn the other cheek, go the extra mile, and forgive and even love their enemies who oppose them who have the power to turn the tide against evil. So look for the privileged opportunity to perform acts of kindness today to bring the light of Christ to others. 🌿 *JOE STOWELL*

Lord, teach me the folly of trying to repay evil for evil. May I be so grateful to You for the loving acts of kindness that You have shown me that I gladly look to share good deeds with others as well!

Light up your world with an act of kindness.

Memory Loss

Sometimes when we face times of trouble, we may get spiritual amnesia and forget the grace of God. But a good way of reestablishing a thankful heart is to set aside undistracted time and deliberately remember God's past provisions for us and give thanks.

When the children of Israel found themselves in a barren, hot desert, they developed memory loss about the grace of God. They began to wish they were back in Egypt enjoying all its foods (EX. 16:2-3), and later they complained about their water supply (17:2). They had forgotten the mighty acts of God in their deliverance and how He had showered them with wealth (12:36). They were dwelling on their current circumstances and forgetting God's gracious past provision.

> TODAY'S READING
> **Psalm 118:1-14**
>
> **Oh, give thanks to the LORD, for He is good! For His mercy endures forever.** v. 1

The psalmist challenges us: "Oh, give thanks to the LORD, for He is good! For His mercy endures forever" (PS. 118:1). The word *mercy* means "steadfast love." It refers to God's faithfulness. He has promised to be present always to care for His children.

By remembering specific ways God has provided for us in the past, we can change our perspective for the better. God's steadfast love endures forever! 🌿   *DENNIS FISHER*

Wait on the Lord from day to day,
Strength He provides in His own way;
There's no need for worry, no need to fear,
He is our God who is always near. FORTNA

***Remembering God's provision for yesterday
gives hope and strength for today.***

More Than Waiting

don't know how it works where you live, but when I have to call for a repair for one of my appliances, the company says something like, "The repairman will be there between 1:00 p.m. and 5:00 p.m." Since I don't know when the repair person will arrive, all I can do is wait.

Jesus told His followers that He would soon be leaving them and they would need to wait for His return in "a little while" (JOHN 16:16). After His resurrection, they saw Him again and they hoped He would be establishing His kingdom on earth at that time. But He told them, "It is not for you to know times or seasons which the Father has put in His own authority" (ACTS 1:7). They would have to wait even longer.

> TODAY'S READING
> **Acts 1:1-11**
>
> **A little while, and you will not see Me; and again a little while, and you will see Me, because I go to the Father.** John 16:16

But they were to do more than wait. Jesus told His followers that they were to "be witnesses to [Him] in Jerusalem, and in all Judea and Samaria, and to the ends of the earth" (V. 8). And He gave them the Holy Spirit to empower them to do this.

We still wait for Jesus' return. And while we do, it's our delight, in the Holy Spirit's power, to tell and show others who He is, what He has done for all of us through His death and resurrection, and that He has promised to return. 🌿

ANNE CETAS

Dear Lord, we love You so much. We want our words and
our lives to be a witness of Your goodness and grace.
Please use us in ways we never thought possible.

Wait and witness till Jesus returns.

Spiritual Navigation

Dava Sobel's award-winning book *Longitude* describes a dilemma faced by early sailors. They could readily determine their latitude north or south of the equator by the length of the day or height of the sun. Calculating east/west longitude, however, remained complex and unreliable until English clockmaker John Harrison invented the marine chronometer. This was "a clock that would carry the true time from the home port . . . to any remote corner of the world," thus enabling sailors to determine longitude.

TODAY'S READING
Psalm 119:97-106

Your word is a lamp to my feet and a light to my path. v. 105

As we navigate the seas of life, we also have a reliable source of spiritual direction—the Bible. The psalmist wrote, "Oh, how I love Your law! It is my meditation all the day" (PS. 119:97). Rather than occasionally glancing at God's Word, he spoke of pondering the Lord's directions throughout each day: "Your testimonies are my meditation" (V. 99). This was coupled with a commitment to obey the Author: "I have sworn and confirmed that I will keep Your righteous judgments" (V. 106).

Like the mariners of old, we need a constant guide to help us find our way and stay on course. That's what happens when we seek the Lord day by day with an open heart and a willing spirit that says, "Your word is a lamp to my feet and a light to my path." ❧

DAVID MCCASLAND

We need God's guidance from above,
His daily leading and His love;
As we trust Him for direction,
To our course He'll give correction. FITZHUGH

With God as your navigator, you're headed in the right direction.

Life's Darkest Moments

Charles **Whittlesey** was a hero's hero. Leader of the so-called "Lost Battalion" in World War I, he was awarded the Medal of Honor for his bravery when his unit was trapped behind enemy lines. When the Tomb of the Unknown Soldier was dedicated, Charles was chosen to serve as pallbearer for the first soldier laid to rest there. Two weeks later, it is presumed that he ended his own life by stepping off a cruise ship in the middle of the ocean.

> **TODAY'S READING**
> **1 Kings 19:1-8**
>
> **An angel touched [Elijah], and said to him, "Arise and eat."** v. 5

Like Elijah (1 KINGS 19:1-7), Charles was publicly strong, but in the quiet, post-public moments, his feelings of despair set in. People today frequently face situations bigger than they can handle. Sometimes it's temporary despair brought on by fatigue, as in Elijah's case. He had been part of a great victory over the prophets of Baal (18:20-40), but then he feared for his life and ran into the wilderness (19:1-3). But often, it's more than despair and it's more than temporary. That's why it is imperative that we talk about depression openly and compassionately.

God offers His presence to us in life's darkest moments, which enables us, in turn, to be His presence to the hurting. Crying out for help—from others and from God—may be the strongest moment of our lives. 🌱   *RANDY KILGORE*

Father, grant us the candor to admit to each other that
sometimes life overwhelms us. And grant us the courage to help
others find help—and to seek it when we need it.

Hope comes with help from God and others.

A Picture of Humility

During the Easter season, my wife and I attended a church service where the participants sought to model the events that Jesus and His disciples experienced on the night before He was crucified. As part of the service, the church staff members washed the feet of some of the church volunteers. As I watched, I wondered which was more humbling in our day—to wash another person's feet or to have someone else wash yours. Both those who were serving and those being served were presenting distinct pictures of humility.

TODAY'S READING
John 13:1-11

God resists the proud, but gives grace to the humble. James 4:6

When Jesus and His disciples were gathered for the Last Supper (JOHN 13:1-20), Jesus, in humble servanthood, washed His disciples' feet. But Simon Peter resisted, saying, "You shall never wash my feet!" Then Jesus answered, "If I do not wash you, you have no part with Me" (13:8). Washing their feet was not a mere ritual. It could also be seen as a picture of our need of Christ's cleansing—a cleansing that will never be realized unless we are willing to be humble before the Savior.

James wrote, "God resists the proud, but gives grace to the humble" (JAMES 4:6). We receive God's grace when we acknowledge the greatness of God, who humbled Himself at the cross (PHIL. 2:5-11). 🌾

BILL CROWDER

My faith looks up to Thee,
Thou Lamb of Calvary, Savior divine;
Now hear me when I pray, take all my sin away,
O let me from this day be wholly Thine! PALMER

The most powerful position on earth is kneeling before the Lord of the universe.

Terms of Service

f you're like me, you seldom read the full text of contracts for online services before you agree to them. They go on for pages, and most of the legal jargon makes no sense to ordinary people like me.

I was quite surprised, therefore, when a friend from Africa made me aware of this one-of-a-kind service agreement for online software. Instead of a wordy license telling people how *not* to use it, the developer offers a simple blessing urging people to use it for good:

TODAY'S READING
Luke 6:27-37

Forgive, and you will be forgiven. v. 37

May you do good and not evil. May you find forgiveness for yourself and forgive others. May you share freely, never taking more than you give.

At first I thought, *Wow. Imagine if more terms of service agreements were written as blessings instead of legal documents.* Then I thought, *The agreement Jesus makes with us is like that.* He offers us forgiveness of sin, peace with God, and the presence of the Holy Spirit. In return, all He asks is that we do good (GAL. 6:10), forgive as we've been forgiven (LUKE 6:37), and love others as He loves us (JOHN 13:34).

The beauty of Jesus' agreement with us is that even though we fail to live up to the terms, we still receive the blessing. 🌱   *JULIE ACKERMAN LINK*

Bestowed with benefits daily,
Sent from the Father above;
Mercies and blessings abounding,
Gifts of His marvelous love. ANON.

As we have opportunity, let us do good to all. GALATIANS 6:10

Step Up!

When a woodchuck started eating our garage (well, just the trim), I bought a live trap with plans to transplant the little guy to a park. I baited it with an assortment of goodies and opened the trap door. The next morning, I was excited to see a little critter in my trap—until I noticed that it was no woodchuck. I had snared a skunk.

I went online to see how to untrap the skunk without having it . . . well, you know. The solutions were extremely cautious in their descriptions of how to protect yourself while releasing the animal. Plastic bags. Gloves. Tarps. Blankets. Goggles. The task looked daunting and dangerous.

> **TODAY'S READING**
> **2 Chron. 15:1-12**
>
> **[Asa] took courage, and removed the abominable idols from all the land.** v. 8

Then my son-in-law Ewing stepped up. He simply walked over to the trap, opened the door, and coaxed our striped friend on its way with a few sprays from the garden hose.

Sometimes our fears can lead to inaction. We worry so much about protecting ourselves that we fail to simply step up. When King Asa learned that the Lord wanted him to remove the idols from Israel, he "took courage" (2 CHRON. 15:8). He could have had a rebellion on his hands for doing this. But he stepped up, and as a result the nation rejoiced (V. 15).

Facing a spiritual challenge? The Lord will help you step up with courage and trust Him for the outcome. 🌿 *DAVE BRANON*

Let the road be rough and dreary,
And its end far out of sight,
Foot it bravely, strong or weary;
Trust in God and do the right. MACLEOD

Courage is fear that has said its prayers.

The Ultimate Sacrifice

When Deng Jinjie saw people struggling in the water of the Sunshui River in the Hunan province of China, he didn't just walk by. In an act of heroism, he jumped into the water and helped save four members of a family. Unfortunately, the family left the area while he was still in the water. Sadly, Jinjie, exhausted from his rescue efforts, was overwhelmed and swept away by the river current and drowned.

> **TODAY'S READING**
> **1 John 3:16-23**
>
> **By this we know love, because [Jesus] laid down His life for us.** v. 16

When we were drowning in our sin, Jesus Christ gave His life to come to our aid. We were the ones He came to rescue. He came down from heaven above and pulled us to safety. He did this by taking the punishment for all of our wrongdoing as He died on the cross (1 PETER 2:24) and 3 days later was resurrected. The Bible says, "By this we know love, because [Jesus] laid down His life for us" (1 JOHN 3:16). Jesus' sacrificial love for us now inspires us to show genuine love "in deed and in truth" (v. 18) to others with whom we have relationships.

If we overlook Jesus' ultimate sacrifice on our behalf, we'll fail to see and experience His love. Today, consider the connection between His sacrifice and His love for you. He has come for your rescue. 🌿

JENNIFER BENSON SCHULDT

Rescued: By Jesus' love;
Rescued: For life above;
Rescued: To serve my King;
Rescued: My praise to bring. VERWAY

Jesus laid down His life to show His love for us.

I Am Not Forgotten

Waiting is hard at any time; but when days, weeks, or even months pass and our prayers seem to go unanswered, it's easy to feel God has forgotten us. Perhaps we can struggle through the day with its distractions, but at night it's doubly difficult to deal with our anxious thoughts. Worries loom large, and the dark hours seem endless. Utter weariness makes it look impossible to face the new day.

TODAY'S READING
Psalm 13

Our soul waits for the LORD; He is our help and our shield. 33:20

The psalmist grew weary as he waited (PS. 13:1). He felt abandoned—as if his enemies were gaining the upper hand (V. 2). When we're waiting for God to resolve a difficult situation or to answer often-repeated prayers, it's easy to get discouraged.

Satan whispers that God has forgotten us, and that things will never change. We may be tempted to give in to despair. Why bother to read the Bible or to pray? Why make the effort to worship with fellow believers in Christ? But we need our spiritual lifelines most when we're waiting. They help to hold us steady in the flow of God's love and to become sensitive to His Spirit.

The psalmist had a remedy. He focused on all that he knew of God's love, reminding himself of past blessings and deliberately praising God, who would not forget him. So can we. 🌱

MARION STROUD

Lover of my soul, who draws close in the darkest and longest night, please keep me trusting You, talking to You, and leaning on Your promises.

God is worth waiting for; His time is always best.

Not Even a Nod

Traffic was bad and everyone was cranky on that hot afternoon. I noticed a car with two young men waiting to enter traffic from a fast-food restaurant driveway.

I thought it was nice when the driver ahead of me let them in.

But when the "nice" driver ahead of me didn't get a nod or even a thank you wave, he turned ugly. First he rolled down his window and shouted at the driver he had let in. Then he gunned his engine and raced forward as if to ram into his car, honking and yelling as he continued to vent his anger.

> **TODAY'S READING**
> **Luke 17:11-19**
>
> **One of them, when he saw that he was healed, returned, and with a loud voice glorified God.** v. 15

Who was "more wrong"? Did the young driver's ingratitude justify the "nice" driver's angry response? Was he owed a thank you?

Certainly the 10 lepers Jesus healed owed gratitude to Him. How could only one return to say thank you? I'm struck by Jesus' response: "Were there not any found who returned to give glory to God except this foreigner?" (LUKE 17:18). If the King of Kings can get only a 1 in 10 response of thanks, how can we expect more from others? Better to do our deeds to honor God and serve others than to do them to collect gratitude. May the grace of God be seen in us even when our kind acts go unappreciated. 🌿

RANDY KILGORE

Lord, we like to be recognized for the things we do. Help us to
remember that we are not owed any recognition or thanks
but that we owe You a lifetime of gratitude for the salvation
You offer through Jesus.

*Let your light so shine before men, that they may ...
glorify your Father in heaven.* MATTHEW 5:16

Hope to Continue On

The solar-powered airplane Solar Impulse can fly day and night without fuel. Inventors Bertrand Piccard and André Borschberg hope to fly it around the world. While the plane flies all day by solar power, it gathers enough energy to be able to fly all night. When the sun rises, Piccard says, "It brings the hope again that you can continue."

The idea of sunrise bringing us hope makes me think of Lamentations 3 from our Bible reading for today: "This I recall to my mind, therefore I have hope. Through the LORD's mercies we are not consumed, because His compassions fail not. They are new every morning" (VV. 21-23). Even when God's people were in the depths of despair while the city of Jerusalem was being invaded by the Babylonians, the prophet Jeremiah said they had reason to hope—they still had the Lord's mercies and compassions.

> TODAY'S READING
> **Lam. 3:19-33**
>
> **Through the LORD's mercies we are not consumed, because His compassions fail not. They are new every morning.**
> vv. 22-23

Sometimes our struggles seem worse at night, but when sunrise comes it brings hope again that we can continue. "Weeping may endure for a night," the psalmist says, "but joy comes in the morning" (PS. 30:5).

Thank You, Lord, for the hope You send with each sunrise. Your mercies and compassions are new every morning! ❧

ANNE CETAS

New mercies every morning,
Grace for every day,
New hope for every trial,
And courage all the way. MCVEIGH

Each new day gives us new reasons to praise the Lord.

The Barking Lion

Visitors to a zoo were outraged when the "African lion" started barking instead of roaring. Zoo staff said they had disguised a Tibetan mastiff—a very large dog—as a lion because they could not afford the real thing. Needless to say, the zoo's reputation was sullied and people will think twice before visiting it.

Reputation is fragile; once it's damaged, it's hard to restore. It is not uncommon to sacrifice a good reputation on the altar of power, prestige, or profit. This too could be our story. Scripture encourages us: "A good name is to be chosen rather than great riches" (PROV. 22:1). God is telling us that true value must be placed not in what we have but in who we are.

> **TODAY'S READING**
> **Proverbs 22:1-5**
>
> **A good name is to be chosen rather than great riches.** v. 1

Ancient Greek philosopher Socrates said, "The way to gain a good reputation is to endeavor to be what you desire to appear." As followers of Jesus, we bear His name. Because of His love for us, we strive to walk worthy of Him, reflecting His likeness in our words and deeds.

When we fail, He picks us up again by His love. By our example, others around us will be led to praise the God who has redeemed and transformed us (MATT. 5:16)—for the name of the Lord is worthy of glory, honor, and all praise. 🌸

POH FANG CHIA

Lord, I do want to walk worthy of Your name because You
have made me Your own. I know I can't live perfectly,
but I want to reflect to others a little of who You are.
Please show Yourself through me.

The purest treasure mortal times afford is a spotless reputation.

SHAKESPEARE

With Him Forever!

I n 1859, during the turbulent years prior to America's Civil War, Abraham Lincoln had the opportunity to speak to the Agricultural Society in Milwaukee, Wisconsin. As he spoke, he shared with them the story of an ancient monarch's search for a sentence that was "true and appropriate in all times and situations." His wise men, faced with this heady challenge, gave him the sentence, "And this, too, shall pass away."

This is certainly true of our present world—it is constantly in the process of deterioration. And it's not happening just to the world; we also face the reality in our own lives that our days are numbered. James wrote, "For what is your life? It is even a vapor that appears for a little time and then vanishes away" (JAMES 4:14).

> **TODAY'S READING**
> **James 4:11-17**
>
> **For what is your life? It is even a vapor that appears for a little time and then vanishes away.** v. 14

Although our current life is temporary and will pass away, the God we worship and serve is eternal. He has shared that eternity with us through the gift of His Son, Jesus Christ. He promises us a life that will never pass away: "For God so loved the world that He gave His only begotten Son, that whoever believes in Him should not perish but have everlasting life" (JOHN 3:16).

When Christ returns, He will take us home to be with Him forever! 🌿

BILL CROWDER

Awake, my soul and sing
Of Him who died for thee,
And hail Him as thy matchless King
Through all eternity. BRIDGES/THRING

For hope today, remember the end of the story—eternity with God.

Let Me Be Singing

When I asked a friend how his mother was getting along, he told me that dementia had robbed her of the ability to remember a great many names and events from the past. "Even so," he added, "she can still sit down at the piano and, without sheet music, beautifully play hymns by memory."

Plato and Aristotle wrote about the helping, healing power of music 2,500 years ago. But centuries before that, the biblical record was saturated with song.

TODAY'S READING
Psalm 150

Let everything that has breath praise the LORD. v. 6

From the first mention of Jubal, "the father of all those who play the harp and flute" (GEN. 4:21), to those who "sing the song of Moses, the servant of God and the song of the Lamb" (REV. 15:3), the pages of the Bible resonate with music. The Psalms, often called "the Bible's songbook," point us to the love and faithfulness of God. They conclude with an unending call to worship, "Let everything that has breath praise the LORD. Praise the LORD!" (PS. 150:6).

Today we need God's ministry of music in our hearts as much as any time in history. Whatever each day brings, may the evening find us singing, "To You, O my Strength, I will sing praises; for God is my defense, my God of mercy" (59:17). 🌱

DAVID MCCASLAND

Lord, I don't know what will come this day or farther into the future, but I'm grateful that You're by my side. Grant me a spirit of praise and thanksgiving in whatever lies ahead.

Praise to God comes naturally when you count your blessings.

More of Him, Less of Me

While I was pastoring a church early in my ministry, my daughter Libby asked me, "Dad, are we famous?" To which I replied, "No, Libby, we're not famous." She thought for a moment and then said rather indignantly, "Well, we would be if more people knew about us!"

Poor Libby! Only 7 years old and already struggling with what many of us struggle with throughout life: Who recognizes us, and are we getting the recognition we think we deserve?

Our desire for recognition wouldn't be such a problem if it didn't tend to replace Jesus as the focus of our attention. But being absorbed with ourselves crowds Him out of the picture.

> TODAY'S READING
> **Philippians 3:1-11**
>
> **I also count all things loss for the excellence of the knowledge of Christ Jesus my Lord.** v. 8

Life cannot be all about us and all about Jesus at the same time. This makes Paul's statement that he counted "everything as loss because of the surpassing worth of knowing Christ" (PHIL. 3:8 ESV) strategically important. Faced with a choice between himself and Jesus, Paul intentionally discarded the things that would draw attention to himself so he could concentrate on knowing and experiencing Jesus (VV. 7-8,10).

For us, the decision is the same. Will we live to draw attention to ourselves? Or will we focus on the privilege of knowing and experiencing Jesus more intimately? ✹ *JOE STOWELL*

Lord, thank You for reminding me of the value of knowing You more intimately. Help me to keep myself out of the way as I pursue a deeper walk with You.

Do our choices bring honor to God or to us?

Sow What?

On the clock tower of my alma mater is an Art Deco bas-relief sculpture titled *The Sower*. The inscription beneath it is from Galatians 6:7, "Whatsoever a man soweth." Michigan State University remains a leader in agricultural research, but despite many improvements in farming techniques and crop produc-tion, this fact remains: Seeds of corn will not produce a crop of beans.

> **TODAY'S READING**
> **Mark 4:1-20**
>
> **He who sows righteousness will have a sure reward.** Proverbs 11:18

Jesus used many farming meta-phors to explain the kingdom of God. In the parable of the sower (MARK 4), He compared the Word of God to seeds sown in different types of soil. As the parable indicates, the sower sows indiscriminately, knowing that some seed will fall in places where it will not grow.

Like Jesus, we are to sow good seed in all places at all times. God is responsible for where it lands and how it grows. The important thing is that we sow. God does not want us to reap destruction, so He wants us to sow what is good and right (PROV. 11:18). The apostle Paul elaborated on the metaphor when he warned believers not to sow seeds of corruption. Instead, we are to sow seeds that will reap eternal life (GAL. 6:8).

The answer to the question, "Sow what?" is "Sow what you want to reap." To reap a good harvest in your life, start sowing seeds of goodness. ❧   *JULIE ACKERMAN LINK*

Sow a thought, reap an act;
Sow an act, reap a habit;
Sow a habit, reap a character;
Sow a character, reap a destiny. ANON.

A buried seed brings fruit; a selfless life reaps an eternal harvest.

A Work of Peace

The small church in Umbarger, Texas, was an unlikely place for an international work of art. But toward the end of World War II, seven Italian prisoners of war, who were being held at a large camp nearby, were chosen to help decorate the church's plain brick walls.

The prisoners were reluctant to aid their captors, but they agreed on the condition that their efforts be considered a contribution toward Christian brotherhood and understanding. But as they worked on their paintings and a wood-carving of the Last Supper, one of the POWs later recalled, "A spontaneous stream of good feelings began almost at once to flow among us." No one spoke of the war or the past because "we were here for a work of peace and love."

> **TODAY'S READING**
> **James 3:13-18**
>
> **The fruit of righteousness is sown in peace by those who make peace.** V. 18

Our lives are filled with unlikely settings for introducing God's peace. We can feel imprisoned by hard feelings, strained relationships, and confining circumstances. But peace has the power to break out anywhere. James reminded us that "the wisdom that is from above is . . . peaceable, gentle, willing to yield . . . . The fruit of righteousness is sown in peace by those who make peace" (JAMES 3:17-18).

Wherever we are today, let's ask the Lord to use us as His peacemakers. 🍂 *DAVID MCCASLAND*

O Prince of Peace, keep us, we pray,
From strife and enmity;
Help us to speak with loving words
That calm hostility. BRANON

The best peacemakers are those who know the peace of God.

One Amazing Letter

Once in a while my wife and I open the mail to find a letter with no words on it. When we take the "letter" out of the envelope, we see a piece of paper with nothing more on it than a colorful mark made with a felt pen. Those "letters" warm our hearts because they're from our preschool granddaughter Katie, who lives in another state. Even without words, these letters tell us that she loves us and is thinking about us.

We all cherish letters from those we love and those who love us. That's why there is so much encouragement in the fact that our heavenly Father has given us a letter called the Bible. The

> **TODAY'S READING**
> **Psalm 119:9-16**
>
> **I will not forget Your word.** v. 16

value of Scripture goes beyond its words of power, challenge, and wisdom. Amid all of the stories, teaching, and guidance this Book provides, the overriding idea is that God loves us and has planned our rescue. It tells us of His love in overseeing our existence (PS. 139), meeting our needs (MATT. 6:31-34), comforting us (2 COR. 1:3-4), and saving us through the sacrifice of His Son, Jesus (ROM. 1:16-17).

You are loved beyond imagination. God says so in His inspired and inspiring message to you. No wonder the psalmist wrote, "I will not forget Your word" (PS. 119:16). It is one amazing letter! 🌱

DAVE BRANON

Lord, help me to examine the Bible's pages, understand its truths, and apply its teachings to my life. May I be as excited about Your letter to me as I am about a letter, email, or Facebook posting by a friend.

The love of God for us is revealed in His letter to us—the Bible.

Born to Rescue

After the terrorist attack and the collapse of the Twin Towers in New York City on September 11, 2001, Cynthia Otto took care of the search-and-rescue dogs. Years later she established a Working Dog Center where young pups are put through specialized training to prepare them to help victims of disaster.

Otto made this comment about these rescue animals: "There are so many jobs now that dogs are being used for . . . and they can save lives." Otto said that these puppies will one day give vital aid to people in life-threatening circumstances. They are "born" to rescue others.

The Bible tells us of the Messiah who was born to rescue humanity from the penalty of sin. What He did rises

> TODAY'S READING
> **Mark 10:35-45**
>
> **For even the Son of Man did not come to be served, but to serve, and to give His life a ransom for many.** v. 45

above all earthly comparison. Two thousand years ago, God Himself became human in order to do for us what we could not do for ourselves. When Jesus became a man, He understood and proclaimed that He was born to rescue (JOHN 12:27). "For even the Son of Man did not come to be served, but to serve, and to give His life a ransom for many" (MARK 10:45).

Let us praise our wonderful Savior—Jesus Christ—who was born to save all who will accept His offer of salvation. 🍂

DENNIS FISHER

Use us, Lord, and make us humble,
Rescue us from foolish pride;
And when we begin to stumble,
Turn our thoughts to Christ who died. SPER

Christ came to seek and to save the lost.

The Small Giant

The towering enemy strides into the Valley of Elah. He stands 9 feet tall, and his coat of armor, made of many small bronze plates, glimmers in the sunlight. The shaft of his spear is wrapped with cords so it can spin through the air and be thrown with greater distance and accuracy. Goliath looks invincible.

But David knows better. While Goliath may look like a giant and act like a giant, in contrast to the living God he is small. David has a right view of God and therefore a right view of the

TODAY'S READING
1 Samuel 17:32-37

The LORD . . . will deliver me. v. 37

circumstances. He sees Goliath as one who is defying the armies of the living God (1 SAM. 17:26). He confidently appears before Goliath in his shepherd's clothes, armed with only his staff, five stones, and a sling. His confidence is not in what he has but in who is with him (V. 45).

What "Goliath" are you facing right now? It may be an impossible situation at work, a financial difficulty, or a broken relationship. With God all things are small in comparison. Nothing is too big for Him. The words of the hymnwriter Charles Wesley remind us: "Faith, mighty faith, the promise sees, and looks to that alone; laughs at impossibilities, and cries it shall be done." God is able to deliver you if that's His desire, and He may do so in ways you don't expect. ❧

POH FANG CHIA

Not to the strong is the battle,
Not to the swift is the race;
Yet to the true and the faithful
Victory is promised through grace. CROSBY

Don't tell God how big your giants are.
Tell your giants how big your God is.

Think of Them No More

My early years as a believer in Christ were laden with foreboding. I had the impression that when Jesus comes back, all my sins will be portrayed on a giant screen for everyone to see.

I know now that God chooses not to remember against me a single one of my transgressions. Every sin has been buried in the deepest sea, never to be exhumed and examined again.

Amy Carmichael wrote, "A day or two ago I was thinking rather sadly of the past—so many sins and failures and lapses of every kind. I was reading Isaiah 43, and in verse 24 I saw myself: 'You have wearied me with your iniquities.' And then for the first time I noticed that there is no space between verse 24 and verse 25: 'I, even I, am He who blots out your transgressions for My own sake; and I will not remember your sins.'"

> TODAY'S READING
> **Isaiah 43:22-28**
>
> **I, even I, am He who blots out your transgressions for My own sake; and I will not remember your sins.** v. 25

Indeed, when our Lord comes back He will "bring to light the hidden things of darkness and reveal the counsels of the hearts. Then each one's praise will come from God" (1 COR. 4:5). On that day our works will be tried and we may suffer loss, but we will not be judged for sin (3:11-15). God will see what Christ has done for us. He "will not remember [our] sins." ❧

DAVID ROPER

Where no far-reaching tide with its powerful sweep
May stir the dark waves of forgetfulness deep,
I have buried them there where no mortal can see!
I've cast all thy sins in the depths of the sea. ANON.

When God saves us, our sins are forgiven forever.

Gentle Jesus

Charles Wesley (1707–1788) was a Methodist evangelist who wrote more than 9,000 hymns and sacred poems. Some, like "O for a Thousand Tongues to Sing," are great, soaring hymns of praise. But his poem "Gentle Jesus, Meek and Mild," first published in 1742, is a child's quiet prayer that captures the essence of how all of us should seek the Lord in sincere, simple faith.

> *Loving Jesus, gentle Lamb,*
> *In Thy gracious hands I am;*
> *Make me, Savior, what Thou art,*
> *Live Thyself within my heart.*

TODAY'S READING
Matthew 18:1-10

Unless you are converted and become as little children, you will by no means enter the kingdom of heaven. v. 3

When some followers of Jesus were jockeying for position in His kingdom, the Lord "called a little child to Him, set him in the midst of them, and said, 'Assuredly, I say to you, unless you are converted and become as little children, you will by no means enter the kingdom of heaven'" (MATT. 18:2-3).

Not many children seek position or power. Instead, they want acceptance and security. They cling to the adults who love and care for them. Jesus never turned children away.

The last stanza of Wesley's poem shows a childlike desire to be just like Jesus: "I shall then show forth Thy praise / Serve Thee all my happy days; / Then the world shall always see / Christ, the holy Child, in me." 🌱   *DAVID MCCASLAND*

Father, give me the faith of a little child. I want to know Your love and care, and to rest in Your embrace. Grant my desire to be like You in all my ways that I might live for Your honor.

Faith shines brightest in a childlike heart.

The Blame Game

When Jenny's husband left her for another woman, she vowed that she would never meet his new wife. But when she realized that her bitterness was damaging her children's relationship with their father, she asked for God's help to take the first steps toward overcoming bitterness in a situation she couldn't change.

In Genesis 16, we read the story of a couple to whom God later promised a baby. When Sarai suggested that her husband Abram have a child with their servant Hagar, she wasn't fully trusting God for the child He had promised. When the baby was born, Hagar despised Sarai (GEN. 16:3-4), and Sarai became bitter (VV. 5-6).

> **TODAY'S READING**
> **Genesis 16:1-6;**
> **21:8-13**
>
> **My wrong be upon you! . . . The LORD judge between you and me.** 16:5

Hagar had been the slave with no rights and suddenly she was special. How did Sarai react? By blaming others, including Abram (V. 5). God's promise was realized in the birth of Isaac 14 years later. Even his weaning celebration was spoiled by Sarai's attitude (21:8-10).

It may never have been easy for Sarai to have lived with the consequences of their decision to go ahead of God. It may have taken a miracle of grace to change her attitude, but that could have transformed everything. Sarai couldn't reverse the decision, but through God's strength she could have lived with it differently and given God the glory. 🌱 *MARION STROUD*

Thank You, Lord, that though our situations may not change,
Your grace is strong enough to change us in our situations.
Help us as we struggle sometimes to live in this sinful world.

By God's grace, we can reflect His light in the dark times.

A Heart for Prayer

While traveling on an airplane with her 4- and 2-year-old daughters, a young mom worked at keeping them busy so they wouldn't disturb others. When the pilot's voice came over the intercom for an announcement, Catherine, the younger girl, paused from her activities and put her head down. When the pilot finished, she whispered, "Amen." Perhaps because there had been a recent natural disaster, she thought the pilot was praying.

> **TODAY'S READING**
> **Psalm 27:7-14**
>
> **When You said, "Seek My face," my heart said to You, "Your face, LORD, I will seek."** v. 8

Like that little girl, I want a heart that turns my thoughts toward prayer quickly. I think it would be fair to say that the psalmist David had that kind of heart. We get hints of that in Psalm 27 as he speaks of facing difficult foes (V. 2). He said, "Your face, LORD, I will seek" (V. 8). Some say that David was remembering the time he was fleeing from Saul (1 SAM. 21:10) or from his son Absalom (2 SAM. 15:13-14) when he wrote this psalm. Prayer and dependence on God were in the forefront of David's thinking, and he found Him to be his sanctuary (PS. 27:4-5).

We need a sanctuary as well. Perhaps reading or praying this psalm and others could help us to develop that closeness to our Father-God. As God becomes our sanctuary, we'll more readily turn our hearts toward Him in prayer. 🌾　　*ANNE CETAS*

Teach me, Father, what it means to run to You and have You as my sanctuary. Help me not to worry about the words I say, but just to express my heart to You and to nestle down close to You.

In prayer, God can still our hearts and quiet our minds.

Giving It to God

hero to a generation of people who grew up after World War II, Corrie ten Boom left a legacy of godliness and wisdom. A victim of the Nazi occupation of the Netherlands, she survived to tell her story of faith and dependence on God during horrendous suffering.

"I have held many things in my hands," Corrie once said, "and I have lost them all; but whatever I have placed in God's hands, that, I still possess."

Corrie was well acquainted with loss. She lost family, possessions, and years of her life to hateful people. Yet she learned to concentrate on what could be gained spiritually and emotionally by putting everything in the hands of her heavenly Father.

> TODAY'S READING
> **Mark 10:17-22**
>
> **[He] went away sorrowful, for he had great possessions.** v. 22

What does that mean to us? What should we place in God's hands for safekeeping? According to the story of the rich young man in Mark 10, *everything*. He held abundance in his hands, but when Jesus asked him to give it up, he refused. He kept his possessions and he failed to follow Jesus—and as a result he "went away sorrowful" (V. 22).

Like Corrie ten Boom, we can find hope by putting everything in God's hands and then trusting Him for the outcome. ❀

DAVE BRANON

All to Jesus I surrender,
All to Him I freely give;
I will ever love and trust Him,
In His presence daily live. VAN DE VENTER

No life is more secure than a life surrendered to God.

Love to Tell His Story

When noted author Studs Terkel was looking for a topic for his next book, one of his friends suggested "death." While he was resistant at first, the idea gradually began to take shape, but its voice became all too real when Mr. Terkel's wife of 60 years passed away. Now the book was also a personal search: a yearning to know what lies beyond, where his loved one had just gone. Its pages are a poignant reminder of our own search for Jesus and the questions and concerns we have about eternity while we walk our faith journey.

TODAY'S READING
1 Chron. 16:7-13

Oh, give thanks to the LORD! Call upon His name; make known His deeds among the peoples! v. 8

I'm thankful for the assurance we can have that we will be with Jesus after we die if we have trusted in Him to forgive our sin. There is no greater hope. It is now our privilege to share that hope with as many as we can. First Peter 3:15 encourages us: "... always be ready to give a defense to everyone who asks you a reason for the hope that is in you, with meekness and fear." We have the opportunity from God, as David said, to "call upon His name; make known His deeds among the peoples" (1 CHRON. 16:8).

The stories of so many people we love are not yet ended, and the privilege to tell them about the love of Jesus is a gift most precious. ❧

RANDY KILGORE

I love to tell the story; more wonderful it seems
Than all the golden fancies of all our golden dreams.
I love to tell the story, it did so much for me;
And that is just the reason I tell it now to thee. HANKEY

***Let our days be filled with a longing—and the opportunities—
to tell our story of Jesus.***

On Being Known

One of the most difficult inner conflicts we have is our desire to be known versus our fear of being known. As beings created in the image of God we are made to be known—known by God and also by others. Yet due to our fallen nature, all of us have sins and weaknesses that we don't want others to know about. We use the phrase "dark side" to refer to aspects of our lives that we keep hidden. And we use slogans like "put your best foot forward" to encourage others to show their best side.

One reason we are unwilling to risk being known is that we fear rejection and ridicule. But when we discover that God knows us, loves us, and is willing to forgive even the worst thing we have done, our fear of being known by God begins to fade away. And when we find a community of believers who understands the dynamic relationship between forgiveness and confession, we feel safe confessing our sins to one another (JAMES 5:16).

> **TODAY'S READING**
> **James 5:16-20**
>
> I acknowledged my sin to You . . . . I said, "I will confess my transgressions to the LORD," and You forgave the iniquity of my sin. Psalm 32:5

The life of faith is not about showing only our good side. It's about exposing our dark side to the light of Christ through confession to God and also to others. In this way we can receive healing and live in the freedom of forgiveness. 🌿

JULIE ACKERMAN LINK

Lord, help me to expose my sin,
Those secret wrongs that lurk within;
I would confess them all to Thee;
Transparent I would always be. D. DEHAAN

The voice of sin may be loud, but the voice of forgiveness is louder.

D. L. MOODY

Rooted

Joash must have been confused and frightened when he was told about the evil deeds of his grandmother Athaliah. She had murdered his brothers to usurp the power of the throne in Judah. But baby Joash had been safely hidden away by his aunt and uncle for 6 years (2 CHRON. 22:10-12). As he grew, he enjoyed the love and instruction of his caregivers. When Joash was only 7 years old, he was secretly crowned king and his grandmother was overthrown (23:12-15).

TODAY'S READING
2 Chron. 24:15-22

Joash did what was right in the sight of the LORD all the days of Jehoiada the priest. 24:2

Young King Joash had a wise counselor by his side—his very own Uncle Jehoiada (CHS. 22–25). Joash was one of the rare "good kings" of Judah, and while his uncle was alive he obeyed the Lord by doing right (24:2). But once his uncle was no longer there to teach and lead by example, Joash fell away and his life ended badly (24:15-25). It seems that the roots of his faith did not run very deep. He even began to worship idols. Perhaps Joash's "faith" had been more his uncle's than his own.

Others can teach us the principles of their faith, but each of us must come individually to a lasting and personal faith in Christ. For faith to be real, it must become our own. God will help us walk with Him and become rooted and established in the faith (COL. 2:6-7). 🌿 *CINDY HESS KASPER*

> I am Thine, O Lord, I have heard Thy voice,
> And it told Thy love to me;
> But I long to rise in the arms of faith
> And be closer drawn to Thee. CROSBY

***The faith that continues to the end gives proof
that it was genuine in the beginning.***

Medieval Meal

A **while ago I attended** a conference on the Middle Ages. In one seminar we actually prepared several foods that would have been common in medieval times. We used pestle and mortar to grind cinnamon and fruit to make jam. We cut orange rinds and broiled them with honey and ginger to produce a sweet snack. We crushed almonds with water and other ingredients to create almond milk. And, finally, we prepared a whole chicken to serve as a main dish with rice. As we sampled these dishes, we enjoyed a tasty culinary experience.

> **TODAY'S READING**
> **Psalm 19:7-14**
>
> **How sweet are Your words to my taste, sweeter than honey to my mouth!** 119:103

When it comes to spiritual food for our souls, God has given us a varied menu that we can chew on and savor. In doing so, we can be filled and satisfied. The historic books, poetry, wisdom literature, prophecy, and other parts of the Bible strengthen us when we are weak, give us wisdom and encouragement, and nourish us for the day's journey (PS. 19:7-14; 119:97-104; HEB. 5:12). As the psalmist tells us: "How sweet are Your words to my taste, sweeter than honey to my mouth!" (PS. 119:103).

So what are we waiting for? God has set before us a banquet of delectable spiritual food and calls us to come and dine. We are all invited! 🌼

DENNIS FISHER

Thank You, Lord, that You call me to Your table to feast on Your Word. I know that I need it for my spiritual nourishment and to grow close to You. I open my heart to You now.

The Bible is the bread of life, and it never gets stale.

Repeat Warnings

Caution, the moving walkway is ending. Caution, the moving walkway is ending." If you've ever used an automated walkway at an airport, you've heard this kind of announcement repeatedly.

Why do airports repeat this announcement over and over? To ensure safety and to protect them from liability if someone were to be injured.

Repeated announcements can be annoying, but they do have value. As a matter of fact, the apostle Paul thought repeating a warning was so vital that he did it in the text of Galatians. But his statement had value far beyond the danger of tripping at the airport. Paul warned them not to listen to, nor believe, him or an angel from heaven if they preached "any other gospel" than

> TODAY'S READING
> **Galatians 1:6-10**
>
> **I marvel that you are turning away so soon from Him who called you in the grace of Christ, to a different gospel.** v. 6

what they had already heard (1:8). In the next verse, Paul said it again. It was a warning worth repeating. The Galatians had begun to believe that their salvation was dependent on good works instead of the true gospel: faith in Christ's work.

The gospel of Jesus—His death, burial, and resurrection for the forgiveness of sins—is the story that we have the privilege and responsibility to share. When we present the gospel, let's share that the risen Jesus is the only solution to the problem of sin. ❧

DAVE BRANON

He is the way, the truth, the life—
That One whose name is Jesus;
There is no other name on earth
That has the power to save us. SPER

Only one road leads to heaven—Jesus Christ is the way.

An Emergency of the Spirit

n March 2011, a devastating tsunami struck Japan, taking nearly 16,000 lives as it obliterated towns and villages along the coast. Writer and poet Gretel Erlich visited Japan to witness and document the destruction. When she felt inadequate to report what she was seeing, she wrote a poem about it. In a PBS *NewsHour* interview she said, "My old friend William Stafford, a poet now gone, said, 'A poem is an emergency of the spirit.'"

> **TODAY'S READING**
> **2 Samuel 1:17-27**
>
> **David lamented with this lamentation over Saul and over Jonathan his son.** v. 17

We find poetry used throughout the Bible to express deep emotion, ranging from joyful praise to anguished loss. When King Saul and his son Jonathan were killed in battle, David was overwhelmed with grief (2 SAM. 1:1-12). He poured out his soul in a poem he called "the Song of the Bow": "Saul and Jonathan were beloved and pleasant in their lives, and in their death they were not divided. . . . How the mighty have fallen in the midst of the battle!… I am distressed for you, my brother Jonathan; you have been very pleasant to me" (VV. 23-26).

When we face "an emergency of the spirit"—whether glad or sad—our prayers can be a poem to the Lord. While we may stumble to articulate what we feel, our heavenly Father hears our words as a true expression of our hearts. 🍃

DAVID MCCASLAND

> Sometimes I do not pray in words—
> I take my heart in my two hands
> And hold it up before the Lord—
> I am so glad He understands. NICHOLSON

God does more than hear words; He reads hearts.

The Language of Whistling

On La Gomera, one of the smallest of the Canary Islands, a language that sounds like a bird song is being revived. In a land of deep valleys and steep ravines, schoolchildren and tourists are learning how whistling was once used to communicate for distances up to 2 miles. One goat herder who is using this ancient language once again to communicate with his flock said, "They recognize my whistle as they recognize my voice."

> TODAY'S READING
> **Zechariah 10:1-8**
>
> **I will whistle for them and gather them, for I will redeem them.** v. 8

The practice of whistling also shows up in the Bible, where God is described as a shepherd whistling for His sheep. This image could be what the prophet had in mind when he described how God will one day whistle to bring a wandering and scattered people back to Himself (ZECH. 10:8).

Many years later Jesus said, "My sheep hear My voice, and I know them, and they follow Me" (JOHN 10:27). That may be the whistle of a shepherd. Sheep don't understand words, but they know the sound that signals the shepherd's presence.

Misleading voices and distracting noises still compete for our attention (CF. ZECH. 10:2). Yet God has ways of signaling us, even without words. By events that can be alarming or encouraging, He reminds us of His guiding, protecting, and reassuring presence. 🌱

MART DEHAAN

Father, it is a noisy world. Thank You for always calling to us
above the din and ruckus that distracts us. Help us to recognize
Your voice and follow Your leading.

The call of God can always be heard.

The Wise Old Owl

Years ago an anonymous writer penned a short poem about the merits of measuring our words.

A wise old owl sat in an oak;
The more he saw the less he spoke;
The less he spoke the more he heard;
Why can't we all be like that wise old bird?

There is a connection between wisdom and limiting what we say. Proverbs 10:19 says, "In the multitude of words sin is not lacking, but he who restrains his lips is wise."

> **TODAY'S READING**
> **Proverbs 10:17-21**
>
> **He who restrains his lips is wise.** v. 19

We are wise to be careful about what we say or how much we say in certain situations. It makes sense to guard our words when we are angry. James urged his fellow believers, "Be swift to hear, slow to speak, slow to wrath" (JAMES 1:19). Restraining our words can also show reverence for God. Solomon said, "God is in heaven, and you on earth; therefore let your words be few" (ECCL. 5:2). When others are grieving, our silent presence may help more than abundant expressions of sympathy: "No one spoke a word to him, for they saw that his grief was very great" (JOB 2:13).

Although there is a time to be quiet and a time to speak (ECCL. 3:7), choosing to speak less allows us to hear more. 🕊

JENNIFER BENSON SCHULDT

Dear Lord, please grant me wisdom to know when to speak
and when to listen. I want to encourage others and to care
for them as You have cared for me.

Let your speech be better than silence; otherwise be silent.

A Matter of Trust

A **news item from Australia** told the story of Pascale Honore, a paraplegic woman who, after 18 years of being confined to a wheelchair, has taken up surfing. How?

Ty Swan, a young surfer, straps her to his back with duct tape. After getting the balance perfect, Ty paddles out into the ocean so they can catch a wave and Pascale can experience the exhilaration of surfing. This requires a tremendous amount of trust; so many things could go wrong. Yet her confidence in Ty is enough to enable her to enjoy a dream come true, in spite of the danger.

> TODAY'S READING
> **Psalm 5**
>
> **Let all those rejoice who put their trust in You; let them ever shout for joy, because You defend them.** v. 11

Life is like that for the follower of Christ. We live in a dangerous world, filled with unpredictable challenges and unseen perils. Yet, we have joy because we know Someone who is strong enough to carry us through the churning waves of life that threaten to overwhelm us. The psalmist wrote, "Let all those rejoice who put their trust in You; let them ever shout for joy, because You defend them; let those also who love Your name be joyful in You" (PS. 5:11).

In the face of life's great dangers and challenges, we can know a joy borne out of our trust in God. His strength is more than enough! 🕊   *BILL CROWDER*

> I'm so glad I learned to trust Thee,
> Precious Jesus, Savior, Friend;
> And I know that Thou art with me,
> Wilt be with me to the end. STEAD

Our faith is stretched by exchanging our weakness for God's strength.

The Ultimate Reunion

'll never forget the vigil of sitting by my dad's bed as he spent his last few days with us before slipping into eternity. To this day the moment of his passing continues to have a profound effect on me. My dad was always there for me. I could call him whenever I needed counsel. I have great memories of our days fishing together; we would talk about God and the Bible, and I would prompt him to tell those fun stories from his youth on the farm.

> TODAY'S READING
> **1 Thess. 4:13-18**
>
> **We who are alive and remain shall be caught up together with them.** v. 17

But when Dad took his last breath, I became aware of the irreversible finality of death. He was gone from this world. And my heart had a vacancy sign hung on its door.

Yet, even in the midst of such loss and grief, God's Word speaks encouragingly into the emptiness. The apostle Paul teaches us that at the coming of the Lord Jesus, those who have gone on before will rise first and we "shall be caught up together with them . . . . And thus we shall always be with the Lord" (1 THESS. 4:17). Now that's a reunion I'm really looking forward to! Not only to be reunited with my dad, but to be with Jesus forever.

C. S. Lewis said, "Christians never say goodbye." I'm eagerly awaiting that ultimate reunion! ❧   *JOE STOWELL*

Lord, in the midst of our sorrow and loss, remind us of the glorious eternal reunion that is waiting for us. Comfort us in our grief and fill our hearts with joyful anticipation of the day You will return!

O Death, where is your sting?   1 CORINTHIANS 15:55

Every Hardship

Like many towns, Enterprise, Alabama, has a prominent monument. But the monument in Enterprise is unlike any other. The statue doesn't recognize a leading citizen; it celebrates the work of a beetle. In the early 1900s, this boll weevil made its way from Mexico to the southern US. Within a few years it had destroyed entire crops of cotton, the primary source of revenue. In desperation, farmers started growing another crop—peanuts. Realizing they had been dependent on one crop for too long, they credited the beetle with forcing them to diversify, which led to increased prosperity.

TODAY'S READING
2 Cor. 12:7-10

My grace is sufficient for you, for My strength is made perfect in weakness. v. 9

The boll weevil is like things that come into our lives and destroy what we have worked hard to accomplish. Devastation results—sometimes financial, emotional, or physical—and it is frightening. We witness the end of life as we know it. But as the people of Enterprise learned, the loss of what is *old* is an opportunity to discover something *new*. God may use hardship to get us to give up a bad habit or learn a new virtue. He used a thorn in Paul's flesh to teach him about grace (2 COR. 12:7-9).

Instead of striving to preserve old habits that are no longer effective, we can view every hardship as an opportunity for God to cultivate a new virtue in us. ❧   *JULIE ACKERMAN LINK*

O much-tried saint, with fainting heart,
The thorn with its abiding pain,
With all its wearing, ceaseless ache,
Can be the means of priceless gain. ANON.

God often uses bitter experiences to make us better.

Amazing Grace

Pressed into service in the Royal Navy, John Newton was dismissed for insubordination and turned to a career trafficking in slaves. Notorious for cursing and blasphemy, Newton served on a slave ship during the cruelest days of trans-Atlantic slavery, finally working his way up to captain.

TODAY'S READING
Ephesians 2:1-10

For by grace you have been saved through faith. v. 8

A dramatic conversion on the high seas set him on the path to grace. He always felt a sense of undeservedness for his new life. He became a rousing evangelical preacher and eventually a leader in the abolitionist movement. Newton appeared before Parliament, giving irrefutable eyewitness testimony to the horror and immorality of the slave trade. We also know him as the author of the lyrics of perhaps the best-loved hymn of all time, "Amazing Grace."

Newton described any good in himself as an outworking of God's grace. In doing so, he stands with these great heroes—a murderer and adulterer (King David), a coward (the apostle Peter), and a persecutor of Christians (the apostle Paul).

This same grace is available to all who call upon God, for "in Him we have redemption through His blood, the forgiveness of sins, according to the riches of His grace" (EPH. 1:7). ❀

PHILIP YANCEY

Amazing grace—how sweet the sound—
That saved a wretch like me!
I once was lost but now am found,
Was blind but now I see. NEWTON

Lives rooted in God's unchanging grace can never be uprooted.

A Fresh Start

n many countries, health laws prohibit reselling or reusing old mattresses. Only landfills will take them. Tim Keenan tackled the problem and today his business employs a dozen people to extract the individual components of metal, fabric, and foam in old mattresses for recycling. But that's only part of the story. Journalist Bill Vogrin wrote, "Of all the items Keenan recycles . . . it's the people that may be his biggest success" (*The Gazette*, Colorado Springs). Keenan hires men from halfway houses and homeless shelters, giving them a job and a second chance. He says, "We take guys nobody else wants."

> **TODAY'S READING**
> **Luke 5:17-26**
>
> **Those who are well have no need of a physician, but those who are sick.** 5:31

Luke 5:17–26 tells how Jesus healed the body and the soul of a paralyzed man. Following that miraculous event, Levi answered Jesus' call to follow Him and then invited his fellow tax collectors and friends to a banquet in honor of the Lord (VV. 27-29). When some people accused Jesus of associating with undesirables (V. 30), He reminded them that healthy people don't need a doctor—adding, "I have not come to call the righteous, but sinners, to repentance" (V. 32).

To everyone who feels like a "throwaway" headed for the landfill of life, Jesus opens His arms of love and offers a fresh beginning. That's why He came! 🍂 *DAVID MCCASLAND*

The power of God can turn a heart
From evil and the power of sin;
The love of God can change a life
And make it new and cleansed within. FASICK

Salvation is receiving a new life.

The Power of Ritual

When I was growing up, one of the rules in our house was that we weren't allowed to go to bed angry (EPH. 4:26). All our fights and disagreements had to be resolved. The companion to that rule was this bedtime ritual: Mom and Dad would say to my brother and me, "Good night. I love you." And we would respond, "Good night. I love you too."

The value of this family ritual has recently been impressed on me. As my mother lay in a hospice bed dying of lung cancer, she became less and less responsive. But each night when I left her bedside I would say, "I love you,

> **TODAY'S READING**
> **1 Cor. 11:23-34**
>
> **Do this in remembrance of Me.** v. 24

Mom." And though she could say little else, she would respond, "I love you too." Growing up I had no idea what a gift this ritual would be to me so many years later.

Time and repetition can rob our rituals of meaning. But some are important reminders of vital spiritual truths. First-century believers misused the practice of the Lord's Supper, but the apostle Paul didn't tell them to stop celebrating it. Instead he told them, "As often as you eat this bread and drink this cup, you proclaim the Lord's death till He comes" (1 COR. 11:26).

Rather than give up the ritual, perhaps we need to restore the meaning. 🌱   *JULIE ACKERMAN LINK*

Lord, when we observe the Lord's Supper, help us avoid the trap
of letting our observance grow routine. May we always be
moved with gratitude for the wonderful gift of ritual.

*Any ritual can lose meaning, but that does not
make the ritual meaningless.*

In the Storm

storm was brewing—not just on the horizon but also in a friend's home. "When I was in Hong Kong," she shared, "the local meteorological service announced that there was a superstorm approaching. But more than the storm that was looming outside my window, there was a storm brewing at home. While my dad was in the hospital, family members were trying to balance their home and work responsibilities while also traveling to and from the hospital. They were so tired that patience was wearing thin, and the situation at home was tense."

> TODAY'S READING
> **Mark 4:35-41**
>
> [Jesus] said to the sea, "Peace, be still!" v. 39

Life can feel like a storm—tossing us around with winds of misfortune, grief, or stress. Where can we turn? When Jesus' disciples were caught in a great windstorm and wondered if He cared, they still knew where to turn. He demonstrated His power by calming the howling storm (MARK 4:38-39).

But often He does not calm the storm immediately. And, like the disciples, we may feel that He doesn't care. To calm our fears, we can cling to faith in who God is and what He can do. We can take shelter in Him (PS. 91:1). We can find His help to relate to others with grace. We can rest in an all-powerful, all-wise, and all-loving God. He is with us *in* the storm and cradles us *through* the storm. ❧

POH FANG CHIA

Whether the wrath of the storm-tossed sea,
Or demons or men, or whatever it be
No waters can swallow the ship where lies
The Master of the ocean, and earth, and skies. BAKER

One need not cry out very loudly; He is nearer to us than we think.
BROTHER LAWRENCE

Filtered Light

The painting *A Trail of Light* by Colorado Springs artist Bob Simpich shows a grove of aspen trees with golden leaves lit by the autumn sun. The topmost leaves are brilliantly illuminated while the ground beneath the trees is a mixture of sunlight and shadows. The painter said of this contrast, "I can't resist the light filtered through to the forest floor. It weaves a special magic."

TODAY'S READING
2 Cor. 4:1-12

It is the God who commanded light to shine out of darkness, who has shone in our hearts. v. 6

The apostle Paul wrote to the followers of Jesus in Corinth, "For it is the God who commanded light to shine out of darkness, who has shone in our hearts to give the light of the knowledge of the glory of God in the face of Jesus Christ" (2 COR. 4:6). Paul goes on to describe the reality of life in which "we are hard-pressed on every side, yet not crushed; . . . perplexed, but not in despair; persecuted, but not forsaken; struck down, but not destroyed" (VV. 8-9).

There are times when it seems that the light of God's face is dimmed because of our difficulty, sorrow, or loss. Yet, even in these dark shadows, we can see evidence of His presence with us.

If we walk in filtered light today, may we discover anew that God's light—Jesus—is always shining in our hearts. 🌿

DAVID MCCASLAND

Lord, shine the light of Your face on us that we may find our way to Your salvation. Shine Your light into the darkness that envelops our world that we may see who You are and show others the way to You.

In dark circumstances, God's light is still shining in our hearts.

Disposable Culture

More than ever, we live in a disposable culture. Think for a minute about some of the things that are made to be thrown away—razors, water bottles, lighters, paper plates, plastic eating utensils. Products are used, tossed, and then replaced.

This disposable culture is also reflected in more significant ways. Many times true commitment in relationships is seen as optional. Marriages struggle to survive. Long-term employees are discharged just before retirement for cheaper options. A highly revered athlete leaves to join another team. It seems as if nothing lasts.

> **TODAY'S READING**
> **Psalm 136:1-9, 23-26**
>
> **Oh, give thanks to the LORD, for He is good! For His mercy endures forever.** v. 1

Our unchanging God, however, has promised that His loving mercy endures forever. In Psalm 136, the singer celebrates this wonderful promise by making statements about God's wonder, work, and character. He then punctuates each statement about God with the phrase, "For His mercy endures forever." Whether it is the wonder of His creation (vv. 4-9), the rescue of His people (vv. 10-22), or His tender care for His own (vv. 23-26), we can trust Him because His mercy will never fail. In a temporary world, the permanence of God's mercy gives us hope. We can sing with the psalmist, "Oh, give thanks to the LORD, for He is good! For His mercy endures forever" (v. 1). 🌱   *BILL CROWDER*

> I sing of mercies that endure,
> Forever builded firm and sure,
> Of faithfulness that never dies,
> Established changeless in the skies. PSALTER

God's grace is immeasurable; His mercy inexhaustible;
His peace inexpressible.

Pink Sheep

While traveling on a road from Glasgow to Edinburgh, Scotland, I was enjoying the beautiful, pastoral countryside when a rather humorous sight captured my attention. There, on a small hilltop, was a rather large flock of pink sheep.

I know that sheep owners mark their animals with dots of spray paint to identify them—but these sheep really stood out. The owner had fully covered every animal with pink coloring. Everyone knew who those sheep belonged to.

TODAY'S READING
John 10:7-18

> **By this all will know that you are My disciples, if you have love for one another.** 13:35

Scripture calls followers of Christ sheep, and they too have a unique identifying mark. What is the "pink coloring" in a Christ-follower's life? How can someone be identified as Jesus' own?

In the gospel of John, Jesus, the Good Shepherd, told us what that identifier is: love. "Love one another; as I have loved you . . . . By this all will know that you are My disciples, if you have love for one another" (JOHN 13:34-35).

In words and deeds, a believer should show love to all those around. "Beloved," John writes, "if God so loved us, we also ought to love one another" (1 JOHN 4:11). A Christian's love for others should be as obvious as pink wool on a flock of Scottish sheep. ❧

DAVE BRANON

Dear Lord, remind me that this life is not about me and my needs, but about others and how Your love can shine through me to them. May Christlike love be my distinguishing characteristic.

As followers of Christ, our love should make us stand out in a crowd.

A Faithful Helper

As a young boy, my father had to deliver slop to hungry pigs on the farm where he grew up. He hated this job because the hogs would knock him over when he entered their pen. This task might have been impossible except for a faithful helper who accompanied my dad—a German shepherd named Sugarbear. She would maneuver herself between my father and the pigs and hold them back until my dad finished his chore.

TODAY'S READING
Jeremiah 20:7-13

The LORD is with me as a mighty, awesome One. v. 11

The prophet Jeremiah had the difficult job of proclaiming God's messages to the Israelites. This required him to endure physical abuse, verbal attacks, imprisonment, and isolation. Although Jeremiah struggled with deep discouragement, he had a Helper through all of his trouble. God promised him, "I am with you . . . to deliver you" (JER. 1:19).

God did not desert Jeremiah, and He will not desert us. We have His continual aid through the power of the Spirit who lives inside every believer (JOHN 14:16-17). The Helper gives us hope (ROM. 15:13), steers us toward spiritual truth (JOHN 16:13), and pours out God's love in our hearts (ROM. 5:5). We can trust that God faithfully helps us as we endure hardship. We can say with Jeremiah, "The LORD is with me as a mighty, awesome One" (JER. 20:11). 🌱

JENNIFER BENSON SCHULDT

You, God, have been our help forever. And You are our hope now and into eternity. We thank You that You will never desert us. You will be faithful.

Our greatest hope here below is help from God above.

Fly the Flag

Queen Elizabeth II has reigned for more than 60 years. Her monarchy has been characterized by grace and class. She has diligently given her life to serve her people well, and as a result she is deeply loved and highly revered. So, you can understand the importance of the flag flying above Buckingham Palace. When the flag is flying, it means that she is in residence in the heart of London. The flag is a public statement that the queen is present with her people.

TODAY'S READING
Ephesians 5:1-13

Therefore be imitators of God as dear children. v. 1

As I was thinking about that, it occurred to me that our King Jesus is in residence in our hearts as our "never leave you nor forsake you" Monarch (HEB. 13:5). As wonderful as that is to us personally, I wonder if those around us would recognize that He is in residence based on the way we live? If He is within us, that will show on the outside. As Paul says, we are to be "imitators of God" and to "walk in love, as Christ also has loved us" (EPH. 5:1-2). As we do so, we will display joy, peace, patience, kindness, goodness, faithfulness, gentleness, and self-control (GAL. 5:22-23).

So let's fly the flag of His presence—the flag of His grace, righteousness, and love—so that others may see Him through us. 🌿

JOE STOWELL

Lord, remind me that Your presence in my heart is intended to be a public reality. May I so value all the blessings of Your presence that I am willing to share them generously with others.

Fly the flag of Christ's presence to show that the King is in residence in your life.

Learn to Wait on God

Cha Sa-soon, a 69-year-old Korean woman, finally received her driving license after 3 years of trying to pass the written test. She wanted the license so she could take her grandchildren to the zoo.

She was persistent in what is normally an instant world. When we want something and cannot get it, we often complain and demand. At other times, we give up and move on if what we want cannot be quickly gratified. "Wait" is a word we hate to hear! Yet, many times the Bible tells us that God wants us to wait on Him for the right timing.

TODAY'S READING
Psalm 62:1-8

> My soul, wait silently for God alone, for my expectation is from Him. v. 5

Waiting on God means patiently looking to Him for what we need. David recognized why he had to wait on the Lord. First, his salvation came from Him (PS. 62:1). He learned that no one else could deliver him. His only hope was in God (V. 5), for God alone hears our prayers (V. 8).

Our prayers often revolve around asking God to hurry up and bless what we want to do. What if God's answer to us is simply, "Be patient. Wait upon Me"? We can pray with David: "Listen to my voice in the morning, LORD. Each morning I bring my requests to you and wait expectantly" (PS. 5:3 NLT). We can trust His response, even if it doesn't come in the time we expect. 🌸   *C. P. HIA*

When we call out to You, O Lord,
And wait for answers to our prayer,
Give us the patience that we need
And help us sense Your love and care. SPER

The bottom line of every prayer should be, "Your will be done."

What Do You Expect?

I n C. S. Lewis' book *God in the Dock*, he wrote: "Imagine a set of people all living in the same building. Half of them think it is a hotel, the other half think it is a prison. Those who think it a hotel might regard it as quite intolerable, and those who thought it was a prison might decide that it was really surprisingly comfortable." Lewis cleverly used this contrast between a hotel and a prison to illustrate how we view life based on our expectations. He says, "If you think of this world as a place intended simply for our happiness, you find it quite intolerable; think of it as a place of training and correction and it's not so bad."

Sometimes we expect that life should be happy and pain-free. But that is not what the Bible teaches. For the believer, this world is a place of spiritual development through both good times and bad. Jesus was realistic when He explained what to expect in life. He told His disciples, "In the world you will have tribulation; but be of good cheer, I have overcome the world" (JOHN 16:33). In facing life's blessings and bruises, we can have the inner peace that God is orchestrating events according to His sovereign plan.

Christ's presence in our lives enables us to "be of good cheer" even in the midst of pain. 🌿   *DENNIS FISHER*

> He whose heart is kind beyond all measure
> Gives unto each day what He deems best—
> Lovingly, its part of pain and pleasure,
> Mingling toil with peace and rest. BERG

In the midst of troubles, peace can be found in Jesus.

The Lesson of the Hula Hoop

One of my favorite childhood toys is making a come-back—the hula hoop. My friend Suzi and I spent hours on the front lawn perfecting our technique and competing to see which of us could keep a hoop circling our waist longer. This year I relived that part of my childhood. While sitting in a park, I watched as children of all ages and sizes tried their hardest to keep hula hoops from falling to the ground. They twisted and turned with all their strength, but despite their exertion the hoops landed on the ground. Then a

TODAY'S READING
Mark 6:34-44

Let us not grow weary while doing good. Galatians 6:9

young woman picked up a hoop. With hardly any motion, she moved it smoothly and rhythmically up and down from her waist to her shoulders and back to her waist. Her success depended on strategic movement, not vigorous motion.

In our spiritual lives, we can expend all kinds of energy trying to keep up with others in service to God. But working to exhaustion is not a virtue (GAL. 6:9). Before feeding thousands of people with only five loaves and two fish (MARK 6:38-44), Jesus called His disciples away to rest, proving that He doesn't need our frantic exertion to accomplish His work. The truth Jesus taught His disciples, He wants to teach us: Quiet obedience accomplishes more than wild activity. ❀   *JULIE ACKERMAN LINK*

Help me, Lord, not to compare myself and what I do with others.
May I serve where You want me to serve and do it in Your
strength. I love You and give myself to You.

Jesus wants willingness, not weariness.

The Power to Change

Educator and best-selling author Tony Wagner is a firm believer in "disruptive innovation" that changes the way the world thinks and works. In his book *Creating Innovators: The Making of Young People Who Will Change the World*, he says, "Innovation occurs in every aspect of human endeavor," and "most people can become more creative and innovative—given the right environment and opportunities."

TODAY'S READING
Romans 12:1-8

Do not be conformed to this world, but be transformed by the renewing of your mind. v. 2

Paul was a first-century innovator who traveled throughout Asia Minor telling people how they could be transformed by faith in Jesus Christ. To the Christians in Rome, Paul wrote, "Don't copy the behavior and customs of this world, but let God transform you into a new person by changing the way you think" (ROM. 12:2 NLT). He urged them to give themselves fully to God (V. 1). In a self-centered, greedy, and grasping world, Paul nurtured and mentored them in how to live a Christ-centered, giving life.

The world has changed dramatically since Paul's time. But the longings of people for love, forgiveness, and the power to change remain the same. Jesus, the Great Innovator, offers all of these and invites us to experience a new and different life in Him. 🌱

DAVID McCASLAND

I'm thankful for the ways You're changing me, Lord. Help me
to be open to You and to cooperate with Your work in me.
Transform me to be like You.

God takes us as we are but never leaves us that way.

A Sanctuary

Entering a church in Klang, Malaysia, I was intrigued by the sign welcoming us into the building. It declared the place to be "A Sanctuary for the Heavy Laden."

Few things better reflect the heart of Christ than for His church to be a place where burdens are lifted and the weary find rest. This was vital in Jesus' ministry, for He said, "Come to Me, all you who labor and are heavy laden, and I will give you rest" (MATT. 11:28).

> **TODAY'S READING**
> **Matthew 11:25-30**
>
> **Come to Me, all you who labor and are heavy laden, and I will give you rest.** v. 28

Jesus promised to take our burdens and exchange them for His light load. "Take My yoke upon you and learn from Me, for I am gentle and lowly in heart, and you will find rest for your souls. For My yoke is easy and My burden is light" (VV. 29-30).

This promise is backed by His great strength. Whatever burdens we may carry, in Christ we find the strong shoulders of the Son of God, who promises to take our heavy burdens and exchange them for His light load.

Christ, who loves us with an everlasting love, understands our struggles, and can be trusted to provide us with a rest we can never find on our own. His strength is enough for our weakness, making Him our "sanctuary for the heavy laden." 🌿

BILL CROWDER

"Let not your heart be troubled,"
His tender word I hear,
And resting on His goodness,
I lose my doubts and fears. MARTIN

God calls the restless ones to find their rest in Him.

Timely Words

You may have heard the adage, "Timing is everything." According to the Bible, good timing applies to our words and speech too. Think of a time when God used you to bring a timely word to refresh someone, or when you wanted to speak, but it was wiser for you to remain silent.

The Bible says that there is an appropriate time to speak (ECCL. 3:7). Solomon compared properly timed and well-spoken words with golden apples in a silver setting—beautiful, valuable, and carefully crafted (PROV. 25:11-12). Knowing the right time to speak is beneficial for both the speaker and hearer, whether they are words of love, encouragement, or rebuke. Keeping silent also has its place and time. When tempted to deride, belittle, or slander a neighbor, Solomon said that it is wise to hold our tongue, recognizing the appropriate time for silence (11:12-13). When talkativeness or anger tempts us to sin against God or another human being, resistance comes by being slow to speak (10:19; JAMES 1:19).

> TODAY'S READING
> **Proverbs 25:11-15**
>
> **A word fitly spoken is like apples of gold in settings of silver.** v. 11

It's often hard to know what to say and when to say it. The Spirit will help us to be discerning. He will help us use the right words at the right time and in the right manner, for the good of others and for His honor. 🌿 *MARVIN WILLIAMS*

Heavenly Father, thank You for using others to speak
words of encouragement and challenge to me. Help me
to be wise in how and when my words or my silence
may be helpful to someone else.

Timely words are works of art.

A Forever Hello

After a week's vacation with her daughter and 4-month-old grandson, Oliver, Kathy had to say goodbye until she could see them again. She wrote to me saying, "Sweet reunions like we had make my heart long for heaven. There, we won't have to try to capture memories in our mind. There, we won't have to pray for the time to go slowly and the days to last long. There, our hello will never turn into goodbye. Heaven will be a 'forever hello,' and I can't wait." As a first-time grandma, she wants to be with her grandson Oliver as much as possible! She's thankful for any time she can be with him and for the hope of heaven—where the wonderful moments will never end.

> **TODAY'S READING**
> **2 Cor. 4:16–5:8**
>
> **He who has prepared us for this very thing is God, who also has given us the Spirit.** 5:5

Our good days do seem too short, and our difficult days far too long. But both kinds of days cause us to long for even better days ahead. The apostle Paul said that he and the Corinthians longed to be "clothed instead with our heavenly dwelling, so that what is mortal may be swallowed up by life" (2 COR. 5:4 NIV). Although the Lord is with us in this life, we cannot see Him face to face. Now we live by faith, not by sight (V. 7).

God made us for the very purpose of being near to Him always (V. 5). Heaven will be a forever hello. 🌿

ANNE CETAS

Face to face—O blissful moment!
Face to face—to see and know;
Face to face with my Redeemer,
Jesus Christ who loves me so! BRECK

Now we see Jesus in the Bible, but then, face to face.

Seeing Upside Down

I n India I worshiped among leprosy patients. Most of the medical advances in the treatment of leprosy came about as a result of missionary doctors, who were willing to live among patients and risk exposure to the dreaded disease. As a result, churches thrive in most major leprosy centers. In Myanmar I visited homes for AIDS orphans, where Christian volunteers try to replace parental affection the disease has stolen away. The most rousing church services I have attended took place in Chile and Peru, in the bowels of a federal prison. Among the lowly, the wretched, the downtrodden—the rejected of this world—God's kingdom takes root.

TODAY'S READING
Matt. 8:1-4; 9:9-12

Those who are well have no need of a physician, but those who are sick. 9:12

Taking God's assignment seriously means that we must learn to look at the world upside down, as Jesus did. Instead of seeking out people with resources who can do us favors, we look for people with few resources. Instead of the strong, we find the weak; instead of the healthy, the sick. Instead of the spiritual, the sinful. Is not this how God reconciles the world to Himself? "It is not the healthy who need a doctor, but the sick. . . . I have not come to call the righteous, but sinners" (MATT. 9:12-13 NIV).

To gain a new perspective, look at the world upside down as Jesus did. 🌿

PHILIP YANCEY

We know, Jesus, that You sought the lowly ones who were rejected by others. We want to be like You. Open our eyes and show us how. We long to be used by You to bless others.

Do you see a needy world through the eyes of Jesus?

Mysterious Detours

Before my wife and I embarked on a 400-mile road trip, I set up the GPS with our daughter's home in Missouri as the destination. As we traveled through Illinois, the GPS instructed us to get off the Interstate, resulting in a detour through the city of Harvey. After the GPS directed us back to I-80, I was baffled by this mysterious detour. Why were we directed off a perfectly good highway?

I'll never know the answer. We continued on our way, and we trusted the GPS to get us there and home again.

That got me to thinking about detours in life. We may seem to be traveling on a smooth pathway. Then for some reason, God redirects us into an unfamiliar area. Perhaps it is an illness, or a crisis at work or school, or an unexpected tragedy occurs. We don't understand what God is doing.

> **TODAY'S READING**
> **Gen. 12:1-10; 13:1**
>
> **Our fathers trusted in You; they trusted, and You delivered them.** Psalm 22:4

Abraham faced a mysterious detour when God told him, "Get out of your country, from your family and from your father's house" (GEN. 12:1). Surely Abraham must have wondered why God was routing him to the Negev desert. But he trusted God and His good purposes.

A GPS may make mistakes, but we can trust our unfailing God (PS. 22:4). He will guide us through all our mysterious detours and lead us where He wants us to go. 🕊 *DAVE BRANON*

We seek Your guidance, Lord, but we understand that our path won't always be without challenges. Help us to trust You through the detours—knowing that You have our best interests and Your honor at heart.

We don't need to see the way when we stay close to the One who does.

From Peeker to Seeker

When our daughter was too young to walk or crawl, she created a way to hide from people when she wanted to be left alone or wanted her own way. She simply closed her eyes. Kathryn reasoned that anyone she couldn't see also couldn't see her. She used this tactic in her car seat when someone new tried to say hello; she used it in her highchair when she didn't like the food; she even used it when we announced it was bedtime.

Jonah had a more grown-up strategy of hiding, but it wasn't any more effective than our daughter's. When God asked him to do something he

TODAY'S READING
Jonah 1:1–2:2

I cried out to the LORD because of my affliction, and He answered me. 2:2

didn't want to do, he ran in the opposite direction. But he found out pretty quickly there is no place God couldn't find him. In fact, Scripture is full of stories of God finding people when they didn't necessarily want to be found (EX. 2:11-3:6; 1 KINGS 19:1-7; ACTS 9:1-19).

You may have tried to hide from God or think even God can't see you. Please know this: If God sees and hears the prayer of a rebellious prophet in the belly of a big fish, then He sees and hears you wherever you are, whatever you've done. But that's nothing to be afraid of. It's actually a great comfort. He's always there, and He cares! 🌿   *RANDY KILGORE*

Thank You, God, that You are there for us. We hear Your words:
"You will seek Me and find Me, when you search for Me
with all your heart" (JER. 29:13).

*We need not fear the troubles around us as long as
the eye of the Lord is on us.*

A Genuine Friend

n the novel *Shane*, a friendship forms between Joe Starrett, a farmer on the American frontier, and Shane, a mysterious man who stops to rest at the Starrett home. The men first bond as they work together to remove a giant tree stump from Joe's land. The relationship deepens as Joe rescues Shane from a fight and Shane helps Joe improve and guard his farmland. The men share a sense of mutual respect and loyalty that reflects what Scripture says: "Two are better than one . . . . If they fall, one will lift up his companion" (ECCL. 4:9-10).

> **TODAY'S READING**
> **1 Samuel 20:32-42**
>
> **Two are better than one.** Eccl. 4:9

Jonathan and David modeled this principle as well. Circumstances tested their friendship when David suspected that King Saul wanted him dead. Jonathan doubted this, but David believed it to be true (1 SAM. 20:2-3). Eventually, they decided David would hide in a field while Jonathan questioned his father about the matter. When Saul's deadly intent became clear, the friends wept together and Jonathan blessed David as he fled (V. 42).

You have a genuine friend in Jesus if you have accepted His offer of salvation—a friend who is always loyal; one who lifts you when you stumble. He has shown you the greatest love one friend can have for another—love that led Him to sacrifice His life for you (JOHN 15:13) 🌿   *JENNIFER BENSON SCHULDT*

What a friend we have in Jesus,
All our sins and griefs to bear!
What a privilege to carry
Everything to God in prayer! SCRIVEN

Jesus is your most trusted Friend.

The Right Foundation

've got bad news for you," said the builder, who was renovating an old house I had inherited. "When we started to convert the back half of the garage for your office, we found that the walls had almost no foundation. We will have to demolish them, dig proper foundations, and start again."

"Do you have to do that?" I pleaded, silently calculating the extra cost. "Can't you just patch it up?" But the builder was adamant. "Unless we go down to the proper depth, the building inspector won't approve it. The right foundation is vital."

The right foundation makes the difference between something that lasts and something temporary. Jesus knew that though foundations are invisible, they are vitally important to

> TODAY'S READING
> **Matthew 7:24-29**
>
> **Whoever hears these sayings of Mine, and does them, I will liken him to a wise man who built his house on the rock.** v. 24

the strength and stability of the house (MATT. 7:24-25), especially when it is battered by the elements. He also knew the hearts of His listeners. They would be tempted to take the easy way, find shortcuts, or do things by halves to gain their objectives.

Other foundations may be quicker and easier. Building our lives on the right foundation is hard work, but God's truth is the only bedrock worth building on. When the storms of life hit, houses built on and held together by Him stand firm. 🌿

MARION STROUD

Father, the winds of life's storms can be powerful and threatening.
Thank You for the foundation of the truth of Your faithfulness.
Help me to rely on Your strength in my storms.

The wise man builds his house upon the Rock.

A War of Words

On July 28, 1914, Austria-Hungary declared war on Serbia in response to the assassination of Archduke Francis Ferdinand and his wife, Sophie. Within 90 days, other European countries had taken sides to honor their military alliances and pursue their own ambitions. A single event escalated into World War I, one of the most destructive military conflicts of modern time.

TODAY'S READING
Proverbs 15:1-23

A soft answer turns away wrath, but a harsh word stirs up anger. v. 1

The tragedy of war is staggering, yet our relationships and families can begin to fracture with only a few hateful words. James wrote, "See how great a forest a little fire kindles!" (JAMES 3:5). A key to avoiding verbal conflict is found in Proverbs: "A soft answer turns away wrath, but a harsh word stirs up anger" (15:1).

A small comment can start a large fight. When we, by God's grace, choose not to retaliate with our words, we honor Jesus our Savior. When He was abused and insulted, He fulfilled the prophetic words of Isaiah, "He was oppressed and He was afflicted, yet He opened not His mouth" (ISA. 53:7).

Proverbs urges us to speak the truth and seek peace through our words. "A wholesome tongue is a tree of life, . . . and a word spoken in due season, how good it is!" (15:4,23). 🌱

DAVID MCCASLAND

A careless word may kindle strife,
A cruel word may wreck a life;
A timely word may lessen stress,
A loving word may heal and bless. ANON.

Lord, make me an instrument of your peace.
Where there is hatred, let me sow love.

Undeserved Praise

Even before I could afford a self-cleaning oven, I managed to keep my oven clean. Guests even commented on it when we had them over for a meal. "Wow, your oven is so clean. It looks like new." I accepted the praise even though I knew I didn't deserve it. The reason my oven was clean had nothing to do with my meticulous scrubbing; it was clean because I so seldom used it.

> **TODAY'S READING**
> **Luke 5:27-32**
>
> **I have not come to call the righteous, but sinners, to repentance.** v. 32

How often, I wonder, am I guilty of accepting undeserved admiration for my "clean" life? It's easy to give the impression of being virtuous; simply do nothing difficult, controversial, or upsetting to people. But Jesus said we are to love people who don't agree with us, who don't share our values, who don't even like us. Love requires that we get involved in the messy situations of people's lives. Jesus was frequently in trouble with religious leaders who were more concerned about keeping their own reputations clean than they were about the spiritual condition of those they were supposed to care for. They considered Jesus and His disciples unclean for mingling with sinners when they were simply trying to rescue people from their destructive way of life (LUKE 5:30-31).

True disciples of Jesus are willing to risk their own reputations to help others out of the mire of sin. ❧

JULIE ACKERMAN LINK

Dear Lord, give me a heart of compassion for those who are lost in sin. Help me not to be concerned about what others think of me but only that Your holy name will be honored.

Christ sends us out to bring others in.

One Who Understands

My friend's husband was in the last stages of dementia. In his first introduction to the nurse who was assigned to care for him, he reached out for her arm and stopped her. He said he wanted to introduce her to his best friend—one who loved him deeply.

Since no one else was in the hall, the nurse thought he was delusional. But as it turned out he was speaking of Jesus. She was deeply touched but had to hurry on to care for another patient. When she returned, the darkness had closed in again and the man was no longer lucid.

> **TODAY'S READING**
> **Psalm 139:7-12**
>
> **The LORD searches all hearts and understands all the intent of the thoughts.**
>
> 1 Chronicles 28:9

Even though this man had descended into the darkness of dementia, he knew that the Lord was his best Friend. God dwells in the fathomless depth that is our soul. He can pierce the darkest mind and assure us of His tender, loving care. Indeed, the darkness shall not hide us from Him (PS. 139:12).

We do not know what the future holds for us or those we love. We too may descend into the darkness of mental illness, Alzheimer's, or dementia as we age. But even there the Lord's hand will lead us and His right hand will hold us tight (V. 10). We cannot get away from His love and personal care. ✿

DAVID ROPER

God knows each winding way I take,
And every sorrow, pain, and ache;
And me He never will forsake—
He knows and loves His own. BOSCH

Jesus loves me. This I know.

Clean the Closet

To this day I can still hear my mother telling me to go and clean up my room. Dutifully, I would go to my room to start the process, only to get distracted by reading the comic book that I was supposed to put neatly in the stack. But soon the distraction was interrupted by my mother warning that she would be up in 5 minutes to inspect the room. Unable to effectively clean the room in that time, I would proceed to hide everything I didn't know what to do with in the closet, make the bed, and then wait for her to come in—hoping that she wouldn't look in the closet.

> **TODAY'S READING**
> **Psalm 139:13-24**
>
> **Search me, O God, and know my heart.** v. 23

This reminds me of what many of us do with our lives. We clean up the outside of our lives hoping that no one will look into the "closet" where we have hidden our sins by rationalization and excuses and by blaming others for our own faults.

The problem is that while looking good on the outside, we remain well aware of the mess on the inside. The psalmist encourages us to submit to the cleansing inspection of God: "Search me, O God, and know my heart; try me, and know my anxieties; and see if there is any wicked way in me, and lead me in the way everlasting" (PS. 139:23-24). Let's invite Him to inspect and cleanse every corner of our lives. 🌼   *JOE STOWELL*

Lord, forgive me for looking good on the outside while attempting to hide my faults and failings. I desire for You to cleanse my life so that I may walk with You in full integrity.

We can own up to our wrongs—
because we can't hide them from God anyway.

Tiny Island

Singapore is a tiny island. It's so small that one can hardly spot it on the world map. (Try it, if you don't already know where Singapore is.) Because it is densely populated, consideration of others is especially important. A man wrote to his fiancée who was coming to Singapore for the first time: "Space is limited. Therefore . . . you must always have that sense of space around you. You should always step aside to ensure you are not blocking anyone. The key is to be considerate."

TODAY'S READING
Titus 3:1-7

Speak evil of no one, . . . be peaceable, gentle, showing all humility to all men. v. 2

The apostle Paul wrote to Titus, a young pastor: "Remind the people . . . to be obedient, to be ready to do whatever is good, to slander no one, to be peaceable and considerate, and always to be gentle toward everyone" (TITUS 3:1-2 NIV). It has been said, "Our lives may be the only Bible some people read." The world knows that Christians are supposed to be different. If we are cantankerous, self-absorbed, and rude, what will others think about Christ and the gospel we share?

Being considerate is a good motto to live by and is possible as we depend on the Lord. And it is one way to model Christ and demonstrate to the world that Jesus saves and transforms lives. 🌿

POH FANG CHIA

Dear Lord, help us to be gracious, kind, and considerate not only in the church but also in our community. May the world who watches see transformed people and believe in Your transforming power.

Your witness is only as strong as your character.

First Response

When my husband, Tom, was rushed to the hospital for emergency surgery, I began to call family members. My sister and her husband came right away to be with me, and we prayed as we waited. Tom's sister listened to my anxious voice on the phone and immediately said, "Cindy, can I pray with you?" When my pastor and his wife arrived, he too prayed for us (JAMES 5:13-16).

Oswald Chambers wrote: "We tend to use prayer as a last resort, but God wants it to be our first line of defense. We pray when there's nothing else we can do, but God wants us to pray before we do anything at all."

> **TODAY'S READING**
> **James 5:13-16**
>
> **Be anxious for nothing, but . . . let your requests be made known to God.** Philippians 4:6-7

At its root, prayer is simply a conversation with God, spoken in the expectation that God hears and answers. Prayer should not be a last resort. In His Word, God encourages us to engage Him in prayer (PHIL. 4:6). We also have His promise that when "two or three are gathered together" in His name, He will be "there in the midst of them" (MATT. 18:20).

For those who have experienced the power of the Almighty, our first inclination often will be to cry out to Him. Nineteenth-century pastor Andrew Murray said: "Prayer opens the way for God Himself to do His work in us and through us." 🌸

CINDY KASPER

When I come before His presence
In the secret place of prayer,
Do I know the wondrous greatness
Of His power to meet me there? HALLEN

Pray first!

All Together

For years my wife's piano and my banjo had an uncomfortable and infrequent relationship. Then, after Janet bought me a new guitar for my birthday, she expressed an interest in learning to play my old guitar. She is a very capable musician, and soon we were, together, playing songs of praise on our guitars. I like to think that a new kind of "praise connection" has filled our home.

When the psalmist was inspired to write of worshiping God, he began with this exhortation: "Shout joyfully to the LORD, all the earth; break forth in song, rejoice, and sing praises" (PS. 98:4). He called for us to "sing to the LORD" with instruments such as harps and trumpets and horns (VV. 5-6). He commanded all of the earth to "shout joyfully to the LORD" (V. 4). In this mighty orchestration of praise, the rolling sea is to roar with exaltation, the rivers are to clap their hands, and the hills are to sing out in joy. All the human race and creation are together called to praise the Lord in "a new song" of praise, "for He has done marvelous things" (V. 1).

> TODAY'S READING
> **Psalm 98:1-9**
>
> **Shout joyfully to the LORD, all the earth; break forth in song, rejoice, and sing praises.** v. 4

Today let your heart connect with others and God's creation in singing songs of praise to the mighty Creator and Redeemer. ❧

DENNIS FISHER

Let us celebrate together,
Lift our voice in one accord,
Singing of God's grace and mercy
And the goodness of the Lord. SPER

God can use ordinary instruments to produce a concert of praise.

New to the Family

While on a ministry trip with a Christian high school chorale to Jamaica, we witnessed an illustration of God's love in action. On the day we visited an orphanage for disabled children and teens, we learned that Donald, one of the boys our kids had interacted with—a teen with cerebral palsy—was going to be adopted.

When the adopting couple arrived at the "base" where we were staying, it was a joy to talk to them about Donald. But what was even better was what happened later. We were at the base when Donald and his new parents arrived just after they had picked him up at the orphanage. As the brand-new mom embraced her son, our students gathered around her and sang praise songs. Tears of joy flowed, and Donald was beaming!

> TODAY'S READING
> **Luke 15:3-7**
>
> **There will be more joy in heaven over one sinner who repents than over ninety-nine just persons who need no repentance.** v. 7

Later, one of the students said to me, "This reminds me of what it must be like in heaven when someone is saved. The angels rejoice because someone has been adopted into God's family." Indeed, it was a picture of the joy of heaven when someone new joins God's forever family by faith in Christ. Jesus spoke of that grand moment when He said, "There will be . . . joy in heaven over one sinner who repents" (LUKE 15:7).

Praise God that He has adopted us into His family. No wonder the angels rejoice! 🖤   *DAVE BRANON*

The One who made the heavens,
Who died on Calvary,
Rejoices with His angels
When one soul is set free. FASICK

Angels rejoice when we repent.

Working for the Wind

Howard Levitt lost his $200,000 Ferrari on a flooded Toronto highway. He had driven into what seemed like a puddle before realizing that the water was much deeper and rising quickly. When the water reached the Ferrari's fenders, its 450-horsepower engine seized. Thankfully he was able to escape the car and get to high ground.

> **TODAY'S READING**
> **Eccl. 5:10-17**
>
> **What profit has he who has labored for the wind?** v. 16

Howard's soggy sports car reminds me of Solomon's observation that "riches perish through misfortune" (ECCL. 5:14). Natural disasters, theft, and accidents may claim our dearest belongings. Even if we manage to protect them, we certainly can't haul them with us to heaven (v. 15). Solomon asked, "What profit has he who has labored for the wind?" (v. 16). There is futility in working only to acquire belongings that will ultimately disappear.

There is something that doesn't spoil and we can "take with us." It is possible to store up eternal heavenly treasure. Pursuing virtues such as generosity (MATT. 19:21), humility (5:3), and spiritual endurance (LUKE 6:22-23) will yield lasting rewards that can't be destroyed. Will the kind of treasure you seek expire on earth? Or, are you seeking "those things which are above, where Christ is, sitting at the right hand of God"? (COL. 3:1). 🌱

JENNIFER BENSON SCHULDT

Dear God, please give me a passion for the unseen,
eternal rewards that You offer. Make me indifferent
to the temporary pleasures of this world.

Treasures on earth can't compare with the treasures in heaven.

Shadowed

Someone was shadowing me. In a darkened hallway, I turned the corner to go up a flight of stairs and was alarmed by what I saw, stopping dead in my tracks. It happened again a few days later. I came around the back of a favorite coffee shop and saw the large shape of a person coming at me. Both incidents ended with a smile, however. I'd been frightened by my own shadow!

TODAY'S READING
Jeremiah 42:1-12

The LORD is my light and my salvation; whom shall I fear? Psalm 27:1

The prophet Jeremiah talked about the difference between real and imagined fears. A group of his Jewish countrymen asked him to find out whether the Lord wanted them to stay in Jerusalem or return to Egypt for safety because they feared the king of Babylon (JER. 42:1-3). Jeremiah told them that if they stayed and trusted God, they didn't need to be afraid (VV. 10-12). But if they returned to Egypt, the king of Babylon would find them (VV. 15-16).

In a world of real dangers, God had given Israel reason to trust Him in Jerusalem. He had already rescued them from Egypt. Centuries later, the long-awaited Messiah died for us to deliver us from our own sin and fear of death. May our Almighty God show us today how to live in the security of His shadow, rather than in shadowy fears of our own making. ❀

MART DEHAAN

Trust when your skies are darkening,
Trust when your light grows dim,
Trust when the shadows gather,
Trust and look up to Him. ANON.

*Under the protecting shadow of God's wing,
the little shadows of life lose their terror.*

Music and Megaphone

Christopher Locke buys old trumpets, trombones, and French horns and transforms them into acoustic amplifiers for iPhones and iPads. His creations are modeled on the trumpetlike speakers used in the first phonographs during the late 1800s. Music played through Christopher's AnalogTelePhonographers has a "louder, cleaner, richer, deeper sound" than what is heard from the small speakers in the digital devices. Along with being interesting works of art, these salvaged brass instruments require no electrical power as they amplify the music people love to hear.

Paul's words to the followers of Jesus in Corinth remind us today that in living for Christ and sharing Him with others, we are not the music but only a megaphone. "For we do not preach ourselves," Paul wrote, "but Christ Jesus the Lord, and ourselves your bondservants for Jesus' sake" (2 COR. 4:5). Our purpose is not to become the message, but to convey it through our lives and our lips. "We have this treasure in earthen vessels, that the excellence of the power may be of God and not of us" (V. 7).

If an old horn can amplify music, then perhaps our flawed lives can magnify the goodness of God. We're the megaphone; the music and the power come from Him! 🍂

> **TODAY'S READING**
> **2 Cor. 3:17–4:7**
>
> **We have this treasure in earthen vessels, that the excellence of the power may be of God and not of us.** 4:7

DAVID MCCASLAND

Thank You, Lord, that You can take our lives and use them in ways we never thought possible. Help us to be the instruments that convey the music of Your love.

Nothing is unusable in God's hands.

What Love Is

Years ago I asked a young man who was engaged to be married, "How do you know that you love her?" It was a loaded question, intended to help him look at his heart's motives for the upcoming marriage. After several thoughtful moments, he responded, "I know I love her because I want to spend the rest of my life making her happy."

We discussed what that meant—and the price tag attached to the self-lessness of constantly seeking the best for the other person, rather than putting ourselves first. Real love has a lot to do with sacrifice.

That idea is in line with the wisdom of the Bible. In the Scriptures there are several Greek words for love, but the highest form is *agape* love—love

> TODAY'S READING
> **Romans 5:1-8**
>
> **God demonstrates His own love toward us, in that while we were still sinners, Christ died for us.** v. 8

that is defined and driven by self-sacrifice. Nowhere is this more true than in the love our heavenly Father has shown us in Christ. We are deeply valued by Him. Paul stated, "God demonstrates His own love toward us, in that while we were still sinners, Christ died for us" (ROM. 5:8).

If sacrifice is the true measure of love, there could be no more precious gift than Jesus: "For God loved the world so much that he gave his one and only Son" (JOHN 3:16 NLT). 🌼

BILL CROWDER

Amazing love!
How can it be
That Thou, my God,
Shouldst die for me? WESLEY

The measure of love is what you are willing to give up for it.

Mosaic

For 3 weeks every fall season, our city becomes an art gallery. Nearly 2,000 artists from around the world display their creations in galleries, museums, hotels, parks, city streets, parking lots, restaurants, churches, and even in the river.

Among my favorite entries are mosaics made from small pieces of colored glass. The winning entry in 2011 was a 9 x 13-foot stained-glass mosaic of the crucifixion by artist Mia Tavonatti. While viewing the artwork, I heard the artist discuss how many times she had cut herself while shaping the pieces of glass for her mosaic.

> TODAY'S READING
> **Ephesians 2:10-22**
>
> **We are His workmanship, created in Christ Jesus for good works.** v. 10

As I gazed at the beautiful rendition of what was a horrific event, I saw more than a representation of the crucifixion—I saw a picture of the church, the body of Christ. In each piece of glass I saw an individual believer, beautifully shaped by Christ to fit together into the whole (EPH. 2:16,21). In the artist's story, I recognized the shedding of Jesus' blood so that this unity could take place. And in the finished artwork, I saw the act of love required to complete the project despite pain and sacrifice.

We who believe in Christ are a work of art created by God to show the greatness of a Savior who makes something beautiful out of the broken pieces of our lives. 🌿

JULIE ACKERMAN LINK

The church's one foundation
Is Jesus Christ her Lord,
She is His new creation,
By water and the Word. STONE

Christ gave everything to make something beautiful of His church.

Hands Off!

I remember bobbing for apples when I was a child, a game that required me to have my hands tied behind my back. Trying to grab a floating apple with my teeth without the use of my hands was a frustrating experience. It reminded me of the vital importance of our hands—we eat with them, greet with them, and use them to do just about anything that is vital to our existence.

When I read Psalm 46:10, I find it interesting that God says, "Be still, and know that I am God." The Hebrew word for "still" means to "cease striving," or, literally, "to put our hands at our side." At first glance this seems to be a rather risky piece of advice, since our first instinct in trouble is to keep our hands on the situation and control it to our advantage. God in essence is saying, "Hands off! Let Me deal with your problem, and rest assured that the outcome is in My hands."

TODAY'S READING
Psalm 46

Be still, and know that I am God. v. 10

But knowing when to take our hands off and let God work can make us feel vulnerable. Unless, that is, we believe that God is indeed "our refuge and strength, a very present help in trouble" (V. 1) and that "the LORD of hosts is with us; the God of Jacob is our refuge" (V. 7). In the midst of trouble, we can rest in God's care. ❧

JOE STOWELL

Lord, forgive me for always wanting to manage my own affairs.
Teach me to trust in Your wise and timely intervention in my life
and to keep my hands out of Your way.

When we put our problems in God's hands,
He puts His peace in our hearts.

Does God Care?

Minnie and **George Lacy** were faced with some questions: "Is Jesus enough? Is our relationship with Christ sufficient to sustain us? Will He be enough to help us want to go on living? Does He care?"

While serving as missionaries in 1904, the Lacys' youngest daughter fell ill. Then in rapid succession, all five of their children died from scarlet fever, none living to see the new year. In letters to the mission board George Lacy wrote about their deep loneliness and grief: "Sometimes it seems more than we can bear." But then he added, "The Lord is with us and is wonderfully helping us." In this, their darkest time, they found that Jesus was near and He was enough.

> **TODAY'S READING**
> **Psalm 30**
>
> **Hear, O LORD, and have mercy on me; LORD, be my helper!** v. 10

Many of us will face moments when we will wonder if we can go on. If our health fails, if our job disappears, if we lose those closest to us, will we find our relationship with the Lord real enough to keep us pressing forward?

The psalmist reminds us of God's presence and faithfulness (PS. 30). When he was deeply depressed, he cried out, "Hear, O LORD, and have mercy on me; LORD, be my helper!" (V. 10). God gave Him healing and comfort (VV. 2-3).

As believers in Jesus, we will never lack what we need to persevere. The Lord will always be near. 🌿   *RANDY KILGORE*

> Though tempted and sadly discouraged,
> My soul to this refuge will flee
> And rest in the blessed assurance,
> "My grace is sufficient for thee." ANON.

Faith in an all-sufficient Christ enables us to press on.

Perception or Reality?

We often hear it said, "Perception is reality." That idea for Americans may have dawned on September 26, 1960—the date of the first televised debate between two presidential candidates. In front of the cameras, John Kennedy appeared composed; Richard Nixon appeared nervous. The perception was that Kennedy would be a stronger leader. The debate not only turned that election, but it also changed the way politics is done in the US. Politics by perception became the rule of the day.

> **TODAY'S READING**
> **Mark 4:35-41**
>
> **Teacher, do You not care that we are perishing?** v. 38

Sometimes perception is reality. But not always—especially our perceptions about God. When Jesus and His disciples were crossing the Sea of Galilee in a small fishing vessel, a sudden storm threatened to sink the boat. With Jesus asleep and the disciples on the verge of panic, they began to stir Him, asking, "Teacher, do You not care that we are perishing?" (MARK 4:38).

Their question sounds similar to questions I've asked. At times I perceive God's apparent inactivity as a lack of care. But His care for me goes well beyond what I can see or measure. Our God is deeply concerned for what concerns us. He urges us to place all our care upon Him, "for He cares for [us]" (1 PETER 5:7). That is true reality.

BILL CROWDER

O yes, He cares; I know He cares!
His heart is touched with my grief;
When the days are weary, the long nights dreary,
I know my Savior cares. GRAEFF

Even when we don't sense God's presence, His loving care is all around us.

Less Than the Least

Unlike those who think highly of themselves, Jacob knew that he had been ruined by sin (GEN. 32:10). He thought himself a man unworthy of God's grace. He had cheated his brother Esau out of his birthright (CH. 27), and his brother hated him for it. Now, years later, Jacob was going to face Esau again.

"I am not worthy of the least of all the mercies," Jacob prayed, using a word for "least" that suggests the tiniest object. "Deliver me, I pray" (32:10-11).

How odd to see those phrases side by side: *I am unworthy of Your mercies . . . . Deliver me!* Yet Jacob could pray for mercy because his hope lay not in his own worth, but in God's promise to look with favor on those who throw themselves at His feet. Humility and contrition are the keys that open the heart of God. Someone has said that the best disposition for praying is being stripped of everything. It is crying out of the depths. It comes from the soul that knows its deep depravity.

Such prayers are offered by those who are thoroughly convicted of their sin and shame, but, at the same time, are convinced of God's grace that goes out to undeserving sinners. God hears best those who cry out: "God, be merciful to me a sinner!" (LUKE 18:13). ❧

DAVID ROPER

> TODAY'S READING
> **Genesis 32:3-12**
>
> **I am not worthy of the least of all the mercies and of all the truth which You have shown Your servant.** v. 10

Lord, I am like Jacob, in need of Your mercy. I have failed You, and I bow at Your feet today. Thank You for being a merciful God, ready and able to forgive and restore me.

It is fitting for a great God to forgive great sinners.

Horse Power

Think for a moment of the power, beauty, and majesty of a galloping horse—his head held high, his mane flying in the wind, and his legs working in unison to provide speed, power, and abandon.

What a wonderful example of God's magnificent creation is the horse! God created it not just for our amazement and enjoyment but also as a complement to the human race (JOB 39). Properly trained, the horse is fearless when we need a courageous companion. The horse was used to carry the soldier faithfully into conflict with speed (V. 24) and anticipation (V. 25).

> TODAY'S READING
> **Job 39:19-25**
>
> **I will praise You, for I am fearfully and wonderfully made.** Psalm 139:14

Although God was using creation to teach Job about His sovereignty, we can also be reminded through this passage about our own value in God's world. We are created not simply as a beautiful creature with a job to do but also as a creature made in God's image. The power of the horse is amazing, but the value of each human transcends all other creatures.

God created us uniquely to have a relationship with Him and to live with Him forever. While we praise God for the magnificence of the creatures of nature, we also stand in awe that we are "fearfully and wonderfully made" (PS. 139:14). 🌱

DAVE BRANON

Thank You, our Almighty God and Father, for Your creation.
You have provided so many majestic creatures for us to enjoy,
but help us to recognize with thankfulness the special place
we have in creation.

Of all God's creation, only humans can experience re-creation.

Multiply It

Amy had battled cancer for 5 years. Then the doctor told her that the treatments were failing and she had just a few weeks to live. Wanting some understanding and assurance about eternity, Amy asked her pastor, "What will heaven be like?"

He asked her what she liked most about her life on earth. She talked about walks and rainbows and caring friends and the laughter of children. "So, then, are you saying I will have all of that there?" she asked longingly.

TODAY'S READING
Revelation 22:1-5

There shall be no more curse. v. 3

Amy's pastor replied, "I believe that your life there will be far more beautiful and amazing than anything you ever loved or experienced here. Think about what's best here for you and multiply it over and over and over. That's what I think heaven will be."

The Bible doesn't describe in detail what life in eternity will be like, but it does tell us that being with Christ in heaven is "far better" than our present circumstance (PHIL. 1:23). "There shall be no more curse, but the throne of God and of the Lamb shall be in it, and His servants shall serve Him" (REV. 22:3).

Best of all, we will see the Lord Jesus face to face. Our deepest yearnings will be fully satisfied in Him. 🌱 *ANNE CETAS*

We're thankful, Lord, for Your presence now in our lives.
But what an amazing day it will be when we meet You face to
face! Life with You in heaven will be greater by far.

To be with Jesus forever is the sum of all happiness.

Oranges or Milk?

When I told my young daughter that a 3-month-old baby boy was coming to our house for a visit, she was delighted. With a child's sense of hospitality, she suggested that we share some of our food with the baby; she thought he might enjoy a juicy orange from the bowl on our kitchen counter. I explained that the baby could drink only milk, but that he might like oranges when he was older.

> **TODAY'S READING**
> **Hebrews 5:5-14**
>
> **Solid food belongs to those who are of full age.** v. 14

The Bible uses a similar concept to describe a believer's need for spiritual food. The basic truths of Scripture are like milk—they help new Christians thrive and grow (1 PETER 2:2-3). In contrast, "Solid food belongs to those who are of full age" (HEB. 5:14). Believers who have had time to digest and understand the basics can move on to investigate other biblical concepts and begin to teach others these truths. The rewards of spiritual maturity are discernment (V. 14), godly wisdom (1 COR. 2:6), and the ability to communicate God's truth to others (HEB. 5:12).

Like a loving parent, God wants us to grow spiritually. He knows that feeding only on spiritual milk is not in our best interest. He wants us to move on so we can enjoy the taste of solid food. 🌱

JENNIFER BENSON SCHULDT

Dear Lord, please deepen my understanding of Your Word.
Let Your Holy Spirit guide me and enlighten my heart as I pursue
Your truth so that I might walk in Your ways.

Spiritual growth occurs when faith is cultivated.

Tear Down the Wall

The years following World War II were labeled the Cold War as nations exchanged threats and jockeyed for power. The Berlin Wall, built in August 1961, stood for almost 3 decades as one of the most powerful symbols of the smoldering animosity. Then, on November 9, 1989, it was announced that citizens could cross freely from East to West Berlin. The entire wall was demolished the following year.

TODAY'S READING
Genesis 50:15-21

He comforted them and spoke kindly to them. v. 21

The familiar Old Testament story of Joseph follows a favorite son whose brothers hated him (GEN. 37–50). Yet Joseph refused to build a wall of hatred between himself and his brothers who sold him into slavery. When a famine brought them face to face after many years, Joseph treated his brothers with kindness, saying, "You meant evil against me; but God meant it for good . . . . And he comforted them and spoke kindly to them" (50:20-21), helping to restore the relationship between them.

Over 25 years ago, an oppressive man-made barrier was opened, offering freedom and reuniting families and friends. If we've built walls of anger and separation between ourselves and others, the Lord is willing and able to help us begin tearing them down today. 🌿

DAVID MCCASLAND

Heavenly Father, examine my heart; reveal to me where I have erected walls in relationships. Show me the way to start tearing them down that there might be reconciliation.

Anger builds walls; love breaks them down.

The Honor of Following

While visiting Jerusalem, a friend of mine saw an old rabbi walking past the Wailing Wall. The interesting thing about the aged rabbi was the five young men walking behind him. They too were walking bent over, limping—just like their rabbi. An Orthodox Jew watching them would know exactly why they were imitating their teacher. They were "followers."

TODAY'S READING
Matthew 4:18-22

Then [Jesus] said to them, "Follow Me." v. 19

Throughout the history of Judaism, one of the most honored positions for a Jewish man was the privilege of becoming a "follower" of the local rabbi. Followers sat at the rabbi's feet as he taught. They would study his words and watch how he acted and reacted to life and others. A follower would count it the highest honor to serve his rabbi in even the most menial tasks. And, because they admired their rabbi, they were determined to become like him.

When Jesus called His disciples to follow Him (MATT. 4:19), it was an invitation to be changed by Him, to become like Him, and to share His passion for those who need a Savior. The high honor of being His follower should show in our lives as well. We too have been called to catch the attention of the watching world as we talk, think, and act just like Jesus—the rabbi, the teacher, of our souls. 🌱   *JOE STOWELL*

Thank You, Lord, for the high honor of being called to follow You.
May my life so imitate You that others will know that You are the
pursuit of my life and the rabbi of my soul.

Follow Jesus and let the world know He is your rabbi.

The Drinking Gourd

Prior to the American Civil War (1861–1865), fugitive slaves found freedom by following the Underground Railroad, a term for the secret routes from the South to the North and the abolitionists who helped them along the way. Slaves would travel at night for many miles, keeping on track by following the light of the "Drinking Gourd." This was a code name for the collection of stars known as the Big Dipper, which points to the North Star. Some believe the fugitives also used encoded directions in the lyrics of the song "Follow the Drinking Gourd" to keep them from getting lost as they traveled.

> TODAY'S READING
> **Philippians 2:12-18**
>
> **Shine as lights in the world, holding fast the word of life.** vv. 15-16

Both the abolitionists and the "drinking gourd" served as points of light directing the slaves to freedom. The apostle Paul says that believers are to shine as "lights in the world" to show the way to those seeking God's truth, redemption, and spiritual liberation (PHIL. 2:15).

We live in a dark world that desperately needs to see the light of Jesus Christ. Our calling is to shine forth God's truth so that others can be directed to the One who redeems and is the path to liberty and life. We point the way to Jesus, the One who is the way, the truth, and the life (JOHN 14:6). 🌾

DENNIS FISHER

Dear Lord, thank You for redeeming me and giving me new life.
Give me compassion for those who are still lost in spiritual
darkness. Use me to be a light that points others to You,
the Light of the world.

Light up your world by reflecting the light of Jesus.

The Final Picture

What started as an empty 11-acre field in Belfast, Northern Ireland, ended up as the largest land portrait in the British Isles. *Wish*, by artist Jorge Rodriguez-Gerada, is made from 30,000 wooden pegs, 2,000 tons of soil, 2,000 tons of sand, and miscellaneous items such as grass, stones, and string.

> **TODAY'S READING**
> **Isaiah 40:21-31**
>
> **Lift up your eyes on high, and see who has created these things.** v. 26

At the beginning, only the artist knew what the final artwork was going to look like. He hired workers and recruited volunteers to haul materials and move them into place. As they worked, they saw little indication that something amazing was about to emerge. But it did. From the ground, it doesn't look like much. But from above, viewers see a huge portrait—the smiling face of a little girl.

God is doing something on a grander scale in the world. He's the artist who sees the final picture. We're His "fellow workers" (1 COR. 3:9) who are helping to make it a reality. Through the prophet Isaiah, God reminded His people that it is He who "sits above the circle of the earth" and "stretches out the heavens like a curtain" (ISA. 40:22). We can't see the final picture, but we continue on in faith, knowing that we're part of an amazing work of art—one that is being created on earth but will be best seen from heaven. ❡ *JULIE ACKERMAN LINK*

While sometimes I think I can see the big picture, Lord,
my heart knows it sees so little. I'm thankful that You are working
out Your beautiful will in this world, and I can trust You.

God is using us to help create a masterpiece.

Creeping Christmas?

I love Christmas. The celebration of the birth of Christ and the beauty and wonder of the season make it "the most wonderful time of the year" for me. In recent years, however, the season has been accompanied by a growing irritation. Every year "Christmas stuff" comes out earlier and earlier—creeping all the way back to early fall.

Christmas used to be limited to December, but now we find radio stations playing Christmas music in early November. Stores start advertising Christmas specials in October, and Christmas candy appears in late September. If we're not careful, this growing deluge can numb us—even sour us to what should be a season of gratitude and awe.

TODAY'S READING
Galatians 4:1-7

Thanks be to God for His indescribable gift!
2 Corinthians 9:15

When that irritation begins to rise in my spirit, I try to do one thing: Remember. I remind myself what Christmas means, who Jesus is, and why He came. I remember the love and grace of a forgiving God who sent us rescue in the Person of His Son. I remember that, ultimately, only one gift really matters—God's "indescribable gift!" (2 COR. 9:15). I remember that the salvation Christ came to provide is both the gift and the Giver all wrapped up in one.

Jesus is our life all year long, and He is the greatest wonder. "O come, let us adore Him!" 🌸

BILL CROWDER

Living God, I thank You for the unspeakable gift of Your Son.
Draw my heart to Your own, that my worship to and gratitude
for Your Son will never be diminished by the distractions of the
world around me.

Jesus is our life throughout the year.

Heartbreak and Hope

When American country singer George Jones died at the age of 81, his fans remembered his remarkable voice and his hard life and personal struggles. While many of his songs reflected his own despair and longing, it was the way he sang them that touched people deeply. *Chicago Tribune* music critic Greg Kot said, "His voice was made for conveying heartbreak."

> TODAY'S READING
> **Lam. 3:1-6,16-25**
>
> **The LORD is good to those who wait for Him.** v. 25

The book of Lamentations records Jeremiah's anguish over the nation of Judah's stubborn refusal to follow God. Often called "the weeping prophet," he witnessed the destruction of Jerusalem and saw his people carried into captivity. He wandered the streets of the city, overwhelmed by grief (LAM. 1:1-5).

Yet, in Jeremiah's darkest hour, he said, "This I recall to my mind, therefore I have hope. Through the LORD's mercies we are not consumed, because His compassions fail not. They are new every morning; great is Your faithfulness" (3:21-23).

Whether we suffer for our own choices or from those of others, despair may threaten to overwhelm us. When all seems lost, we can cling to the Lord's faithfulness. "'The LORD is my portion,' says my soul. 'Therefore I hope in Him!'" (V. 24). 🌱

DAVID MCCASLAND

I'm thankful for Your faithfulness, Father, even in the times when I am unfaithful. Help me to remember, like Jeremiah, that my hope comes from You, not from my circumstances.

The anchor of God's faithfulness holds firm in the strongest storms.

Windfall

Upon winning **$314 million** in a 2002 lottery, a happy business owner expressed noble desires. He wanted to start a charitable foundation, put laid-off workers back on the job, and do nice things for his family. Already wealthy, he told reporters the big win wouldn't change him.

A few years later, a follow-up arti- cle described a different outcome. Since winning the biggest of all lotteries, the man had run into legal problems, lost his personal reputation, and gambled away all of his money.

> TODAY'S READING
> **Proverbs 30:1-9**
>
> **Give us this day our daily bread.**
> Matthew 6:11

A thoughtful man by the name of Agur wrote words that anticipate such heartbreak. Brought low by the awareness of his own natural inclinations (PROV. 30:2-3), Agur saw the dangers of having too much or too little. So he prayed, "Give me nei- ther poverty nor riches—feed me with the food allotted to me; lest I be full and deny You, and say, 'Who is the LORD?' Or lest I be poor and steal, and profane the name of my God" (VV. 8-9).

Agur saw the special challenges that come both with wealth and poverty, but also with our own tendencies. Each gives us reason for caution. Together they show our need for the One who taught us to pray, "Give us this day our daily bread." ❧ *MART DEHAAN*

Lord, as we seek Your face today to ask for what we need, help us to keep in mind that You are as wise in what You don't give us as what You do give us. So often, You rescue us from our own sinful tendencies. Thank You.

*Discontentment makes rich people poor,
while contentment makes poor people rich.*

Amazing Guide

When actors and actresses make a movie, it's the director who sees the "big picture" and the overall direction. Actress Marion Cotillard admits she didn't understand everything the director was doing in one of her recent films. She said, "I found it very interesting to allow myself to be lost, because I knew that I had this amazing guide.... You abandon yourself for a story and a director that will make it all work."

I think Joshua could have said something similar about the director of his life. In today's Scripture passage, the newly commissioned leader of Israel is standing at the threshold of the Promised Land. More than 2 million Israelites are looking to him to lead them. How would

> **TODAY'S READING**
> **Joshua 1:1-9**
>
> **Not a word failed of any good thing which the LORD had spoken.** 21:45

he do it? God didn't give him a detailed script, but He gave him the assurance that He would go with him.

God said, "I will be with you. I will not leave you" (JOSH. 1:5). He commanded Joshua to study and practice everything written in His Word (VV. 7-8), and He promised to be with Joshua wherever he went. Joshua responded with complete devotion and surrender to his amazing Guide, and "not a word failed of any good thing which the LORD had spoken" (21:45).

We too can abandon ourselves to our Director and rest in His faithfulness. 🌿

POH FANG CHIA

He leadeth me! O blessed thought!
O words with heavenly comfort fraught!
Whate'er I do, where'er I be,
Still 'tis God's hand that leadeth me. GILMORE

Faith never knows where it is being led; it knows and loves the One who is leading. OSWALD CHAMBERS

Defeated Adversary

The roaring lion is the legendary "king of the jungle." But the only lions many of us see are the lethargic felines that reside in zoos. Their days are filled with lots of rest, and their dinner is served to them without the lions having to lift a single paw.

In their natural habitat, however, lions aren't always living a laid-back life. Their hunger tells them to go hunting, and in doing so they seek the young, weak, sick, or injured. Crouching in tall grasses, they slowly creep forward. Then with a sudden pounce, they clamp their jaws to the body of their victim.

TODAY'S READING
Ephesians 6:10-18

Be sober, be vigilant; because your adversary the devil walks about like a roaring lion, seeking whom he may devour. 1 Peter 5:8

Peter used "a roaring lion" as a metaphor for Satan. He is a confident predator, looking for easy prey to devour (1 PETER 5:8). In dealing with this adversary, God's children must be vigilant at putting "on the whole armor of God" and thus they can "be strong in the Lord and in the power of His might" (EPH. 6:10-11).

The good news is that Satan is a defeated adversary. While he is a powerful foe, those who are protected by salvation, prayer, and the Word of God need not be paralyzed in fear at this roaring lion. We are "kept by the power of God" (1 PETER 1:5). James 4:7 assures us: "Resist the devil and he will flee from you." ❧   *CINDY HESS KASPER*

Lord, we know that our enemy seeks to devour us. Please protect us from him. We believe Your Word that He who is in us is greater than he who is in the world.

No evil can penetrate the armor of God.

Rooted Love

When I think of all the wonders of God's magnificent creation, I am especially awed by the giant sequoia tree. These amazing behemoths of the forest can grow to around 300 feet tall with a diameter that exceeds 20 feet. They can live over 3,000 years and are even fire resistant. In fact, forest fires pop the sequoia cones open, distributing their seeds on the forest floor that has been fertilized by the ashes. Perhaps the most amazing fact is that these trees can grow in just 3 feet of soil and withstand high winds. Their

TODAY'S READING
Hebrews 13:15-25

Do not forget to do good and to share. v. 16

strength lies in the fact that their roots intertwine with other sequoias, providing mutual strength and shared resources.

God's plan for us is like that. Our ability to stand tall in spite of the buffeting winds of life is directly related to the love and support we receive from God and one another. And then, as the writer of Hebrews says, we are to "do good and to share" (13:16). Think of how tough it would be to withstand adversity if someone were not sharing the roots of their strength with us.

There is great power in the entwining gifts of words of encouragement, prayers of intercession, weeping together, holding each other, and sometimes just sitting with one another sharing the presence of our love. 🌱   JOE STOWELL

Lord, thank You for entwining Your strength into my life.
Lead me today to someone who needs the love of shared
strength from resources that You have given to me.

***Let the roots of God's love in your life be entwined
with others who need your support.***

Goodbye

When **Max Lucado** participated in a half-Ironman triathlon, he experienced the negative power of complaint. He said, "After the 1.2-mile swim and the 56-mile bike ride, I didn't have much energy left for the 13.1-mile run. Neither did the fellow jogging next to me. He said, 'This stinks. This race is the dumbest decision I've ever made.' I said, 'Goodbye.'" Max knew that if he listened too long, he would start agreeing with him. So he said goodbye and kept running.

> TODAY'S READING
> **Numbers 11:1-10**
>
> **When the people complained, it displeased the LORD; for the LORD heard it, and His anger was aroused.** V. 1

Among the Israelites, too many people listened too long to complaints and began to agree with them. This displeased God, and for good reason. God had delivered the Israelites from slavery, and agreed to live in their midst, but they still complained. Beyond the hardship of the desert, they were dissatisfied with God's provision of manna. In their complaint, Israel forgot that the manna was a gift to them from God's loving hand (NUM. 11:6). Because complaining poisons the heart with ingratitude and can be a contagion, God had to judge it.

This is a sure way to say "goodbye" to complaining and ingratitude: Each day, let's rehearse the faithfulness and goodness of God to us. 🌐   *MARVIN WILLIAMS*

Lord, You have given us so much. Forgive us for our short memories and bad attitudes. Help us to remember and be grateful for all that You have provided. And help us to tell others of the good things You have done for us.

Proclaiming God's faithfulness silences discontentment.

Can You Help?

The administrators of the high school in Barrow, Alaska, were tired of seeing students get into trouble and drop out at a rate of 50 percent. To keep students interested, they started a football team, which offered them a chance to develop personal skills, teamwork, and learn life lessons. The problem with football in Barrow, which is farther north than Iceland, is that it's hard to plant a grass field. So they competed on a gravel and dirt field.

> **TODAY'S READING**
> **James 2:14-20**
>
> **Faith by itself, if it does not have works, is dead.** v. 17

Four thousand miles away in Florida, a woman named Cathy Parker heard about the football team and their dangerous field. Feeling that God was prompting her to help, and impressed by the positive changes she saw in the students, she went to work. About a year later, they dedicated their new field, complete with a beautiful artificial-turf playing surface. She had raised thousands of dollars to help some kids she didn't even know.

This is not about football—or money. It is about remembering "to do good and to share" (HEB. 13:16). The apostle James reminds us that we demonstrate our faith by our actions (2:18). The needs in our world are varied and overwhelming but when we love our neighbor as ourselves, as Jesus said (MARK 12:31), we reach people with God's love. 🌿   *DAVE BRANON*

Open our eyes, dear Father, to those in need. Allow us to find ways—momentarily and otherwise—to help meet those needs. Help us to take the focus off ourselves and to place it on those who can use our assistance.

Open your heart to God to learn compassion
and open your hand to give help.

Dealing with Distractions

A restaurant owner in the village of Abu Ghosh, just outside Jerusalem, offered a 50-percent discount for patrons who turned off their cell phones. Jawdat Ibrahim believes that smartphones have shifted the focus of meals from companionship and conversation to surfing, texting, and business calls. "Technology is very good," Ibrahim says. "But . . . when you are with your family and your friends, you can just wait for half an hour and enjoy the food and enjoy the company."

TODAY'S READING
Matthew 13:14-22

The cares of this world . . . choke the word. v. 22

How easily we can be distracted by many things, whether in our relationship with others or with the Lord.

Jesus told His followers that spiritual distraction begins with hearts that have grown dull, ears that are hard of hearing, and eyes that are closed (MATT. 13:15). Using the illustration of a farmer scattering seed, Jesus compared the seed that fell among thorns to a person who hears God's Word but whose heart is focused on other things. "The cares of this world and the deceitfulness of riches choke the word, and he becomes unfruitful" (V. 22).

There is great value in having times throughout each day when we turn off the distractions of mind and heart and focus on the Lord. 🌱   *DAVID MCCASLAND*

O Lord, help me to turn off all the distractions around
me and focus on You. May my heart be good soil for the
seed of Your Word today.

Focusing on Christ puts everything else in perspective.

The Warmth of the Sun

On a **November day** in 1963, the Beach Boys' Brian Wilson and Mike Love wrote a song quite unlike the band's typically upbeat tunes. It was a mournful song about love that's been lost. Mike said later, "As hard as that kind of loss is, the one good that comes from it is having had the experience of being in love in the first place." They titled it "The Warmth of the Sun."

Sorrow serving as a catalyst for songwriting is nothing new. Some of David's most moving psalms were penned in times of deep personal loss, including Psalm 6. Though we aren't told the events that prompted its writing, the lyrics are filled with grief: "I am weary with my groaning; all night I make my bed swim, I drench my couch with my tears. My eye wastes away because of grief" (vv. 6-7).

> **TODAY'S READING**
> **Psalm 6**
>
> **I am weary with my groaning; all night I make my bed swim; I drench my couch with my tears.** v. 6

But that's not where the song ends. David knew pain and loss, but he also knew God's comfort. And so he wrote, "The LORD has heard my supplication; the LORD will receive my prayer" (v. 9).

In his grief, David not only found a song, he also found reason to trust God, whose faithfulness bridges all of life's hard seasons. In the warmth of His presence, our sorrows gain a hopeful perspective. 🌿

BILL CROWDER

Heavenly Father, life can be so wonderful, but also so hard.
Help us to seek You in the good times as well as the bad.
Help us to always be mindful that You are our sure hope in a
world that doesn't always seem to care.

*A song of sadness can turn our hearts to the God
whose joy for us is forever.*

Outlasting Bitterness

During the Second World War, Corrie ten Boom's family owned a watchmaking business in the Netherlands, and they actively worked to protect Jewish families. Eventually, the entire ten Boom family was sent to a concentration camp, where Corrie's father died 10 days later. Her sister Betsie also died in the camp. While Betsie and Corrie were in the camp together, Betsie's faith helped to strengthen Corrie's.

TODAY'S READING
Colossians 3:12-17

If anyone has a complaint against another; even as Christ forgave you, so you also must do. v. 13

That faith led Corrie to forgive even the ruthless men who served as guards during her concentration camp days. While hate and the desire for revenge continued to destroy many lives long after the concentration camps were gone, Corrie knew the truth: Hate hurts the hater more than the hated, no matter how justified it may seem.

Like Corrie, we each have the opportunity to love our enemy and choose forgiveness. Forgiveness doesn't excuse the offense, but when we forgive we show Christ to the world. "Be kind to one another, tenderhearted, forgiving one another, even as God in Christ forgave you" (EPH. 4:32).

God will help you let go of every angry grudge as you watch the Spirit build into you a place where others see the Savior. 🌿

RANDY KILGORE

The love of God within our hearts
Enables us to show
Forgiveness that is undeserved
So others too might know. SPER

*When we forgive someone, we look more like Jesus
than at any other moment in our life.*

Hope in Suffering

When I opened my Bible to read Jeremiah 1 through 4, the subhead ascribed to the book startled me: "Hope in Time of Weeping." I almost cried. The timing was perfect, as I was walking through a season of weeping over the death of my mom.

I felt much the same way after hearing my pastor's sermon the day before. The title was "Joy in Suffering," taken from 1 Peter 1:3-9. He gave us an illustration from his own life: the one-year anniversary of his father's death. The sermon was meaningful for many, but for me it was a gift from God. These and other events were indications backed up by His Word that God would not leave me alone in my grief.

> **TODAY'S READING**
> **1 Peter 1:3-9**
>
> In this [living hope] you greatly rejoice, though now . . . you have been grieved by various trials. v. 6

Even though the way of sorrow is hard, God sends reminders of His enduring presence. To the Israelites expelled from the Promised Land due to disobedience, God made His presence known by sending prophets like Jeremiah to offer them hope—hope for reconciliation through repentance. And to those He leads through times of testing, He shows His presence through a community of believers who "love one another fervently with a pure heart" (1 PETER 1:22). These indications of God's presence during trials on earth affirm God's promise of the living hope awaiting us at the resurrection. 🌱

JULIE ACKERMAN LINK

Does Jesus care when I've said goodbye
To the dearest on earth to me,
And my sad heart aches till it nearly breaks,
Is it aught to Him? Does He see? O yes, He cares! GRAEFF

We need never be ashamed of our tears. DICKENS

Resting in God

t was our last holiday together as a family before our eldest son went off to college. As we filled the back pew in the little seaside church, my heart filled with love as I glanced along the row of my five reasonably tidy children. "Please protect them spiritually and keep them close to You, Lord." I prayed silently, thinking of the pressures and challenges each of them faced.

The final hymn had a rousing chorus based on the words of 2 Timothy 1:12. "I know whom I have believed, and am persuaded that He is able to keep what I have committed to Him." It brought a sense of peace as I was assured that God would keep their souls.

Years have passed since then. There have been times of wandering for some of my children, and outright rebellion for others. Sometimes I've wondered about God's faithfulness. Then I remember Abraham. He stumbled but never failed in his trust in the promise he'd received (GEN. 15:5-6; ROM. 4:20-21). Through years of waiting and mistaken attempts to help things along, Abraham hung on to God's promise until Isaac was born.

> TODAY'S READING
> **Romans 4:16-22**
>
> **He did not waver ... through unbelief ... being fully convinced that what [God] had promised He was also able to perform.** vv. 20-21

I find this reminder to trust encouraging. We tell God our request. We remember that He cares. We know He is powerful. We thank Him for His faithfulness. ❧

MARION STROUD

Lord, my patience is often lacking and my timetable often does not match Yours. Forgive me for my times of doubt, and help me to trust You more. Thank You for Your faithfulness.

Some lessons of patience take a long time to learn.

God Whispers "Fish"

A number of years ago our sons and I enjoyed some days together drifting and fishing the Madison River in Montana with two fishing guides who also served as our boatmen.

The guide I drew was a man who had lived on the river all his life and knew where the big trout held. He was a quiet man who spoke scarcely two dozen words in all the time he was with us, but his few words enlivened my days.

> **TODAY'S READING**
> **Luke 5:1-10**
>
> **From now on you will catch men.** v. 10

We were fishing with small flies in choppy water. My eyesight was not what it once was, and I was missing most of the takes. My guide—who was also a soul of patience— began to alert me by murmuring "fish" when he saw a trout rising under the fly. When I heard his cue, I lifted the tip of my rod and . . . voilà! A trout on the end of my line!

I've often thought of that guide and Jesus' declaration to His fishermen-disciples, "From now on you will catch men" (LUKE 5:10). There are great opportunities that come our way every day—people circling around us, searching for that elusive "something" for which their souls crave—occasions to show the love of Christ and speak of the hope that is in us. These are opportunities we might miss if not alerted.

May the Great Angler, who knows every heart, whisper "fish" in our ears and may we have ears to hear. 🌸 *DAVID ROPER*

All through this day, O Lord, let me touch as many lives as possible for You—through the words I speak, the prayers I breathe, the letters I write, and the life I live.

When the Spirit prompts, take action.

A Lesson in Praise

P salm 150 is not only a beautiful expression of praise, it's also a lesson in praising the Lord. It tells us where to praise, why we're to praise, how we're to praise, and who should offer praise.

Where do we praise? In God's "sanctuary" and "mighty firmament" (V. 1). Wherever we are in the world is a proper place to praise the One who created all things.

Why do we praise? First, because of what God does. He performs "mighty acts." Second, because of who God is. The psalmist praised Him for "His excellent greatness" (V.2). The all-powerful Creator is the Sustainer of the universe.

> TODAY'S READING
> **Psalm 150**
>
> **Praise the LORD!** v. 1

How should we praise? Loudly. Softly. Soothingly. Enthusiastically. Rhythmically. Boldly. Unexpectedly. Fearlessly. In other words, we can praise God in many ways and on many occasions (VV. 3-5).

Who should praise? "Everything that has breath" (V. 6). Young and old. Rich and poor. Weak and strong. Every living creature. God's will is for everyone to whom He gave the breath of life to use that breath to acknowledge His power and greatness.

Praise is our enthusiastic expression of gratitude to God for reigning in glory forever. 🌿

JULIE ACKERMAN LINK

Let every creature rise and bring
Peculiar honors to our King;
Angels descend with songs again,
And earth repeat the loud amen! WATTS

Praise is the overflow of a joyful heart.

Amani

Amani, which means "peace" in Swahili, is the name of a Labrador retriever pup that has some special friends. Amani lives with two young cheetahs at the Dallas Zoo. Zoologists placed the animals together so the cheetahs could learn Amani's relaxed ways. Since dogs are generally at ease in public settings, the experts predict that Amani will be a "calming influence" in the cheetahs' lives as they grow up together.

TODAY'S READING
1 Samuel 16:14-23

> God has not given us a spirit of fear, but of power and of love and of a sound mind.
>
> 2 Timothy 1:7

David was a soothing influence in King Saul's life when a "distressing spirit" troubled him (1 SAM. 16:14). When Saul's servants learned of his problem, they thought music might ease his affliction. One servant summoned David, who was a skilled harpist. Whenever the king became troubled, David would play the harp. "Then Saul would become refreshed and well" (V. 23).

We crave refreshment and well-being when we are plagued by anger, fear, or sadness. The God of the Bible is a "God of peace" (HEB. 13:20-21), One who gives His Holy Spirit to everyone who believes in Him. When we're agitated or anxious, we can remember that God's Spirit produces power, love, and self-control (2 TIM. 1:7). God's influence in our lives can create a calming effect—one that leads to comfort and wholeness. 🌱

JENNIFER BENSON SCHULDT

We're grateful, Father, for the peace that You offer for our hearts. Nothing has the power to take that away. Thank You that Your peace has come to stay.

Peace I leave with you, My peace I give to you;
not as the world gives do I give to you. JESUS

Happy Ending

n its "plot," the story of the Bible ends up very much where it began. The broken relationship between God and human beings has healed over at last, and the curse of Genesis 3 is lifted. Borrowing images from Eden, Revelation pictures a river and a tree of life (REV. 22:1-2). But this time a great city replaces the garden setting—a city filled with worshipers of God. No death or sadness will ever darken that scene. When we awake in the new heaven and new earth, we will have at last a happy ending.

> **TODAY'S READING**
> **Revelation 21:1-7**
>
> I saw a new heaven and a new earth. v. 1

Heaven is not an afterthought or an optional belief. It is the final justification of all creation. The Bible never belittles human tragedy and disappointment—is any book more painfully honest?—but it does add one key word: *temporary*. What we feel now, we will not always feel. The time for re-creation will come.

For people who feel trapped in pain or in a broken home, in economic misery or in fear—for all of us—heaven promises a timeless future of health and wholeness and pleasure and peace. The Bible begins with the promise of a Redeemer in the book of Genesis (3:15) and ends with that same promise (REV. 21:1-7)—a guarantee of future reality. The end will be the beginning. ❦   *PHILIP YANCEY*

Beyond earth's sorrows, the joys of heaven;
Eternal blessings with Christ my Lord;
Earth's weeping ended, earth's trials over,
Sweet rest in Jesus, O blest reward! GILMORE

The gains of heaven will more than compensate us for the losses of earth.

For Sale—"As Is"

A house listed for sale "As Is" usually means the seller is unable or unwilling to spend any money to repair it or make it attractive. Any necessary repairs or desired improvements are the responsibility of the buyer after the purchase is complete. "As Is" on a real estate listing is equivalent to saying, "Buyer beware. Home may require significant further investment."

TODAY'S READING
Revelation 5:1-12

For You were slain, and have redeemed us to God by Your blood. v. 9

How remarkable that when Jesus died, He paid the highest price for each of us, regardless of our condition. Revelation 5 describes a scene in heaven where only "The Lion of the tribe of Judah, the Root of David" is found worthy to open and read a sealed scroll (VV. 3-5). He appears as a Lamb and becomes the object of praise in a new song, "For You were slain, and have redeemed us to God by Your blood out of every tribe and tongue and people and nation, and have made us kings and priests to our God; and we shall reign on the earth" (VV. 9-10).

Jesus Christ willingly purchased us for God with His blood. We were bought "as is," faults, defects, needed renovation included. By faith we are now under His ownership, in the process of remodeling for God's glory. How wonderful that God knew us, loved us, and bought us just as we are. ✿

DAVID MCCASLAND

Jesus paid it all,
All to Him I owe.
Sin had left a crimson stain;
He washed it white as snow. HALL

God knows us inside and out. No renovation project is too big for Him.

Struggling with Addiction

Eric was struggling with an addiction, and he knew it. His friends and family members encouraged him to stop. He agreed that it would be best for his health and relationships, but he felt helpless. When others told him how they had quit their bad habits, he replied, "I'm happy for you, but I can't seem to stop! I wish I had never been tempted in the first place. I want God to take the desire away right now."

TODAY'S READING
Hebrews 4:14-16

God is faithful.
1 Corinthians 10:13

Immediate deliverance may happen for some, but most face a daily battle. While we don't always understand why the temptation doesn't go away, we can turn to God on whatever path we find ourselves. And perhaps that is the most important part of our struggle. We learn to exchange our futile efforts to change for complete dependence on God.

Jesus was tempted also, just as we are, so He understands what we're feeling (MARK 1:13). He sympathizes with our struggles (HEB. 4:15), and we can "come boldly to the throne of grace, that we may obtain mercy and find grace to help in time of need" (V. 16). He also uses others, including trained professionals, that we can lean on along the way.

Whatever battles we may be facing today, we know this— God loves us much more than we can imagine, and He is faithful to come to our assistance. 🌸   *ANNE CETAS*

FOR FURTHER THOUGHT
Read Matthew 4:1–11 about how Jesus handled temptations.
Also read 1 Corinthians 10:11–13 to learn how He can help us
when we are tempted.

We are not tempted because we are evil;
we are tempted because we are human.

Losing Our Way

An online survey conducted by a New York law firm reveals that 52 percent of Wall Street traders, brokers, investment bankers, and other financial service professionals have either engaged in illegal activity or believe they may need to do so in order to be successful. The survey concludes that these financial leaders "have lost their moral compass" and "accept corporate wrong-doing as a necessary evil."

In mentoring young Timothy, the apostle Paul warned that the love of money and the desire to get rich had caused some to lose their way. They had yielded to temptations and embraced many "foolish and harmful" desires (1 TIM. 6:9). Paul saw "the love of money" (not money itself) as a source of "all kinds of evil" (V. 10), especially the evil of trusting in money rather than depending on Christ.

> **TODAY'S READING**
> **1 Timothy 6:6-10**
>
> **The love of money is a root of all kinds of evil, for which some have strayed from the faith in their greediness.** v. 10

As we learn to see that Christ is the source of all we have, we will find contentment in Him rather than in material possessions. When we seek godliness rather than riches, we will gain a desire to be faithful with what we have been given.

Let's deliberately cultivate an attitude of contentment in God, and faithfully submit to Him, for our Provider will care for us. ❧

MARVIN WILLIAMS

Father, it's easy to see the problem that others have with
loving money. But I know I have my own struggles too. I need
Your help to learn thankfulness for all that You have given.
Grow in me an attitude of contentment in You.

To love money is to lose sight of the Source of life.

Whose Side Are You On?

In the heat of the American Civil War, one of President Lincoln's advisors said he was grateful that God was on the side of the Union. Lincoln replied, "Sir, my concern is not whether God is on our side; my greatest concern is to be on God's side, for God is always right."

TODAY'S READING
Psalm 73

It is good for me to draw near to God. v. 28

What a great challenge for us who assume that God is there to support our plans, our perspectives, our decisions, and our desires. However, Lincoln's reply reminds us that even our best plans may not be near to what God desires.

Clearly the psalmist wants to be on God's side when he pleads, "Search me, O God, and know my heart; . . . and see if there is any wicked way in me, and lead me in the way everlasting" (PS. 139:23-24). When we follow the psalmist's example to "draw near to God" (73:28), we can be certain that we are on His side, as His Spirit helps us measure every thought and action by His ways that are always right.

So, let's ask ourselves: Are we on the Lord's side? Being on His side means that we will reflect His love to the world around us in the way we interact with others. We will forgive, treat others justly, and seek peace. God's ways are always best. 🌿

JOE STOWELL

Father, teach us to search Your ways so that we may know
how to be on Your side of the critical issues in life.
Thank You that when we draw near to You, You draw near
to us with gifts of wisdom and discernment.

When you draw near to God, you are sure to be on His side.

Called by Name

At the beginning of the academic year, a school principal in our city pledged to learn the names of all 600 students in her school. Anyone who doubted her ability or resolve could look at her track record. During the previous year she had learned the names of 700 students, and prior to that, 400 children in a different school. Think of what it must have meant to these students to be recognized and greeted by name.

TODAY'S READING
Luke 19:1-10

[Jesus] looked up and saw him, and said to him, "Zacchaeus, make haste and come down, for today I must stay at your house." v. 5

The story of Zacchaeus and Jesus (LUKE 19:1-10) contains a surprising element of personal recognition. As Jesus passed through the city of Jericho, a wealthy tax collector named Zacchaeus climbed a tree in order to see Him. "When Jesus came to the place, He looked up and saw him, and said to him, 'Zacchaeus, make haste and come down, for today I must stay at your house'" (V. 5). Instead of ignoring Zacchaeus or saying "Hey, you in the tree," Jesus called him by name. From that moment on, his life began to change.

When it seems that no one knows you or cares who you are, remember Jesus. He knows us by name and longs for us to know Him in a personal way. Our Father in heaven sees us through His eyes of love and cares about every detail of our lives. 🌼

DAVID MCCASLAND

Father, thank You that my value in Your eyes is not determined by what I do but simply by the fact that You created me. Help me to recognize that same value in others as I represent You to the world.

Jesus knows you by name and longs for you to know Him.

Human Chess

Chess is an ancient game of strategy. Each player begins with 16 pieces on the chessboard with the goal of cornering his opponent's king. It has taken different forms over the years. One form is human chess, which was introduced around AD 735 by Charles Martel, duke of Austrasia. Martel would play the game on giant boards with real people as the pieces. The human pieces were costumed to reflect their status on the board and moved at the whim of the players—manipulating them to their own ends.

Could this human version of the game of chess be one that we sometimes play? We can easily become so driven by our goals that people become just one more pawn that we use to achieve them. The Scriptures, however, call us to a different view of those around us. We are to see people as created in the image of God (GEN. 1:26). They are objects of God's love (JOHN 3:16) and deserving of ours as well.

> **TODAY'S READING**
> **1 John 4:7-12**
>
> **Beloved, let us love one another, for love is of God; and everyone who loves is born of God and knows God.** v. 7

The apostle John wrote, "Beloved, let us love one another, for love is of God; and everyone who loves is born of God and knows God" (1 JOHN 4:7). Because God first loved us, we are to respond by loving Him and the people He created in His image. 🌿   *BILL CROWDER*

Open my eyes, Lord, to people around me,
Help me to see them as You do above;
Give me the wisdom and strength to take action,
So others may see the depth of Your love. KURT DEHAAN

People are to be loved, not used.

Better Than Before

As infants, my children had nearly perfect skin. Their flesh was soft—they had no dry elbows or rough patches on their feet. Smooth and new, it contrasted with mine, which was marked by years of various scars and callouses.

As a mighty warrior and the commander of the Syrian army, Naaman may have had scuffed skin and battle scars, but he also had a serious skin disease—leprosy. When a servant suggested that the prophet Elisha could heal him, Naaman visited him. He followed Elisha's instructions, and his diseased flesh became "like the flesh of a little child" (2 KINGS 5:14). This cure left Naaman better off both physically and spiritually. After being healed, he proclaimed, "Now I know that there is no God in all the earth, except in Israel" (V. 15). Through this miraculous experience, he learned that there is only one true God (1 COR. 8:6).

> TODAY'S READING
> **2 Kings 5:1-15**
>
> **[Naaman's] flesh was restored like the flesh of a little child.** v. 14

Like Naaman, we can learn important lessons about God as a result of our life experiences. Receiving a blessing may show us about His mercy and goodness (MATT. 7:11). Surviving or enduring a trial may help us see God's sufficiency and care. Growing in knowledge of Him (2 PETER 3:18) will always leave us better off spiritually than we were before. 🌱

JENNIFER BENSON SCHULDT

Father, help me to learn more about You as I travel through this world. Let this knowledge inspire fresh praise in my heart and a desire to become more like You.

Lessons about God are embedded in life experiences.

Johnny's Race

When 19-year-old Johnny Agar finished the 5k race, he had a lot of people behind him—family members and friends who were celebrating his accomplishment.

Johnny has cerebral palsy, which makes physical activity difficult. But he and his dad, Jeff, have teamed up to compete in many races— Dad pushing and Johnny riding. But one day, Johnny wanted to finish by himself. Halfway through the race, his dad took him out of his cart, helped him to his walker, and assisted Johnny as he completed the race on his own two feet.

> **TODAY'S READING**
> **Hebrews 10:19-25**
>
> **Comfort each other and edify one another.**
> 1 Thessalonians 5:11

That led to a major celebration as friends and family cheered his accomplishment. "It made it easier for me to do it with them behind me," Johnny told a reporter. "The encouragement is what drove me."

Isn't that what Christ-followers are meant to do? Hebrews 10:24 reminds us, "Let us consider how we may spur one another on toward love and good deeds" (NIV). As we model the love of our Savior (JOHN 13:34-35), imagine the difference it could make if we all set out to encourage each other— if we always knew that behind us we had a group of friends cheering us on. If we took the words "comfort each other and edify one another" (1 THESS. 5:11) seriously, the race would be easier for all of us. ❧ *DAVE BRANON*

Help us, Lord, not to think that we can go through life without others. Cure us of our independent spirit. Use us to bless others and humble us to accept encouragement.

A word of encouragement can make the difference between giving up or going on.

Stones Cry Out

Every year it seems that Christmas becomes more and more commercialized. Even in nations where the majority of people call themselves "Christian," the season has become more about shopping than worshiping. The pressure to buy gifts and plan elaborate parties makes it increasingly difficult to stay focused on the real meaning of the holiday—the birth of Jesus, God's only Son, the Savior of the world.

But every holiday I also hear the gospel coming from surprising places—the very places that so commercialize Christmas—shopping malls. When I hear "Joy to the World! The Lord is come" ringing from public address systems, I think of the words Jesus said to the Pharisees who told Him to silence the crowds who were praising Him. "If they keep quiet," Jesus said, "the stones will cry out" (LUKE 19:40 NIV).

> **TODAY'S READING**
> **Luke 19:28-40**
>
> I tell you that if these should keep silent, the stones would immediately cry out. v. 40

At Christmas we hear stones cry out. Even people spiritually dead sing carols written by Christians long dead, reminding us that no matter how hard people try to squelch the real message of Christmas, they will never succeed.

Despite the commercialism that threatens to muddle the message of Christ's birth, God will make His good news known as "far as the curse is found." ❧

JULIE ACKERMAN LINK

No more let sins and sorrows grow,
Nor thorns infest the ground;
He comes to make His blessings flow
Far as the curse is found. WATTS

*Keeping Christ out of Christmas
is as futile as holding back the ocean's tide.*

Our Life Is a Primer

The New England Primer was published in the late 1600s. Throughout the colonies that would later become the United States, the book became a widely used resource.

This early American textbook was based largely on the Bible, and it used pictures and rhymes based on Scripture to help children learn to read. It also included prayers like this one: "Now I lay me down to sleep, I pray the Lord, my soul to keep. If I should die before I wake, I pray the Lord my soul to take."

In Colonial America, this became a way that one generation was able to pass along their faith to the next generation. It fit well with what God wanted of His people, the ancient Israelites, as recorded in Deuteronomy 6:6–7, "These words which I command you today shall be in your heart. You shall teach [God's commandments] diligently to your children, and shall talk of them . . . when you walk by the way, when you lie down, and when you rise up."

TODAY'S READING
Deuteronomy 6:4-9

You shall teach them diligently to your children . . . when you walk by the way, when you lie down, and when you rise up. v. 7

As we talk about who God is, what He has done for us, and how He desires our love and obedience, our lives can become primers to the next generation. We can be teaching tools that God will use to help people in their walk with Him. 🍂

DENNIS FISHER

Lord, we love You. We want to learn to love You with all our
heart, soul, and strength. Use our lives and our words to point
others to You, who first loved us.

When we teach others, we're not just spending time, we're investing it.

Wonders of the Heart

O ur heart beats about 100,000 times every day, pumping blood to every cell in our bodies. This adds up to about 35 million beats a year and 2.5 billion beats in an average lifetime. Medical science tells us that every contraction is similar to the effort it would take for us to hold a tennis ball in our palm and give it a good hard squeeze.

Yet as amazing as our heart is, it is only one example of a natural world that is designed to tell us something about our Creator. This is the idea behind the story of a man named Job.

TODAY'S READING
Job 38:1-11

By You I have been upheld from birth.
Psalm 71:6

Broken by a series of mounting troubles, Job felt abandoned. When God finally spoke, He didn't tell Job why he was suffering. Nor did the Creator tell him that someday He would suffer for Job. Instead, He drew Job's attention to a series of natural wonders that are always whispering to us—and sometimes shouting—about a wisdom and power far greater than our own (JOB 38:1-11).

So what can we learn from the complexity of this hard-working muscle, the heart? The message may be similar to the sound of waves coming to shore and stars quietly shining in the night sky. The power and wisdom of our Creator give us reason to trust Him. 🌿

MART DEHAAN

> Lord, we are Yours, You are our God;
> We have been made so wondrously;
> This human frame in every part
> Your wisdom, power, and love we see. ANON.

**When we reflect on the power of God's creation,
we see the power of His care for us.**

Snake in a Box

At a nature center, I watched my friend's rosy-cheeked toddler pat the side of a large glass box. Inside the box, a bull snake named Billy slithered slowly, eyeing the little girl. Billy's body was as thick as my forearm and he sported brown and yellow markings. Although I knew Billy could not escape from his container, seeing a menacing-looking creature so close to a small child made me shudder.

> **TODAY'S READING**
> **Isaiah 11:1-9**
>
> **The earth shall be full of the knowledge of the LORD.** v. 9

The Bible speaks of a time in the future when fierce animals will fail to threaten each other or human beings. "The wolf . . . shall dwell with the lamb" and "the nursing child shall play by the cobra's hole" (ISA. 11:6,8). All the inhabitants of the world will experience total harmony and peace.

The Lord will establish this safe environment when He restores the world with His wisdom, might, and knowledge. At that time, He will judge the world with righteousness and justice (11:4). And everyone will acknowledge His greatness: "The earth shall be full of the knowledge of the Lord" (11:9).

We live in a broken world. Unfairness and discord, fear and pain are a very real part of our daily lives. But one day God will change everything, and "the Sun of Righteousness shall arise with healing in His wings" (MAL. 4:2). Then Jesus will rule the world in righteousness. 🌱 *JENNIFER BENSON SCHULDT*

> Be still, my soul: the hour is hast'ning on
> When we shall be forever with the Lord.
> When disappointment, grief, and fear are gone,
> Sorrow forgot, love's purest joys restored. VON SCHLEGEL

Leave final justice in the hands of a just God.

Snug As a Bug in a Rug!

When I was a child, my family lived in a house my father built in the cedar breaks west of Duncanville, Texas. Our house had a small kitchen-dinette area, two bedrooms, and a great room with a large stone fireplace in which we burned 2-foot-long cedar logs. That fireplace was the center of warmth in our home.

> **TODAY'S READING**
> **Psalm 91:9-16**
>
> **I will both lie down in peace, and sleep; for You alone, O LORD, make me dwell in safety.** 4:8

There were five people in our family: my father and mother, my sister, my cousin, and me. Since we had only two bedrooms, I slept year-round on a porch with canvas screens that rolled down to the floor. Summers were delightful; winters were cold.

I remember dashing from the warmth of the living room onto the porch, tiptoeing across the frost-covered plank floor in my bare feet, leaping into bed and burrowing under a great mountain of blankets. Then, when hail, sleet, or snow lashed our house and the wind howled through the eaves like a pack of wolves, I snuggled down in sheltered rest. "Snug as a bug in a rug," my mother used to say. I doubt that any child ever felt so warm and secure.

Now I know the greatest security of all: God Himself. I can "lie down in peace, and sleep" (PS. 4:8), knowing that He is my shelter from the stinging storms of life. Enveloped in the warmth of His love, I'm snug as a bug in a rug. 🌼 *DAVID ROPER*

> Leaning, leaning,
> Safe and secure from all alarms;
> Leaning, leaning,
> Leaning on the everlasting arms. HOFFMAN

No one is more secure than those who are in God's hands.

Another Hero of Christmas

or most of my life, I missed the importance of Joseph in the Christmas story. But after I became a husband and father myself, I had a greater appreciation for Joseph's tender character. Even before he knew how Mary had become pregnant, he decided that he wasn't going to embarrass or punish her for what seemed to be infidelity (MATT. 1:19).

I marvel at his obedience and humility, as he not only did what the angel told him (V.24) but also refrained from physical intimacy with Mary until after Jesus was born (V.25). Later we learn that Joseph was willing to flee his home to protect Jesus (2:13-23).

> **TODAY'S READING**
> **Matthew 1:18-25**
>
> Joseph her husband, being a just man, and not wanting to make her a public example, was minded to put her away secretly. v. 19

Imagine the pressure Joseph and Mary must have felt when they learned that Jesus would be theirs to raise and nurture! Imagine the complexity and pressure of having the Son of God living with you every moment of every day; a constant call to holiness by His very presence. What a man Joseph must have been to be trusted by God for this task! What a wonderful example for us to follow, whether we're raising our own children or those born to others who are now entrusted to us.

May God grant us the strength to be faithful like Joseph, even if we don't fully understand God's plan. 🌱 *RANDY KILGORE*

We know, Father, that Your wisdom is far above our limited understanding. We thank You that we can rely on You to carry out Your good plans for us. You are worthy of our faithfulness.

The secret of true service is absolute faithfulness wherever God places you.

A Special Birth

n the pages of Scripture, several baby-boy births stand out. Cain, the firstborn after creation. Isaac, the hope of Israel's future. Samuel, the answer to a mother's fervent prayer. All extremely important. All joyously expected. And all described exactly the same by the chroniclers of Scripture: In each case, we are told that the mother conceived and bore a son (GEN. 4:1; 21:2-3; 1 SAM. 1:20).

TODAY'S READING
Isaiah 7:10-15

Behold, the virgin shall conceive and bear a Son, and shall call His name Immanuel. v. 14

Now consider one more baby boy's birth. The description of this arrival was much more greatly detailed: a few words were clearly not enough to tell of Jesus' birth. In Micah, we were told where He would be born—Bethlehem (5:2). In Isaiah, that His mother would be a virgin (7:14), and that He was coming to save people from their sin (CH. 53).

In the New Testament, we were given such key information as what His name would be and why (MATT. 1:21), where He was born in fulfillment of prophecy (2:6), and how both His birth mother and His adoptive father were part of God's plan (1:16).

Jesus' birth stands above all births. His coming changed the world and can change our lives. Let's celebrate Him! 🌼

DAVE BRANON

Mild He lays His glory by,
Born that man no more may die.
Born to raise the sons of earth,
Born to give them second birth. WESLEY

Christ is the greatest gift known to man.

Story Stewards

Many people take great care to make sure their resources are used well after they die. They set up trusts, write wills, and establish foundations to guarantee that their assets will continue to be used for a good purpose after their life on earth is done. We call this good stewardship.

Equally important, however, is being good stewards of our life story. God commanded the Israelites not only to teach their children His laws but also to make sure they knew their family history. It was the responsibility of parents and grandparents to make sure their children knew the stories of how God had worked in their behalf (DEUT. 4:1-14).

> **TODAY'S READING**
> **Deuteronomy 4:1-9**
>
> **Take heed . . . lest you forget the things your eyes have seen. . . . And teach them to your children and your grandchildren.** v. 9

God has given each of us a unique story. His plan for our lives is individualized. Do others know what you believe and why? Do they know the story of how you came to faith and how God has worked in your life to strengthen your faith? Do they know how God has shown Himself faithful and has helped you through doubts and disappointments?

The faithfulness of God is a story that we have the privilege to pass on. Record it in some way and share it. Be a good steward of the story that God is telling through you. ❀

JULIE ACKERMAN LINK

How great, O God, Your acts of love!
Your saving deeds would now proclaim
That generations yet to come
May set their hope in Your great name. D. DEHAAN

A life lived for God leaves a lasting legacy.

A Ukrainian Christmas

The people of Ukraine include many wonderful elements in their observance of Christmas. Sometimes wisps of hay are placed on the dinner table as a reminder of the Bethlehem manger. Another portion of their celebration echoes the events of the night when the Savior entered the world. A Christmas prayer is offered and then the father in the household offers the greeting, "Christ is born!" The family then responds, "Let us glorify Him!"

> TODAY'S READING
> **Luke 2:6-14**
>
> **Glory to God in the highest, and on earth peace, goodwill toward men!** v. 14

These words draw my mind to the appearance of the angels in the sky over Bethlehem on the night Christ was born. The angel of the Lord declared, "For there is born to you this day in the city of David a Savior, who is Christ the Lord" (LUKE 2:11). The heavenly host responded, "Glory to God in the highest, and on earth peace, goodwill toward men!" (V. 14).

Those twin messages give such depth of meaning to this wonderful time of year. The Savior has come bringing forgiveness and hope—and He is deserving of all the worship we can give Him.

May all who know the wonder of His gift of eternal life join with the voices of that angelic host declaring, "Glory to God in the highest!" ✿
BILL CROWDER

> With th'angelic hosts proclaim,
> "Christ is born in Bethlehem!"
> Hark! the herald angels sing,
> "Glory to the newborn King!" WESLEY

***The spectacular glory of God's love for us
was revealed in the coming of Jesus.***

A Work in Progress

Pablo Casals was considered to be the preeminent cellist of the first half of the 20th century. When he was still playing his cello in the middle of his tenth decade of life, a young reporter asked, "Mr. Casals, you are 95 years old and the greatest cellist that ever lived. Why do you still practice 6 hours a day?"

Mr. Casals answered, "Because I think I'm making progress."

What a great attitude! As believers in Christ, we should never be satisfied to think we have reached some self-proclaimed pinnacle of spiritual success, but rather continue to "grow in the grace and knowledge of our Lord and Savior Jesus Christ" (2 PETER 3:18). Jesus reminds us in John 15:16 that He chose us to "go and bear fruit." The result of healthy growth is continuing to bear spiritual fruit throughout our lives. Our Lord promises: "I am the vine, you are the branches. He who abides in Me, and I in him, bears much fruit" (V. 5).

> **TODAY'S READING**
> **John 15:9-17**
>
> **Grow in the grace and knowledge of our Lord and Savior Jesus Christ.**
> 2 Peter 3:18

In a steady and faithful progression to become more and more like the One we love and serve, we can be confident that He who began "a good work" in us will continue it until it is finally finished on the day when He returns (PHIL. 1:6). 🕊

CINDY HESS KASPER

Closer yet I'd cling, my Savior,
You're the all-sufficient Vine;
You alone can make me fruitful,
Blessed source of strength divine. BOSCH

God's unseen work in our hearts produces fruit in our lives.

My Friends and I

John Chrysostom (347–407), archbishop of Constantinople, said this about friendship: "Such is friendship, that through it we love places and seasons; for as . . . flowers drop their sweet leaves on the ground around them, so friends impart favor even to the places where they dwell."

Jonathan and David illustrate the sweetness of a true friendship. The Bible records an intimate and immediate bond between them (1 SAM. 18:1). They kept their friendship alive by demonstrating their loyalty to each other (18:3; 20:16, 42; 23:18), as well as nurturing it by expressions of concern. Jonathan gave gifts to David (18:4) and watched out for him through many difficulties (19:1-2; 20:12-13).

> **TODAY'S READING**
> **1 Samuel 18:1-4; 23:15-18**
>
> **Then Jonathan and David made a covenant, because he loved him as his own soul.** 1 Samuel 18:3

In 1 Samuel 23:16, we see the highest moment of their friendship. When David was on the run from Saul, "Jonathan, Saul's son, arose and went to David in the woods and strengthened his hand in God." Friends help you find strength in God during the low points of life.

In a world where most relationships are about what we can get, let us be the type of friends who focus on what we can give. Jesus, our perfect Friend, demonstrated for us that "greater love has no one than this, than to lay down one's life for his friends" (JOHN 15:13).

POH FANG CHIA

Thank You, Lord, for the friends You've given me to love me in spite of my failures and weaknesses. Let me treat them as You treated Your friends. Bind us together in You and enable us to help one another.

The glory of life is to love, not to be loved; to give, not to get; to serve, not to be served.

The Heart of Christmas

Charles Dickens' novel *A Christmas Carol* was released on December 19, 1843, and has never been out of print. It tells the story of Ebenezer Scrooge, a wealthy, sour, stingy man who says, "Every idiot who goes about with 'Merry Christmas,' on his lips, should be boiled with his own pudding!" Yet, one Christmas Eve, Scrooge is radically changed into a generous and happy man. With great humor and insight, Dickens' book captures the universal longing for inner peace.

TODAY'S READING
1 Timothy 1:12-17

The grace of our Lord was exceedingly abundant, with faith and love which are in Christ Jesus. v. 14

As a young man, the apostle Paul opposed Jesus and His followers with a vengeful spirit. He "made havoc of the church, entering every house, and dragging off men and women, committing them to prison" (ACTS 8:3). But one day he encountered the risen Christ, and his life became a different story (9:1-16).

In a letter to Timothy, his son in the faith, Paul described that life-changing event by saying, even though he was "a blasphemer, a persecutor, and an insolent man . . . the grace of our Lord was exceedingly abundant, with faith and love which are in Christ Jesus" (1 TIM. 1:13-14).

Jesus was born into our world and gave His life so that we can be forgiven and transformed through faith in Him. This is the heart of Christmas! ❦   *DAVID MCCASLAND*

Then let us all with one accord
Sing praises to our heavenly Lord,
That hath made heaven and earth of naught,
And with His blood mankind hath bought.   ENGLISH CAROL

A change in behavior begins with Jesus changing our heart.

In Jesus' Name

One of my favorite collections of photos is of a family dinner. Preserved in an album are images of Dad, his sons and their wives, and his grandchildren in a time of thanksgiving and intercession.

Dad had suffered a series of strokes and was not as verbal as usual. But during that time of prayer, I heard him say with heartfelt conviction: "We pray in Jesus' name!" About a year later, Dad passed from this world into the presence of the One in whose name he placed such trust.

> **TODAY'S READING**
> **John 14:12-21**
>
> **Until now you have asked nothing in My name. Ask, and you will receive, that your joy may be full.** 16:24

Jesus taught us to pray in His name. The night before He was crucified, He gave a promise to His disciples: "Until now you have asked nothing in My name. Ask, and you will receive, that your joy may be full" (JOHN 16:24). But the promise of asking in Jesus' name is not a blank check that we might get anything to fulfill our personal whims.

Earlier that evening, Jesus taught that He answers requests made in His name so that He will bring glory to the Father (JOHN 14:13). And later that night, Jesus Himself prayed in anguish, "O My Father, if it is possible, let this cup pass from Me; nevertheless, not as I will, but as You will" (MATT. 26:39).

As we pray, we yield to God's wisdom, love, and sovereignty, and we confidently ask "in Jesus' name." 🕊 *DENNIS FISHER*

Father in heaven, help us worry less about what we can get
from You and more about what we can learn from You.
As Your followers said, "Increase our faith" (LUKE 17:5).

*Nothing lies beyond the reach of prayer except that
which lies outside the will of God.*

Just the Right Time

The conductor stood on the podium, his eyes scanning the choir and orchestra. The singers arranged the music in their folders, found a comfortable position for standing, and held the folder where they could see the conductor just over the top. Orchestra members positioned their music on the stand, found a comfortable position in their seats, and then sat still. The conductor waited and watched until everyone was ready. Then, with a downbeat of his baton, the sounds of Handel's "Overture to Messiah" filled the cathedral.

TODAY'S READING
Hebrews 9:11-22

Christ came as High Priest of the good things to come. v. 11

With the sound swirling around me, I felt I was immersed in Christmas—when God, at just the right moment, signaled the downbeat and set in motion an overture that started with the birth of the Messiah, the "High Priest of the good things to come" (HEB. 9:11).

Every Christmas, as we celebrate Christ's first coming with glorious music, I'm reminded that God's people, like choir and orchestra members, are getting ready for the next downbeat of the conductor when Christ will come again. On that day, we will participate with Him in the final movement of God's symphony of redemption—making all things new (REV. 21:5). In anticipation, we need to keep our eyes on the Conductor and make sure we are ready. 🌱 *JULIE ACKERMAN LINK*

Sound the soul-inspiring anthem,
Angel hosts, your harps attune;
Earth's long night is almost over,
Christ is coming—coming soon! MACOMBER

The advent of Christ celebrates His birth and anticipates His return.

Remember the Wrapping

At our house some Christmas events are the same each year. Among them is my wife Martie's appeal to the kids and grandkids as they attack their gifts: "Save the paper, we can use it next year!" Martie loves to give nice gifts, but she also appreciates the wrapping. Presentation is part of the beauty of the gift.

It makes me think of the wrapping Christ chose when He came as a redemptive gift to rescue us from our sinful selves. Jesus could have wrapped Himself in a mind-boggling show of power, lighting up the sky with His presence in a celestial show of glory. Instead, in a beautiful reversal of Genesis 1:26, He chose to wrap Himself "in the likeness of men" (PHIL. 2:7).

> **TODAY'S READING**
> **Philippians 2:5-11**
>
> **[Jesus] made Himself of no reputation . . . coming in the likeness of men.** v. 7

So why is this wrapping so important? Because, being like us, He is no stranger to our struggles. He experienced deep loneliness and the betrayal of a dear friend. He was publicly shamed, misunderstood, and falsely accused. In short, He feels our pain. As a result, the writer of Hebrews tells us that we can "come boldly to the throne of grace, that we may obtain mercy and find grace to help in time of need" (HEB. 4:16).

When you think of the gift of Jesus this Christmas, remember to keep the "wrapping" in mind! 🌱　　*JOE STOWELL*

Lord, thank You for wrapping Yourself in our likeness! Remind us that You understand our struggles and that we can confidently take advantage of the mercy and grace You offer to make us victorious.

Don't disregard the wrapping of the best Christmas gift of all.

What Really Matters

When our children were living at home, one of our most meaningful Christmas morning traditions was very simple. We would gather our family around the Christmas tree where, in sight of the gifts we were receiving from one another, we would read the Christmas story together. It was a gentle reminder that the reason we give gifts is not because the Magi brought gifts to the Christ-child. Rather, our gifts of love for one another were a reflection of God's infinitely greater Gift of love to us.

TODAY'S READING
2 Cor. 9:10-15

Thanks be to God for His indescribable gift!
v. 15

As we rehearsed the familiar story of angels, shepherds, and the manger scene, it was our hope that the magnitude of what God had done that first Christmas would overshadow our best attempts at displaying our love for each other.

Nothing could ever match the gift God has given us in His Son, a reality which echoes in Paul's words to the church at Corinth, "Thanks be to God for His indescribable gift!" (2 COR. 9:15).

Clearly, God's willingness to send His Son to be our rescue is a gift that words cannot fully comprehend. This is the gift that we celebrate at Christmas—for Christ Himself is truly what matters most. 🌱

BILL CROWDER

'Twas a humble birthplace, but O how much
God gave to us that day;
From the manger bed what a path has led,
What a perfect, holy way! NEIDLINGER

Jesus Himself is the greatest Christmas gift ever given.

Lasting Peace

O n Christmas Eve 1914, during the First World War, the guns fell silent along a 30-mile stretch of the Western Front. Soldiers peered cautiously over the tops of trenches while a few emerged to repair their positions and bury the dead. As darkness fell, some German troops set out lanterns and sang Christmas carols. Men on the British side applauded and shouted greetings.

TODAY'S READING
Ephesians 2:13-19

He Himself is our peace, who has made both one, and has broken down the middle wall of separation. v. 14

The next day, German, French, and British troops met in no man's land to shake hands, share food, and exchange gifts. It was a brief respite from war that soon ended when the artillery and machine guns roared to life again. But no one who experienced "The Christmas Truce," as it became known, would ever forget how it felt and how it fueled their longing for lasting peace.

In Isaiah's prophecy of the coming Messiah we read, "His name will be called Wonderful, Counselor, Mighty God, Everlasting Father, Prince of Peace" (ISA. 9:6). By His death on the cross, Jesus removed the "no man's land" between us and God. "For He Himself is our peace" (EPH. 2:14).

In Jesus we can find lasting peace with God and harmony with each other. This is the life-changing message of Christmas! 🌿

DAVID MCCASLAND

Hark! The herald angels sing,
"Glory to the newborn King;
Peace on earth, and mercy mild,
God and sinners reconciled!" WESLEY

Only in Christ can true peace be realized.

The Smells of the Stable

A **stable?** What a place to give birth to the Messiah! The smells and sounds of a barnyard were our Savior's first human experience. Like other babies, He may even have cried at the sounds of the animals and the strangers parading around His temporary crib.

If so, they would have been the first of many tears. Jesus would come to know human loss and sorrow, the doubts his brothers and family had about Him, and the pain His mother experienced as she saw Him tortured and killed.

All these hardships—and so much more—awaited the baby trying to sleep that first night. Yet from His very first moments, Jesus was "God with us" (MATT. 1:23), and He knew what it meant to be human. This would continue for over three decades, ending at His death on the cross.

> TODAY'S READING
> **Luke 2:15-20**
>
> **They shall call His name Immanuel, which is translated, "God with us."** Matthew 1:23

Because of His love for you and me, Jesus became fully human. And being human allows Him to identify with us. Never again can we say that no one understands us. Jesus does.

May the Light that entered the world that night cast its brilliance into the deepest corners of our souls this Christmas, giving us the peace on Earth of which the angels spoke so long ago. 🍂

RANDY KILGORE

Father, help our hearts to know the love of Christ and to honor Him with our unyielding devotion in this and every season. We love You.

Jesus understands.

In the Neighborhood

t was the buzz of our neighborhood. A famous professional football player had moved in just two houses down from where we lived. We had seen him on television and read about his great skills on the field, but we never thought he would choose to reside in our neighborhood. Initially, our expectations were that we would wel-come him into the neighborhood and we would all become great friends. But his life was obviously far too busy for any of us to get to know him personally.

TODAY'S READING
John 1:1-14

The Word became flesh and dwelt among us. v. 14

Imagine this: Jesus—the Lord of the universe and Creator of all things—chose to dwell among us! He left heaven and came to this earth. As John says, "We beheld His glory, the glory as of the only begotten of the Father" (JOHN 1:14). Jesus chose to become intimately involved with all who will come to Him. And, even more significant, for those of us who have received His redeeming love, the Holy Spirit has now set up residence in our hearts to comfort, counsel, convict, lead, and teach us.

When you think of the Babe in the manger, remember how special it is that He not only moved into our "neighbor-hood," but that He did it so He could bless us with the inti-mate privileges of His residence within us. ❀   *JOE STOWELL*

Lord, I'm amazed that You, the greatest One of all,
would take up residence within us! Help us to treasure
the gift of Your presence as our ultimate joy.
Draw us to Yourself to enjoy intimacy with You.

Take advantage of the gift of God's presence.

Out of Egypt

One year when our family was traveling through Ohio on the way to Grandma's house, we arrived in Columbus just as a tornado warning was issued. Suddenly everything changed as we feared that our children might be in danger.

I mention that story to help us imagine what it was like for Joseph's family as he, Mary, and their young child traveled to Egypt. Herod, not a tornado, threatened them as he sought to kill their little boy. Imagine how frightening it was for them, knowing that "Herod [sought] the young Child to destroy Him" (MATT. 2:13).

TODAY'S READING
Matthew 2:13-21

Take the young Child and His mother, flee to Egypt. v. 13

We usually take a more idyllic view of Christmastime—lowing cattle and kneeling shepherds in a peaceful scene. But there was no peace for Jesus' family as they sought to escape Herod's horror. Only when an angel told them it was safe did the family go out of Egypt and back home to Nazareth (VV. 20-23).

Consider the awe we should feel for the incarnation. Jesus, who enjoyed the majesty of heaven in partnership with the Father, set it all aside to be born in poverty, to face many dangers, and to be crucified for us. Coming out of Egypt is one thing, but leaving heaven for us—that's the grand and amazing part of this story! 🌿 *DAVE BRANON*

Jesus our Savior left heaven above,
Coming to Earth as a Servant with love;
Laying aside all His glory He came,
Bringing salvation through faith in His name. HESS

Jesus came to Earth for us so we could go to heaven with Him.

Is Jesus Still Here?

Ted Robertson's home in Colorado was one of more than 500 destroyed by the Black Forest Fire in June 2013. When he was allowed to return and sift through the ash and rubble, he was hoping to find a precious family heirloom made by his wife—a tiny ceramic figurine of baby Jesus about the size of a postage stamp. As he searched the charred remains of their home, he kept wondering, "Is the baby Jesus still here?"

> **TODAY'S READING**
> **Romans 8:31-39**
>
> **[Nothing] shall be able to separate us from the love of God which is in Christ Jesus our Lord.** vv. 38-39

When our lives are rocked by disappointment and loss, we may wonder if Jesus is still here with us. The Bible's answer is a resounding Yes! "Neither death nor life, nor angels nor principalities nor powers, nor things present nor things to come . . . shall be able to separate us from the love of God which is in Christ Jesus our Lord" (ROM. 8:38-39).

In a corner of what used to be his garage, Ted Robertson discovered the burned remnants of a nativity scene and there he found the baby Jesus figurine undamaged by the flames. He told KRDO NewsChannel 13, "[We've] gone from apprehension to hope . . . that we're going to recover some parts of our life that we thought were lost."

Is Jesus still here? He is indeed, and that is the everlasting wonder of Christmas. ❧

DAVID MCCASLAND

> When all around me is darkness
> And earthly joys have flown,
> My Savior whispers His promise
> Never to leave me alone. ANON.

If you know Jesus, you'll never walk alone.

Delay May Not Mean Denial

My sons' birthdays are in December. When they were small, Angus quickly learned that if he didn't receive a longed-for toy for his birthday at the beginning of the month, it might be in his Christmas stocking. And if David didn't receive his gift for Christmas, it might appear for his birthday 4 days later. Delay didn't necessarily mean denial.

It was natural for Martha and Mary to send for Jesus when Lazarus became seriously ill (JOHN 11:1-3). Perhaps they looked anxiously along the road for signs of His arrival, but Jesus didn't come. The funeral service had been over for 4 days when Jesus finally walked into town (V. 17).

Martha was blunt. "If You had been here," she said, "my brother would not have died" (V. 21). Then her faith flickered into certainty, "Even now I know that whatever You ask of God, God will give You" (V. 22). I wonder what she expected. Lazarus was dead, and she was wary about opening the tomb. And yet at a word from Jesus, Lazarus' spirit returned to his decaying body (VV. 41-44). Jesus had bypassed simply healing His sick friend, in order to perform the far greater miracle of bringing him back to life.

Waiting for God's timing may also give us a greater miracle than we had hoped for.

MARION STROUD

> **TODAY'S READING**
> **John 11:21-35**
>
> When [Jesus] heard that [Lazarus] was sick, He stayed two more days in the place where He was. 11:6

My Savior hears me when I pray,
Upon His Word I calmly rest;
In His own time, in His own way,
I know He'll give me what is best. HEWITT

Time spent waiting on God is never wasted.

He Leads Me

n Istanbul, Turkey, in 2005, one sheep jumped off a cliff and then nearly 1,500 others followed! In the end, about one-third of them died. Not knowing which way to go, sheep mindlessly follow other members of the flock.

No better word picture than sheep can be found to illustrate our need for a trustworthy leader. We are all, Isaiah wrote, like sheep (ISA. 53:6). We tend to go our own way, yet we desperately need the sure direction of a shepherd.

TODAY'S READING
Psalm 23

He leads me beside the still waters. v. 2

Psalm 23 describes the trustworthiness of our Good Shepherd. He cares for us (V. 1); He provides for our physical needs (V. 2); He shows us how to live holy lives (V. 3); He restores us, comforts us, heals us, and bountifully blesses us (VV. 3-5); and He will not abandon us (V. 6).

What a comfort to know that God gently but firmly leads us! He does so through the urging of the Holy Spirit, the reading of His Word, and through prayer. God is the reliable leader we need.

In acknowledgment of our dependence on the Lord, we can say with the psalmist, "The LORD is my shepherd; I shall not want. He makes me to lie down in green pastures; He leads me beside the still waters." ❧

DAVE EGNER

> Like sheep that sometimes wander from the flock
> In tangled paths of life to lose their way,
> I need my Shepherd's hand and watchful eye
> To keep me always, lest I go astray. SANDERS

The Lamb who died to save us is the Shepherd who lives to guide us.

Standing on the Edge

My little girl stood apprehensively at the pool's edge. As a nonswimmer, she was just learning to become comfortable in the water. Her instructor waited in the pool with outstretched arms. As my daughter hesitated, I saw the questions in her eyes: Will you catch me? What will happen if my head goes under?

TODAY'S READING
Joshua 3:9-17

The Israelites may have wondered what would happen when they crossed the Jordan River. Could they trust God to make dry ground appear in the river-bed? Was God guiding their new leader, Joshua, as He had led Moses? Would God help His people defeat the threatening Canaanites who lived just across the river?

[The Israelites] set out . . . to cross over the Jordan, with the priests bearing the ark of the covenant before [them]. v. 14

To learn the answers to these questions, the Israelites had to engage in a test of faith—they had to act. So they "set out from their camp to cross over the Jordan, with the priests bearing the ark of the covenant before [them]" (JOSH 3:14). Exercising their faith allowed them to see that God was with them. He was still directing Joshua, and He would help them settle in Canaan (VV. 7,10,17).

If you are facing a test of faith, you too can move forward based on God's character and His unfailing promises. Relying on Him will help you move from where you are to where He wants you to be. ❧ *JENNIFER BENSON SCHULDT*

Lord, we're prone to quickly forget Your goodness and care for us.
May we trust You today and into the new year—whatever
uncertainties we face. You are the God who can be trusted.

Fear fades when we trust our Father.

Rescued

There was a young mountaineer who was so full of self-reliance that he believed he needed nothing and no one. He certainly had no need of God. But one night he stood on the edge of a sheer cliff 1,000 feet above the valley floor, rope gone, best friend missing and presumed dead, rain pouring down, and the pitch black of night engulfing him. With everything he had relied upon gone, and with no hope of survival, he came face-to-face with the certainty that he was about to die. Then the rock he was standing on began to collapse, and he knew he had seconds to live.

He was unprepared for death, and in his hopelessness this unbelieving, arrogant man cried out to God to save him. He needed a God that could move heaven and earth (an all-powerful God), and a God who would move heaven and earth for someone who didn't even believe in Him (a compassionate, loving, and forgiving God). He also needed a God who would act quickly, without him having to earn His affection. He needed a God who was zealous and passionate in His love for him, a God who was concerned about him as an individual.

I certainly would not have helped a person like that, but thankfully God is not like me because He did help. I know, because that man was me. I asked a God I didn't believe in to rescue me, and as I stepped off the mountainside a rope that I could not see was in my hand. After that, He guided me down a sheer rock wall in pitch black darkness, negotiating rotten granite and a waterfall, until I reached the bottom—without even a scratch! That's not just improbable; it's impossible! (Ask any climber.) Yet my God is the God of the impossible.

God Is All-Powerful and All-Loving

Only the God of the Bible is both all-powerful and all-loving (SEE JOB 28-39; 1 JOHN 4:7-21). No other religion or faith system can make this claim. He is powerful enough to move heaven and earth, and He loves us so much that He sent His Son, Jesus, to give His life for us.

God is holy and His standard is perfection (MATT. 5:48; 1 PETER 1:15-16). All the wrong things that each and every person has ever done—our sins—have separated us from Him. We need someone to pay for our wrongdoings because we cannot pay the price ourselves (ROM. 3:10,23).

God sent Jesus to earth to rescue us from sin and bring us into a relationship with Himself. Jesus lived a perfect life on earth and then endured death on a cross to pay for our wrong-doings (JOHN 1:1-14; 3:16). When we ask God to forgive us, He puts all our blame onto Jesus and He puts all the righteousness of Jesus onto us so that we can stand before a holy God clean and pure (ROM. 3:24-26; 5:8-9; 2 COR. 5:21). This is a truly remarkable event, borne out of the greatest love ever known and paid for with the greatest suffering ever imaginable.

Call Out to God

Are you in need of rescue? Admit to the Lord that you are a sinner and cannot save yourself. Then accept His free gift of salvation that promises forgiveness and life with Him forever. 🌿

Russell Fralick, author of *Over the Top* by Discovery House Publishers.

About the Publisher

Our Daily Bread Ministries

Our Daily Bread Ministries is a nondenominational, nonprofit organization with more than 600 staff and 1,000 volunteers serving in 37 countries. Together we distribute more than 60 million resources every year in over 150 countries. Our mission is to make the life-changing wisdom of the Bible understandable and accessible to all.

Beginning in 1938 as a Bible class aired on a small radio station in Detroit, Michigan, USA, Our Daily Bread Ministries now offers radio and television programs; devotional, instructional, evangelistic, and apologetic print and digital resources; and a biblical correspondence ministry. You can access our online resources at ourdailybread.org. Our signature publication, *Our Daily Bread*, is published in nearly 50 languages and is read by people in almost every country around the world.

Discovery House Publishers

Discovery House Publishers was founded in 1988 as an extension of Our Daily Bread Ministries. Our goal is to produce resources that feed the soul with the Word of God, and we do this through books, music, video, audio, software, greeting cards, and downloadable content. All our materials focus on the never-changing truths of Scripture, so everything we produce shows reverence for God and His Word, demonstrates the relevance of vibrant faith, and equips and encourages people in their everyday lives.

Our Daily Bread
Ministries™ Offices
Europe

For information on our resources, visit **ourdailybread.org**. Alternatively, please contact the office nearest you from the list below, or go to **ourdailybread.org/locations** for the complete list of offices.

BELARUS
Our Daily Bread Ministries, PO Box 82, Minsk, Belarus 220107
belarus@odb.org ‖ (375-17) 2854657; (375-29) 9168799

IRELAND
Our Daily Bread Ministries, YMCA, Claremont Road, Dublin 4
ireland@odb.org ‖ +3531 (01)667 8428

RUSSIA
MISSION Our Daily Bread, PO Box "Our Daily Bread",
str.Vokzalnaya 2, Smolensk, Russia 214961
russia@odb.org ‖ 8(4812)660849; +7(951)7028049

UKRAINE
Christian Mission Our Daily Bread, PO Box 533, Kiev, Ukraine 01004
ukraine@odb.org ‖ +380964407374; +380632112446

United Kingdom (Europe Regional Office)
Our Daily Bread Ministries, PO Box 1, Carnforth, Lancashire, LA5 9ES
europe@odb.org ‖ 015395 64149

Topic Index

Topic Index

Topic Index